New Directions in Aesthetics, Creativity, and the Arts

Edited by

Paul Locher
Montclair State University

Colin Martindale
University of Maine

Leonid Dorfman
Perm Institute of Art and Culture

Foundations and Frontiers in Aesthetics
Series Editors: Colin Martindale and Arnold Berleant

Baywood Publishing Company, Inc.
AMITYVILLE, NEW YORK

Baywood Publishing Company, Inc.
P.O. Box 337
26 Austin Avenue
Amityville, NY 11701
(800) 638-7819
E-mail: baywood@baywood.com
Web site: baywood.com

Library of Congress Catalog Number: 2005053617
ISBN: 0-89503-305-4 (cloth)

BH
301
P78
N 49
2006

Library of Congress Cataloging-in-Publication Data

New directions in aesthetics, creativity, and the arts / edited by Paul Locher, Colin
    Martindale, and Leonid Dorfman.
        p. cm. -- (Foundations and frontiers in aesthetics series)
    Includes bibliographical references and index.
    ISBN 0-89503-305-4 (cloth)
    1. Aesthetics--Psychological aspects. 2. Creation (Literary, artistic, etc.) 3.
Arts--Psychological aspects. I. Locher, Paul, 1941- II. Martindale, Colin. III. Dorfman, L.
IA. (Leonid IAKovlevich), 1951- IV. Series

    BH301.P78N49 2005
    111'.85019--dc   2005053617

Table of Contents

PART II
NEW DIRECTIONS IN CREATIVITY

PART III
ART AND COGNITION

PART IV
ART, AFFECT, AND PERSONALITY

Preface

The purpose of this volume is to show the different ways scholars who are preeminent in their fields are currently thinking about the processes that underlie creativity and aesthetic experience. The authors describe not only the established theory and research in their respective fields, but provide creative speculation on future problems for inquiry and new approaches to conceptualize and investigate phenomena. The book contains many new findings that have not been published before, or are new by virtue of the novel context in which they have been incorporated in the chapters. Thus, the chapters present new approaches to old problems and new problems not heretofore explored by the leading scholars in the areas covered in this volume.

The volume is divided into four major sections. Part I is devoted to the understanding of the nature of the aesthetic processes that occur during encounters with visual art stimuli. The authors bring a variety of research methodologies, ranging from traditional experimental procedures to naturalistic research approaches, to bear on phenomenon of common interest. In the first chapter Hochberg and Brooks present an overview of how the experimental study of the way movies work helps cognitive psychologists, neurophysiologists, and aestheticians learn more about human perceptual mechanisms that have real-life consequences. Specifically, their chapter is concerned with explanations of how objects integrate across views in moving pictures and how scenes integrate across cuts. They point out that future research in this field must focus on ways to identify and measure factors that contribute to the maintenance and integration of protracted perceptual inquiry when one watches a film. In the next chapter Locher describes how "brass instrument" techniques, such as recording eye fixation patterns of observers of art, are used to subject to empirical scrutiny the writings of art theoreticians about the influence of pictorial balance on the perception of visual art. The research findings presented demonstrate the valuable contribution traditional experimental approaches make not only to our understanding of why balance is such an important design principle but also to their potential to reveal perceptual/cognitive processes that occur during an aesthetic episode with art. The central theme of Cutting's chapter is that the mere exposure phenomenon helps shape aesthetic preferences for art. He presents the findings of naturalistic investigations of the effects of cultural exposure on preferences for images drawn from the French Impressionist canon and explains how everyday exposure of individuals to artworks helps to establish and maintain an artistic canon. His research involves a most innovative procedure to determine image frequency of art stimuli and his findings demonstrate that the laboratory phenomenon mere exposure can be generalized to broader cultural behaviors such as aesthetic preferences. Smith and Smith's chapter focuses on their model of aesthetic fluency, which they define as the knowledge that a person has acquired about art and aspects of life closely related to art. The model was developed on the basis of their extensive research on people's behavior in art museums and they describe how the naturalistic study of what happens in museums contributes to an understanding of the development of aesthetic fluency. The study of museum behavior has not found its way to any great extent into the visual aesthetics or creativity literature. Yet, as Smith and Smith make clear in their chapter, both theory construction and research in the field of museology share considerable overlap with the more traditional approaches to visual aesthetics and creativity. Hence the editors thought it important to expand the variety of topics in this section to include this newly emerging dimension of the psychology of art. In the last chapter of Part I, Washburn illustrates how anthropological approaches to the study of art and aesthetic responses enhance our understanding about cross-cultural aesthetic universals in cultural perception and practice. She describes the nature of the aesthetic response to beauty that people from different cultures find in certain symmetrical arrangements of design. She explains how it should be possible to access and confirm such a deeply seated aesthetic using preference tests for symmetrical pattern configurations she and others are developing.

The four chapters in Part II discuss new dimensions in the study of creativity. Sternberg reviews the work he and his collaborators are doing in their efforts toward the development of a comprehensive theory of creativity—the *investment theory of creativity*. He provides an overview of a number of issues that a complete theory of creativity must address, such as the confluence of interrelated resources required by creative people and the types of decisions one must make to develop his or her own creativity. Research evidence supporting the theory is provided throughout this very comprehensive description of the investment theory of creativity. In the next chapter Dorfman lays out a systems perspective of creativity that is based on a metaindividual world model. He explains how this perspective can integrate an understanding of the nature of personality and creativity into a unitary systems framework and he presents empirical findings to support the model. Simonton illustrates an analytic strategy that enables an investigator to simultaneously examine the major contributions to a film's cinematic success. He presents the findings of investigations regarding four aspects of cinematic creativity and aesthetics: the relationship between film awards and critical acclaim; creative clusters in cinematic art; budget, box office and aesthetic success, and gender differences in acting contributions. He discusses future directions of empirical research on cinematic creativity and aesthetics. Overbeeke and Forlizzi point out that product design is creative; it is about making innovative products. Since the introduction of electronics in consumer products, design has become more complicated and designers need to understand how human responses to products influence product design. The authors describe how designers now use research in the fields of perception, semiotics, and pre-cognitive and habitual psychological responses to create variations in the appearance and behavior of a new product and how it derives interactive meaning with a user. To understand the complex nature of the creative processes involved in design in this age of electronics, theory and research in this area has had to borrow insights and adopt research approaches from the fields of creativity and visual aesthetics. In so doing, design is emerging as an important area of interest within each of these fields.

In Part III three chapters deal with the application of concepts and models from cognitive psychology to the study of music, literary meaning, and the visual arts, respectively. Deliège outlines a model—the *cue abstraction model*—of the cognitive processes involved in real time listening to a piece of music. She describes the findings of a number of experimental procedures that have been developed to test the validity of the different components and processes of the model. Miall's chapter addresses the question, What are readers doing when they read a literary text? He discusses development of the major systematic experimental approaches to literary reading; the findings obtained from research in this field, and the questions and issues raised by an empirical approach to this topic. In the first part of their chapter Winner and her colleagues describe what research shows about the transfer of learning from the arts to non-arts cognition and they discuss the weakness of these studies. The remainder of the chapter is devoted to the presentation of their current research, which is designed to identify the kinds of thinking skills or habits of mind that emerge from serious study of the visual arts at the high school level.

The four chapters in Part IV focus on the interactive contribution of the personality and affect state of observers to the creation and perception of art. Cupchik elucidates how the relationship between stimulus features of an artwork and the affect state of observers can be viewed as dynamic, bi-directional processes that underlie the pleasure and interest generated by an aesthetic work. He describes the relations between emotion and cognition in aesthetics in terms of the interaction of top-down and bottom-up processes across the time course of an aesthetic episode, be it with visual or literary material. Machotka examines the internal mechanisms by which personality expresses itself during the making of art and when one responds to it. Support for the view that taste is determined in part by personality is provided by the findings of analyses reported in the chapter that compared the themes and forms of art images created by individuals with the clinical picture of each participant obtained from personality interviews. In her chapter Russ reviews the theoretical and research literature that demonstrates the relationship between the affective processes in pretend play and the development of creativity in children. She describes the mechanisms and specific processes in pretend play that account for this relationship and presents techniques to facilitate pretend play that foster creativity. In the final chapter of this volume Gabrielsson reports the findings of his research project that asked participants to describe the strongest, most intense experience of music that they have ever had. His data provide a comprehensive and detailed description of the components— physical, behavioral, perceptual, cognitive, emotional, and social— contained in strong experiences to music and speculates about the "causes" and consequences of such experiences to listeners.

In conclusion, this volume provides a state of the art overview of the richness of work being conducted on aesthetics and creativity. My colleagues and I consider ourselves extremely fortunate to have had the opportunity to edit a volume that contains contributions by scholars who are leading authorities in their fields and we thank them for their participation in this project. We are also very grateful to Stuart Cohen, President of Baywood Publishing Company, for his enthusiastic support of this work.

Paul J. Locher

PART I

VISUAL AESTHETICS

CHAPTER 1

Perception and Moving Pictures: From Brunelleschi and Berkeley to Video and Video Games

*Julian Hochberg
and Virginia Brooks*

How pictures function tells us much about how we perceive the world, and their makers' discoveries guided yesterday's philosophy and science. Today, moving pictures help in raising and answering questions of concern to cognitive psychologists, to neurophysiologists, to aestheticians, and to those computer scientists who automate our interaction with the visual world and its representations. This is increasingly true as we start to learn how meaningful sequences are processed, and how the perceptual system routinely draws on creative anticipatory abilities which can be aroused by filmmakers and other artists, but are not invented by them.

There is obviously still a great deal to learn about moving pictures before we can expect computers to create them with only cursory human supervision; however, if *Pixar*, which is heavily computer-executed, can now make a $400 million profit on a $100 million cost (see Stross, 2004), we are at least on the road. More important to us here, by studying how movies work, we can learn more about human perceptual mechanisms that have real-life consequences. In this chapter, our two main concerns are these: to make a start on how objects integrate across views, and on how scenes integrate across cuts.

First, we sketch yesterday's approach as a backdrop and reminder of what won't work.

HOW WE USED TO EXPLAIN SEEING

Until quite recently (about 50 years ago—recent to some of us) it was widely assumed that the purely *visual* components of what we perceive are tiny points of color at various loci in 2D space, while the rest of our perceptions—shapes, motions, depth, gestures, and above all *the integrated views of the world that span our successive glances*—were all assumed to be clusters of sensory and motor memories. Mapping the photoreceptors' sensitivities, the associative learning curve, etc., and measuring the probabilities with which different aspects of our ecology co-occur (and thereby become associated, in the *likelihood principle*), were all challenging but eminently possible, publishable, and rewarding activities.

The fact that perceived motion could be produced by successions of static pictures, i.e., moving pictures, did not in itself offer the classical view a serious problem (although some writers on film did fuss about uncritical issues, like the phi phenomenon of apparent motion, and "persistence of vision"; to put those in perspective, see Steinman, Pizlo, & Pizlo, 2000, for the first, and Anderson & Anderson, 1983, for the second). Classically, perceived movement was simply considered a perception that was composed of memories of sensations at successive loci in the retinal image, so that was not then a problem in itself.

However, combining the images of objects and scenes, as viewpoints change, was (and is) another story: That we seem able to integrate the glimpses of the world given by successive eye movements was usually explained as compensation for how the eye muscles had moved the eye. Much work was done on this quite difficult question. It came to very little: We do not in fact firmly transfer information about retinal position when moving our eyes (e.g., Jonides, Irwin, & Yantis, 1983). The use of view-changes (cuts) in films and in dioramic slide-shows really told us that by the dawn of the 20th century.

We still do not have a good account of what accrues across glances.

Film makers, on the other hand, have long since (since the early 1900s) shown that one can provide information across viewpoints comprehensibly, so that moving pictures may suggest alternatives to the approach outlined above. And such help is needed because, as we all now know, the classical approach to perception is no longer viable for other reasons as well. Some of those reasons are particularly relevant here.

HOW LOOKING LOOKS NOW

1. Neural structures in eye and brain respond not to individual points, but to extended patterns (even to faces!), so we do not yet know

the full vocabulary with which the visual system analyzes what it receives. It is therefore prudent to include representative stimuli like those we use outside the laboratory as we formulate and test any a new approach.

2. As incoming visual signals enter the earliest cortical region V1, they confront output from various higher cortical levels, including pre-frontal cortex (the top-most and most anticipatory level; see Lennie, 1998), so the brain is not merely a passive associative network.

3. The biggest fact is this: Laboratory experiments show that each *saccade only occurs after a purposeful shift of attention* (see Hoffman & Subramaniam, 1995; Kowler, Anderson, Dosher, & Blaser, 1995). Each new glance is thus *purposefully* directed to some place that is likely to have been seen, but only peripherally, during a previous glance. This vindicates older claims that glances are normally purposeful, and directed by a perceptual question or an anticipation about what information can be found (Hochberg, 1970; Hochberg & Brooks, 1970; see also Cavanagh, Labianca, & Thornton, 2001, Gottesman & Intraub, 2003). We therefore next look briefly at looking as a purposeful behavior.

PURPOSEFUL LOOKING AT OBJECTS
AND SCENES

The fact that real eye movements have two purposeful antecedents—the posing of a visual question, and the likelihood of preceding extrafoveal glimpses—makes them very different from cuts between shots in moving pictures (although cuts can approximate glances in some ways and thereby help investigate the nature of perceptual inquiry).

Saccadic eye movements themselves have usually been studied while stationary viewers read or looked at pictures, but the eyes move quite similarly in many other situations. In fact, a freely moving viewer's gaze touches the sites of planned actions long before those actions are undertaken (Pelz & Canosa, 2001). In as many as 4-5 saccades per second, the eye directs its high-resolution *fovea* to some point that was previously seen by the eye's periphery, which has only extremely low acuity and loses information further by "crowding" (see Tripathy & Cavanagh, 2002). Therefore anything not fixated has little or no detail; in any case, features which do not fit the visual question that the glance is asking are subsequently disregarded as irrelevant (Hochberg, 1970; Hochberg & Brooks, 1970). Furthermore, how scenes are remembered shows signs of what are most likely the preparations for further restricted glances (Gottesman & Intraub, 2003). In short, each individual glance picks up and retains very little (about 4 letters) out of a page full of text, and comparably sparse encodings when viewing brief pictorial displays (see review on sparseness by Intraub, 1997; see Potter, Staub, & O'Connor, 2004, for the time course of response to briefly-exposed pictures; also see Hollingworth, 2004, on the memories of individual meaningful items flagged and looked at within a meaningful scene).

Simply put, what is not attended is likely to be not looked at, likely to be not encoded, and likely to be not remembered. This was a major point in Neisser's 1967 comprehensive initiation of modern cognitive psychology, a concern of other less ambitious theories (Hochberg, 1968; Treisman & Geffen, 1967) and the focus of what Mack and Rock (1998) later called inattentional blindness. (That now-popular term obscures the fact that the supposedly-lost information has detectible consequences, as shown by Becker & Egeth, 2000, so inattentional disregard or neglect is the term used here.) Around that issue, a growing body of research has studied attentional effects on moving pictures of real people, starting with Neisser and Becklen (1975), then using superimposed actions, and now using more natural films (e.g., Levin & Simons, 1997; see review by Simons, 2000).

Such research is certainly interesting and more applicable than the old approach's measures of attentional effects on psychophysical thresholds of spots of light. However, mere data about what viewers can't report is not as informative as data about what else they can report, i.e., what *perceptual couplings* (Hochberg, 1974) or conse-quences they display, as in Figure 1*C*. The figures that follow sketch demonstrations in which attention is directed within and across objects and scenes. (See note before the first caption.)

LEARNING FROM MOVING PICTURES

Figure 1 shows frames from 3 animations, each meant to be attended in succession at two different places. Figures *A*, *B,* and *C* are so designed that where one attends, within the same object or scene, and the perceptual question one asks of the world, determine what motion and structure one sees. Figure 1*A* was modeled after a demonstration (as we remember it) by Slavko Vorkapitch, at the Museum of Modern Art in the mid '60s (Kevles, 1965). In that shot, the woman appeared stationary, showing the importance of Gibsonian motion gradients. Here, we added walking feet and a moving (receding) pavement, so that when attended at *a* the "actress" seemed to step forward. When attended at *b*, her motion is lost, and the bottom becomes a disregarded jumble (which the loss of motion at *b* would seem to imply in any case, given other evidence that distance information is well transmitted by such "nested contact" Meng & Sedgwick, 2001). In Figure 1*B*, a stationary "dancer" appears to move when she is strongly fixated. And in Figure 1*C*, an illusory motion is used to corroborate that the viewer has misread a close relative of the Necker cube, switching without noticing it from a possible structure when fixated at *a*, to an impossible structure at *b*. Motion gradients do not automatically suffice for direct (unmediated, unattentional) perception, unless they receive directed attention when they need it. For an extensive discussion, see Cutting, Alliprandini, and Wang (2000) and Cutting (2004).

It was previously observed (see Brooks, 1984) that choreographed motions as perceived from the screen are not automatically those the camera confronts, because the motion picture frame itself affects the performance space and therefore the depth and magnitude of the perceived movement. As we now see in the surprising independence between parts of a single object, particularly evident in Figure 1*C,* perceived motions within the scene and object are determined more by local conditions than we would expect from any physical models like those on which computer-generated animations are based (or those with which Gestalt psychology tried to replace the classical approach; see Hochberg, 1998). Film-making models should incorporate such knowledge, as we acquire it.

Perceptual psychologists also should pursue such phenomena (assisted by brain imaging). Even when the "Killer Cube" in *C* is less than 4°, the part at *a* goes unparsed when attention shifts to *b*. Attentional parsing, and not poor extrafoveal acuity or crowding must contribute to the phenomenon, and must underlie the astonishing tolerance we have for impossible figures (which Gillam also found in 1979). And given the ease and speed with which mental models have been shown to change (Moore & Engel, 2001), the vanishing of the previously parsed structure is not an isolated phenomenon. (Indeed, we may just have explained why reversible figures, like the Necker cube, reverse.)

Attentive glances not only parse objects in our field of view, they bring new parts of the world into view. Cuts in moving pictures can of course do likewise, and we take a step toward learning from them in Figures 2 and 3.

The demonstrations pictured in Figures 2*B-D* show that the direction of displacement between two brief views is easily seen, at rates like those of rapid glances, if the views contain a salient feature, or landmark (i.e., *B*, *C*, *E*1). That occurs even when masks like *m* in Figure 2*C* are inserted to block any cues that might be provided by potential low-level motion and low-level persistence (Sperling & Lu, 1998). Before

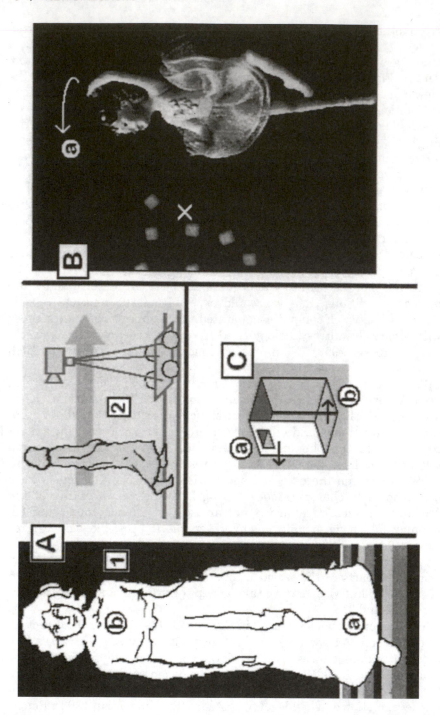

Figure 1. Inattentional disregard: 2 dancers and the Killer Cube.

Note: Figures 1-3 will appear as animations on *inthemindseye.org* as of October 1, 2005. As with many ambiguous figures, knowing that some alternatives may appear is often important for them to do so, so consider that before viewing each demonstration on the web. Further information will appear there, and in Hochberg (In press).

A. When attended at *a*, the woman in the animation sketched at **1** (animated as if filmed by the moving camera at **2**) appears to walk toward the viewer, as the stripes at bottom move away from the viewer in an appropriate motion gradient. When attention is shifted to *b*, she appears stationary, and the stimulus motion at *a* goes unparsed (see text).

B. The doll, while stationary in real space, appears to turn on the screen (arrow *a*). Only if the viewer concentrates on the pattern on the wall at left, striving to see it as an optical expansion pattern around the point **X** at which the camera is heading, does the doll appear stationary in space. (See Cutting *et al*, 2000, for analysis and experimental research on the heading effect that this demonstration exploits.)

C. When attending *a*, the left side of the "Killer Cube" looks solidly nearer, in a perfectly possible structure. If fixation shifts to *b*, while still looking at the cube, the perceived structure soon reverses, and the heavy vertical bar comes forward. Note that a possible structure has become an impossible one overall! If it is in fact parsed overall, which it almost certainly is not, *we cannot claim to understand what is perceived until we can predict how much of any object will act as a unit.*

We know that such reports of nearness and farness are to be taken seriously, because when the cube is set into motion (e.g., as shown by the top arrow) while the heavy lower vertical is attended, the object is seen to move in the opposite direction, as shown by the lower arrow. This is true even when the entire cube falls within the fovea. Such *perceptual coupling* between what looks nearer, on the one hand, and on which way it appears to move (see text), lends credibility to the phenomenon. That phenomenon would seem to raise fewer problems in an approach in which individual focal inquiries, and recognizable local object-parts, rather than overall objects, are perception's functional units (Hochberg, 2003; Peterson, 2003; Peterson & Grant, 2003).

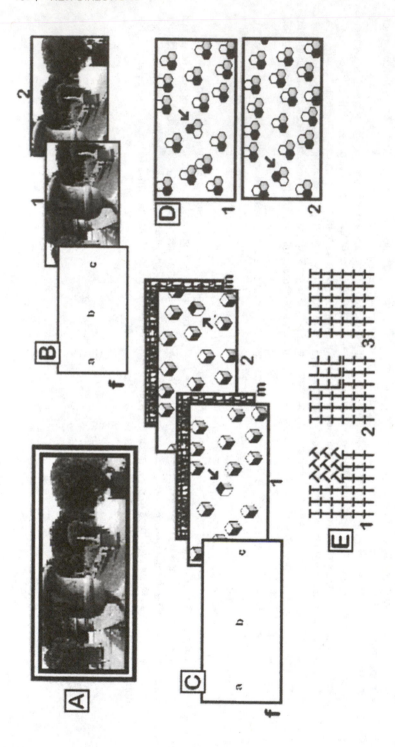

Figure 2. Integrating shots and gluing glances: landmarks act in accordance with their measured salience (so far).

A, B) A selection of scenes with salient landmarks, like *A*, were divided into two overlapping shots (*2, 3*) preceded by a fixation field, *f*, and presented as a sequence. With 200 ms between onset of shots *2* and *3*, a viewer reliably identifies whether the view shifted right or left. That is fast enough for saccadic vision and far faster than normal film demands (see text). These demonstrations were also performed with 50 ms noise masks interposed as in *C* (see text). It seems plausible that this is at least one way we know how to combine our glances at both the real world and at the screen.

C–E) We can use this method to find out what it takes to serves as a landmark across shots (or glances). The series at *C* uses as landmarks the patterns to which small arrows point here (but not in the demonstration itself), which Enns (1990) discovered to stand out saliently from the distractors around them. With SOAs of 200 ms (from onset to onset) between them, the displacement direction (left or right) is visible every time. The control objects in *D* do not do as well (slightly better than chance). Similarly, *E1* does much better than *E2* when either is surrounded by several *E3*s as distractors (the *E*s are from Beck, 1967). This is a first step in studying landmarks (see text), but such salience per se cannot be the whole story, as we see in Figure 3.

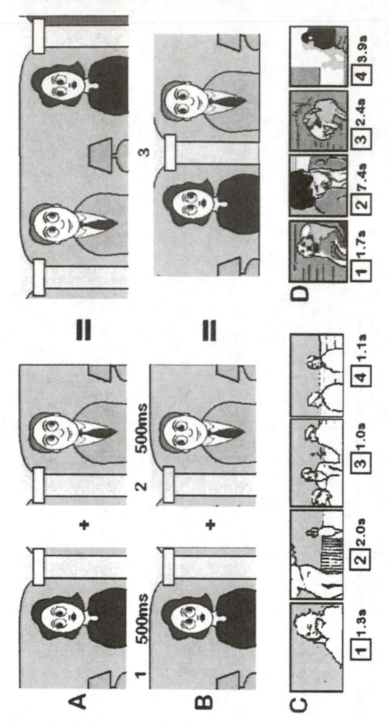

Figure 3. Beyond landmarks: Microstories (e.g., look where I look).

Sequences *A* and *B* are usually perceived to yield the larger scenes here visualized at *A*3 and *B*3, respectively. Either a simple rule (e.g., "next shot shows what the actor is attending") or some tiny story (man and woman are looking at each other) can serve to signal where the new view lies, at least when the landmarks are not too strong. (We are currently trying to titrate such story strength against manipulable landmark prominence.) In **C**, sketched from Chris Marker's "La Jetée," a short film of still shots with voice-over (here modified from Hochberg and Brooks, 1996, with durations estimated from videotape), each shot contains no movement, but the sequence appears as a rightward sweep. The shots at **D** sketched form Warren Beatty's "Reds" (duration estimates from videotape), contain little motion and have no voice-over narrative. They are seen as near each other, but do so more by the situation inferred than by any landmarks (see text).

we can hope to use such procedures in automated Film making, we will have to learn more about the conditions that determine salience, and work on this topic does continue apace in psychology and brain imaging. Beyond anything as tractable as salience, however, the problem of combining views presses the border of short-term narrative, and mapping that border demands a very different line of work.

Most commercial films are carefully edited and assembled in the cutting room, and it is there (after the story board) that the eye-informed decisions are made about the desired integration of successive views. The closest thing that we have to a body of research on maintaining purposeful perceptual inquiry is therefore the body of archived movies now so very available.

In Figure 3, $A2$ appears leftward of $A1$ in the combined scene, as visualized at $A3$; $B2$ appears to the right of $B1$ (see $B3$). The characters' gaze directions have effectively overcome the column-as-landmark in A and the lamp-as-landmark in B. The anticipations that guide such integrations are therefore not driven only by configuration and salience, but by factors like where the actors are looking (or at whom they are likely to be looking)—that is, by an inferred event or story. And in fact, filmmakers tend to avoid successive shots with substantial overlap because low-level apparent motion produces disturbing *jump cuts*, which then need to be separated by *cutaways* (interposed shots which allow the persistence between views to subside). So that tends to mean the use of few or weak landmarks, and the need for other factors to guide integration.

In C, in a series of still shots that have no salient overlap or landmarks, but that clearly progresses from left to right within in an overall field of view, actors' gaze direction seems to determine the resulting overview. (Given the voiceover's needs, we can't judge whether shorter durations would have sufficed.) In D, the views show parts of a shared space, but are clearly integrated by an inferred small story, not by overlap. The relatively long durations may offer the viewer time to access the larger narrative, and to form and test inferences about what will happen next.

CONCLUSION AND PROSPECT

Space does not permit a discussion here of the long-term factors designed to invite protracted perceptual inquiry (like the story that unfolds in book or film, or the structures that provide for successful anticipation and satisfaction when watching dance, listening to music, etc.), especially since they probably do not contribute much at the glance-by-glance level (cf. Dosher & Corbett, 1982; Glanzer, Fischer, &

Dorfman, 1984; McKoon & Ratcliff, 1992). Much smaller attention-based units of social and mechanical movement have been demonstrated (see Heider & Simmel, 1944, and the recent comprehensive review by Scholl & Tremoulet, 2000, for the former, and the "sprites" described by Cavanagh, Labianca, & Thornton, 2001 for the latter). Low-level factors, like cutting rate, affect how viewers watch simple meaningful film sequences (Hochberg & Brooks, 1978), and Krumhansl and her colleagues (Krumhansl & Schenck,1997; Camurri, Krumhansl, Mazzarino, & Volpe, 2004) have recently shown promising techniques that identify viewers' anticipations concerning music and dance.

What we do not have in any of these domains are attempts to measure how they contribute to the maintenance and integration of acts of looking. Unless we can address the question of how the viewer chooses to look (or not to look) directly at any indirectly-glimpsed potential-object-of-attention, and with what intent, we cannot have a science of perception or its applications. Since the "decision" of where to look cannot be based on a full survey, it must involve a creative "satis-ficing" (Simon, 1987) rather than any of the optimization models (e.g., likelihood/simplicity) that were previously pursued (see also Pizlo & Li, in press). We are now trying something like that with methods evolved from that in Figure 2, and will present those findings when they come into sharper focus.

REFERENCES

Anderson, J., & Anderson, B. (1983). The myth of persistence of vision. *Journal of Film and Video, 45,* 3-12.

Beck, J. (1967). Perceptual grouping produced by line figures. *Perception and Psychophysics, 2,* 491-495.

Becker, L., & Egeth, H. (2000). Mixed reference frames for dynamic inhibition of return. *Journal of Experimental Psychology: Human Perception and Performance, 26,* 1167-1177.

Brooks, V. (1984). Why dance films do not look right: A study in the nature of the documentary of movement as visual communication. *Studies in Visual Communication, 10,* 44-67.

Camurri, A., Krumhansl, C., Mazzarino, B., & Volpe, G. (2004). An exploratory study of anticipating human movement in dance. *2nd International Symposium on Measurement, Analysis and Modeling of Human Functions.* Italy: Genova.

Cavanagh, P., Labianca, A., & Thornton, I. (2001). Attention-based visual routines: sprites. *Cognition, 80,* 47-60.

Cutting, J. E. (2004). Perceiving scenes in film and in the world. In H. D. Anderson & B. F. Anderson (Eds.), *Moving image theory: Ecological considerations* (pp. 9-27). Carbondale, IL: University of Southern Illinois Press.

Cutting, J. E., Alliprandini, P. M., & Wang, R. F. (2000). Seeking one's heading through eye movements. *Psychonomic Bulletin & Review, 7*(3), 490-498.

Dosher, B. A., & Corbett, A. T. (1982). Instrument inferences and verb schemata. *Memory and Cognition, 10,* 531-539.

Enns, J. T. (1990). Three dimensional features that pop out in visual search. In D. Brogan (Ed.), *Visual search* (pp. 37-45). London: Taylor & Francis.

Gillam, B. (1979). Even a possible figure can look impossible. *Perception, 8,* 229-232.

Glanzer, M., Fischer, B., & Dorfman, D. (1984). Short-term storage in reading. *Journal of Verbal Learning and Verbal Behavior, 23,* 467-486.

Gottesman, C. V., & Intraub, H. (2003). Constraints on spatial extrapolation in the mental representation of scenes: View-boundaries vs. object-boundaries. *Visual Cognition, 10,* 875-893.

Heider, F., & Simmel, M. (1944). An experimental study of apparent behavior. *American Journal of Psychology, 57,* 243-259.

Hochberg, J. (1968). In the mind's eye. In R. N. Haber (Ed.), *Contemporary theory and research in visual perception* (pp. 309-332). New York: Holt, Rinehart & Winston.

Hochberg, J. (1970). Attention, organization, and consciousness. In D. I. Mostofsky (Ed.), *Attention: Contemporary theory and analysis* (pp. 99-124). New York: Appleton-Century-Crofts.

Hochberg, J. (1974). Higher-order stimuli and interresponse coupling in the perception of the visual world. In R. B. MacLeod & H. L. Pick (Eds.), *Perception: Essays in honor of James J. Gibson* (pp. 7-39). Ithaca: Cornell University Press.

Hochberg, J. (1998). Gestalt theory and its legacy: Organization in eye and brain, in attention and mental representation. In J. Hochberg (Ed.), *Perception and cognition at century's end* (pp. 253-306). San Diego, CA: Academic Press.

Hochberg, J. (2003). Acts of perceptual inquiry: Problems for any stimulus-based simplicity theory. *Acta Psychologica, 114,* 215-228.

Hochberg, J. (in press). Looking ahead (one glance at a time). In M. A. Peterson, B. Gillam, & H. A. Sedgwick (Eds.), *In the mind's eye: Julian Hochberg's contributions to our understanding of the perception of pictures, film, and the world.* New York: Oxford University Press.

Hochberg, J., & Brooks, V. (1970). Reading as intentional behavior. In H. Singer (Ed.), *Theoretical models and processes of reading.* Newark, DE: International Reading Association.

Hochberg, J., & Brooks, V. (1978). Film cutting and visual momentum. In J. W. Senders, D. F. Fisher, & R. A. Monty (Eds.), *Eye-movements and higher psychological functions.* Hillsdale, NJ: Erlbaum.

Hochberg, J., & Brooks, V. (1996). Movies in the mind's eye. In D. Bordwell & N. Carroll (Eds.), *Post-theory: Reconstructing film studies* (pp. 368-387). Madison, WI: University of Wisconsin Press.

Hoffman, J E., & Subramaniam, B. (1995). Saccadic eye movements and visual selective attention. *Perception & Psychophysics, 57,* 787-795.

Hollingworth, A. (2004). Constructing visual representations of natural scenes: The roles of short- and long-term visual memory. *Journal of Experimental Psychology: Human Perception and Performance, 30,* 519–537.

Intraub, H. (1997). The representation of visual scenes. *Trends in Cognitive Sciences, 1*(6), 217-222.

Jonides, J., Irwin, D. E., & Yantis, S. (1983). Failure to integrate information from successive fixations. *Science, 222,* 188.

Kevles, B. L. (1965). Slavko Vorkapich on film as a visual language and as a form of art. *Film Culture, 38,* 1-46.

Kowler, E., Anderson, E., Dosher, B., & Blaser, E. (1995). The role of attention in the programming of saccades. *Vision Research, 35*(13), 1897-1916.

Krumhansl, C., & Schenck, D. (1997). Can dance reflect the structural and expressive qualities of music? A perceptual experiment on Balnchine's choreography of Mozart's Divertimento No. 15. *Musicae Scientiae, 1,* 63-85.

Lennie, P. (1998). Single units and visual cortical organization. *Perception, 27,* 889-935.

Levin, D. T., & Simons, D. J. (1997). Failure to detect changes to attended objects in motion pictures. *Psychonomic Bulletin and Review, 4,* 501–506.

Mack, A., & Rock, I. (1998). *Inattentional blindness.* Cambridge, MA: MIT Press.

Meng, J. C., & Sedgwick, H. A. (2001). Distance perception mediated through nested contact relations among surfaces. *Perception & Psychophysics, 63,* 1-15.

McKoon, G., & Ratcliff, R. (1992). Inference during reading. *Psychological Review, 99,* 440-466.

Moore, C., & Engel, S. A. (2001) Mental models change rapidly with implicitly acquired information about the local environment: A two-tone image study. *Journal of Experimental Psychology: Human Perception and Performance, 27,* 1211-1228.

Neisser, U. (1967). *Cognitive psychology.* New York: Appleton-Century-Crofts.

Neisser, U., & Becklen, R. (1975). Selective looking: Attending to visually specified events. *Cognitive Psychology, 7,* 480-494.

Pelz, J. B., & Canosa, R. (2001). Oculomotor behavior and perceptual strategies in complex tasks. *Vision Research, 41,* 3587-3596.

Peterson, M. A. (2003). Overlapping partial configurations in object memory: An alternative solution to classic problems in perception and recognition. In M. A. Peterson & G. Rhodes (Eds.), *Perception of faces, objects, and scene: Analytic and holistic processes* (pp. 269-294). New York: Oxford University Press.

Peterson, M. A., & Grant, E. S. (2003). Memory and learning in figure-ground perception. In D. Irwin & B. Ross (Eds.), *Cognitive vision, psychology of learning, and motivation series, 42* (pp. 1-34). USA: Elsevier Science.

Pizlo, Z., & Li, Z. (in press). Solving combinatorial problems: 15-puzzle. *Memory & Cognition.*

Potter, M. C., Staub, A., & O'Connor, D. H. (2004). Pictorial and conceptual representation of glimpsed pictures. *Journal of Experimental Psychology: Human Perception and Performance, 30,* 478-489.

Scholl, B. J., & Tremoulet, P. D. (2000). Perceptual causality and animacy. *Trends in Cognitive Science, 4,* 299-309.

Simon, H. (1987). Satisficing. In J. Eatwell, M. Milgate, & P. Newman (Eds.), *The new palgrave: A dictionary of economics* (Vol. 4, pp. 243-245). New York: Macmillan.

Simons, D. (2000). Attentional capture and inattentional blindness. *Trends in Cognitive Sciences, 4,* 147-155.

Sperling, G., & Lu, Z.-L. (1998). A systems analysis of motion perception. In T. Watanabe (Ed.), *High-level motion processing* (pp. 153-183). Cambridge, MA: MIT Press.

Steinman, R., Pizlo, Z., & Pizlo, F. (2000). Phi is not beta, and why Wertheimer's discovery launched the Gestalt revolution. *Vision Research, 40,* 2257-2264.

Stross, R. (2004). Pixar's Mr. Incredible May Yet Rewrite the Apple Story, *New York Times,* Oct. 24, 2004.

Treisman, A., & Geffen, G. (1967). Selective attention: Perception or response? *Quarterly Journal of Experimental Psychology, 19,* 1-17.

Tripathy, S. P., & Cavanagh, P. (2002). The extent of crowding in peripheral vision does not scale with target size. *Vision Research, 42,* 2357–2369.

CHAPTER 2

Experimental Scrutiny of the Role of Balance in the Visual Arts

Paul Locher

A visual image such as a painting is balanced when its elements are grouped or organized in such a way that their perceptual forces compensate one another. Stated another way, pictorial balance is achieved when the elements of a painting are pitted against each other about a balance center so that the parts seem anchored and stable. The weights or forces exerted by the elements of a composition are based on conditional probabilities that derive from the interaction of physical, statistical, and organizational properties of a display and perceptual-cognitive processes within the observer. In perceptual experience, the equipoise among the elements of a painting about a balance center creates a structural framework or skeleton that helps determine the role of each element within the balance system as a whole.

In his treatise on design and expression in the visual arts, Taylor (1964) states, "a work of art is more than an artistic equilibrium; but it is always committed to being at least that. A work which achieves less is artistically incomplete. A work which is committed to achieving less has not the status of art at all" (p. 28). For centuries artists and writers of Western art have asserted, like Taylor, that balance or visual harmony is the primary design principle guiding the distribution of compositional elements within an art work (e.g., Arnheim, 1988, Bouleau, 1980, Kandinsky 1979/1926). Manuals on composition invariably contain at least one chapter that describes the importance of balance to good design and describes technical devices to create it. According to this view, balance is necessary in the visual arts because it unifies the structural elements of a visual display into a cohesive narrative statement thereby creating the essential integrity or meaning of a work. Matisse has put it this way; "In a picture, every part will be visible and will play a role conferred upon it by the artist, be it principal or secondary. All that is not useful in the picture is detrimental. A work of art must be harmonious in its entirety; for superfluous details would, in the mind of the beholder, encroach upon its essential elements" (cited in Stangos, 1994, p. 24).

This chapter presents experimental approaches used by this author and other researchers to subject to empirical scrutiny the philosophical writings about the influence of pictorial balance on the perception of visual art. A common feature of the studies described is that they use as stimuli reproductions of original compositions by renowned artists and experimentally manipulated less well-balanced versions of each. Prior to the availability of computer graphics programs, researchers had to cut paper copies of artists' compositions apart and reposition their pictorial components to experimentally manipulate balance. However, such cut-and-paste methods were often visible to subjects in the form of fine cut marks on perturbed versions (Gordon & Gardner, 1974) and often the manipulation gave an artificial look to the reconstructed images (Nodine, 1982). Researchers recognized these problems as limitations to their findings. Graphics programs have made it possible in recent years to create altered versions that are, except for the manipulated features, indistinguishable in terms of physical properties from their original counterparts. This is accomplished by repositioning one or more of the pictorial elements of a composition deemed by its artist or art experts to be an integral part of the balance structure to a location within the composition that disrupts the equipoise among its elements. No structural information is added to or deleted from (except perhaps for the artist's signature) a composition, and after an element(s) is moved, the background color and pattern are very carefully filled in. Reproductions of the original work and its altered counterpart are then generated from the same graphics program thereby ensuring that color and texture of all versions are consistent. Figure 1 presents renditions of an original painting titled "Still Life, Red Peppers on White Table" by Vallotton and two less-balanced version of the composition created by Locher (2003; Locher, Gray, & Nodine, 1996). An explanation of the changes made to the structural organization of the original to create the two perturbed versions is provided with the figure.

If, as described above, a balanced composition has a very efficient structural organization, that is, it is "visually right," then it is reasonable to expect that its organization should be salient to viewers of the work regardless of their level of sophistication with art. Support for this assertion is provided by Locher et al. (1996). They investigated how the compositional elements of a painting create the impression of balance and if perception of a composition's balance structure requires training in the visual arts. Their stimuli consisted of reproductions of 20th century paintings varying in artistic style and a reconstructed less-balanced version of each (see Figure 1). Participants included adults with no formal training in art, museum professionals, and university faculty who teach courses in design theory. On a copy of each stimulus, they indicated the location of its balance center and assigned "weights" to the pictorial elements and regions that contributed to the perceived location of the balance center. They also rated each picture for balance. Locher et al. found that design and museum professionals and individuals untrained in the visual arts were in good agreement as to the structural framework underlying the balance organization of a painting. For all participants, disruption of the balanced organization of the original compositions led to reliable shifts in the location of the perceived balance centers of the originals compared with their less-balanced perturbations. Additionally, it was observed that particular features as such were not the origin of the balance phenomenon; rather, judgments concerning the balance structure and its center were dependent upon the global integration of information across a wide area of the display field, but especially from its central region. These findings demonstrate that individuals have the ability to detect the induced structural skeleton of a painting resulting from a balanced or visually right design and that this ability does not appear to require knowledge of design principles.

Additional support for this assertion is provided by the findings of a study by Locher, Stappers, and Overbeeke (1999). Their stimuli consisted of reproductions of compositions from which one major element of each composition's balance structure was removed. The resulting unfilled space in each work was then carefully reconstructed by extending the surrounding background features. Participants, who had either no training in art or design, or were novices or experts in design, placed each element in its respective picture at the location where they believed in appears in the original. It was found that participants, regardless of level of design expertise, were in strong agreement among themselves and with the artist as to the location of each element within its pictorial field; the location chosen conformed to its compositional structure but not always to its actual location in the original. Once again, these findings demonstrate that the structural skeleton or network created by a skilled artist is visually right for the composition and that it is salient to any observer regardless of his or her level of sophistication in the visual arts.

Figure 1. Renditions of Vallotton's "Still Life, Red Peppers on White Table" (top) and a slightly (bottom left) and highly (bottom right) less well-balanced version of the original. The orientation of the red peppers and knife in the original conforms to the oval appearance of the table on which they rest. Additionally, the distribution of structural weight is relatively balanced about the composition's vertical midline. Alignment of the elements has been disrupted in the slightly altered perturbation by tilting the pepper at the left side of the table in a more up-right position and by rotating the knife 180 deg., which places its dark wood handle in the right picture field. This combination of modifications increases the perceived structural weight in the right as contrasted to the left picture field. The position of the knife in the highly perturbed version clearly disrupts the global structural organization of that composition and increases the structural weight above the horizontal midline as compared to the lower region.

Locher et al. (1999) point out, however, that their findings throw doubt on a strict interpretation of the visual rightness theory of pictorial composition. That is, there are several locations within the spatial system of a picture at which pictorial features could occur without disturbing the unitary effect of the composition. For example, pictorial balance between two elements within a field can be achieved by placing them at a variety of locations relative to a balance fulcrum. Thus, any location within a composition that conforms to its principal structural network contributes to its theme and helps make the artist's visual statement clear. Given that pictorial space contains a rich variety of elements and features, there are many ways by which the elements of a composition can be arranged within the principal balance network. It is not surprising, therefore, that the location chosen by participants for the free-standing element did not always conform to its actual location in the original, but it did conform to its overall structural framework.

Artists have known for a long time that the juxtaposition of colors within a composition is a major contributing factor to its balance or harmony. Piet Mondrian, for example, addressed the compositional problem of color balance "experimentally" in the series of paintings he produced in the 1920s and 1930s. He spent lengthy periods of time working on and revising compositions during this period to optimize structural balance within each painting. Locher, Overbeeke, and Stappers (2005) used renditions of Mondrian's paintings to examine the color-area-weight relationship among color triads in abstract displays. Specifically, they investigated the interactive contribution of the color and size of the three areas occupied by the primary colors red, yellow, and blue in adaptations of six abstract compositions by Mondrian to the perceived weight of the areas and the location of the compositions' balance centers. Thirty-six art stimuli were created by experimentally changing the colors of the three areas of each original work so that the resulting five variations and the original constituted the six possible spatial arrangements of the three colors in the three locations. Design trained and untrained participants determined the location of the balance center of each composition seen on a computer screen and rated the apparent weight or heaviness of each color area. It was found that for all participants the perceived weight of a color, especially red and yellow, varied as a function of the size of the area it occupied in the pictorial field, with red perceived as significantly heavier than yellow and blue perceived as intermediate in weight between red and yellow. Furthermore, participants perceived significant shifts in the locations of the balance centers between the originals and their altered versions demonstrating the contribution of color to pictorial balance.

Only the trained participants, however, perceived significant shifts in balance centers among the five color variations of the compositions demonstrating their superior sensitivity to color's contribution to balance structure. These findings provide empirical support for the existence of a color-area-weight-relationship among color triads in relatively complex abstract displays and its influence on color balance in abstract art.

Findings cited thus far support the view of theoreticians that the induced compositional structure of a painting resulting from a balanced design ties its visual material into a comprehensive structure that is perceptually salient to all observers. If, as suggested, a balanced composition has a very elegant and efficient organization, then it should be possible for people to discriminate between several articulation possibilities of visually right compositions, like those shown in Figure 1. Some empirical support for this assertion has appeared in the literature. Gordon and Gardner (1974) observed that college students untrained in the visual arts were able to discriminate between reproductions of abstract paintings from an experimentally modified version of each. Accuracy of detection was 62%. McManus, Cheema, and Stoker (1993) found that subjects were slightly but significantly better than expected by chance (hit rate = 55%) at distinguishing computer facsimiles of original Mondrian paintings from perturbed versions of each and that certain original Mondrians could be distinguished more easily from pseudo-Mondrians than was the case for other picture pairs. Locher et al. (1999) reported that design professionals were reliably more successful than individuals untrained in the visual arts at distinguishing between reproductions of original abstract and representational paintings by recognized artists from experimentally reconstructed less well-organized versions of each art stimulus (hit rates were 64% and 55%, respectively).

While the hit rates for originals reported in these studies reflect accuracy significantly greater than chance performance, the values are not greatly above the expected chance level of 50% (discrimination between an original an its altered version). Locher (2003) suggested that the failure of previous research to provide stronger support for the visual rightness theory may be due to the fact that no attempt was made by the researchers to determine whether the way one thinks about an artwork influences his or her ability to accurately discriminate an original composition from structurally altered versions of it. Art is capable of layers of stimulation and interpretation. In thinking about a painting, one may consider its physical and structural properties, its subject matter, or its emotional expressiveness. Intuitively it seems reasonable to expect that if the viewer of a painting focuses her attention on its structural organization, then her ability to discriminate an original artwork from a structurally less well-organized version of it would be greater than if she focused primarily on the work's emotional content. It follows from this that the stylistic quality of a painting may be expected to differentially influence a viewer's experience with it. Representational art invites one to focus attention on its pictorial content and emotional aspects whereas a viewer is forced, in a sense, to attend to the physical and structural features of abstract works, which by definition lack realistic qualities. Locher hypothesized that accuracy of detection of original compositions would be a function of the style of a painting and a viewer's way of thinking about it as determined from his verbal reactions to it.

To test this hypothesis Locher (2003) asked 100 college students untrained in the arts to discriminate between reproductions of original abstract and representational paintings by renowned artists from two experimentally manipulated less well-balanced versions of each art stimulus like those presented in Figure 1. Perturbed stimuli contained either minor or major disruptions in the original's balance structural network. Participants were asked to identify the original composition from among the three versions of each artwork. They then listed as many characteristics or properties of the chosen picture as possible that contributed to their selection of it as the original and described any reaction they had to it. These responses were used to classify participants' reactions to the pictures according to five types or levels of reaction. These were adapted from the reactions to artworks characteristic of the five stages of Parsons' (1987) cognitive developmental account of aesthetic experience. The levels reflect increasing cognitive ability to interpret the content and expressiveness of art works. Specifically, verbal responses were classified by levels as reflecting reactions to (1) the familiarity and favoritism of pictorial elements; (2) the beauty and realism of the elements; (3) expressiveness of the work's content; (4) the style and form of the composition, and (5) statements of personal taste.

Accuracy of detection of the originals was found to be a function of the style of the painting and a viewer's way of thinking about a work as determined from his or her verbal reactions to it. Specifically, hit rates for originals were highest for abstract works when participants focused on their compositional style and form and highest for representational works when their content and realism were the focus of attention. Under these conditions, hit rates for individual abstract and representational works were as high as 76% and 90%, respectively. It was also found that participants were significantly more successful in discriminating between originals and their highly altered, but not slightly altered, perturbations than expected by chance. The hit rates observed by Locher (2003) provide stronger support for the ability of observers to discriminate original compositions from their perturbations than previously reported in the literature. They also suggest that future empirical attempts to study the influence of balance on any aspect of picture perception would profit from observations of the way participants think about art. To date, this has been a neglected variable in most studies of the nature of the aesthetic experience associated with visual art stimuli.

Recording observers' eye movements as they view art stimuli varying in compositional balance has proven to be a very useful tool to verify empirically speculation concerning the influence of pictorial balance on the perceptual encoding of pictures (see Locher, 1996, for a review of this literature). For example, Nodine and McGinnis (1983) used actual variations of balanced compositions painted by recognized artists as stimuli in their study of balance perception. These included two versions of Seurat's "La Grande Jatte," an early less-balanced study and the final version that is acknowledged to epitomize the use of formal, geometric balance. Two very similar renditions of the same subject, the entombment of Christ, by Rubens and Caravaggio, were also used as stimuli. Rubens' composition was based on a study of Caravaggio's "Entombment" and is very similar in structural composition to Caravaggio's work. Subjects, who had no formal training in the arts, looked at each version of the composition for 5 s and then indicated which picture they preferred.

Nodine and McGinnis (1983) observed clear differences in attention patterns between the two versions of each painting. In the case of Seurat's works, the locations of fixations were more evenly distributed across the central region of the final more-balanced painting than was the case for the less balanced sketch version. The relatively slight variation in structural organization of the two versions of "Entombment" also produced a difference in the spatial distribution of the gaze. Specifically, participants tended to concentrate their attention about the visual center to a greater extent when viewing Rubens' versus Caravaggio's version. These differences, however, produced very little shift in the x, y location or pictorial coordinates of the paintings' visual centers and balance lines as determined from the distribution of fixations across the pictorial fields. A key finding of this study was that the distribution of fixations during the first 1.5 s of viewing were very similar to those for the full 5-s viewing period for each of the four paintings. Thus, differences in attention patterns between stimulus pairs were already present shortly after presentation of each painting. For this to be the case, participants must have detected the structural skeleton of a composition rapidly and used this information to guide visual exploration.

In another study, Nodine, Locher, and Krupinski (1993) recorder the eye movements of adults untrained in the visual arts as they evaluated for harmony and beauty reproductions of paintings by renowned artists, such as Seurat, Cezanne, and Mondrian, and an experimentally manipulated more- or less-balanced balanced version of each. The effects of balance on visual exploration of the compositions were examined by determining how much area (percentage) of each artwork was covered by visual exploration. Nodine et al. found that exploration of a composition was indeed influenced by the balance manipulations. Specifically, average coverage of the picture field was 72% for the full set of balanced compositions versus 53% for their less-balanced counterparts. This finding demonstrates that balanced compositions "engage" viewers to a greater degree than do less-balanced works, at least in terms of perceptual analysis. Furthermore, the spatial distribution of fixations over the originals reflected a greater interplay between the eyes and pictorial elements that created the structural skeletons of balanced compositions. On the other hand, the structural organization of poorly balanced compositions was associated with less-well organized scanning of key pictorial elements.

More recently, Locher et al. (1996) recorded the fixation patterns of adults untrained in the visual arts as they examined reproductions of 20th century paintings varying in artistic style and a less-balanced version of each. The participants' task was to determine the location of the balance center of each composition by examining the arrangement of its pictorial elements and considering the contribution each element made to the overall structural organization. The scanning pattern for each observer for each stimulus was quantified by superimposing a 4 × 4 grid over it and measuring the percentage of total fixation time (gaze density) in each cell location. Comparisons of the gaze density distributions between the originals and their altered version revealed that the balance structure of original representational and abstract compositions resulted in different regions of the original and perturbed versions being visually explored.

As mentioned above, a major limitation of experimental aesthetics research, including eye movement investigations, is that researchers have not studied the relationship between the way observers think about an artwork as they explore it. Clearly, knowing how individuals explore *and* think about a picture during an aesthetic episode would provide greater insights into the perceptual-cognitive processes involved in an encounter with art stimuli than would information concerning just one of these factors. Until very recently researchers have not been able to study this relationship because eye-movement recording systems required an observer's head to be immobile to maintain the system's calibration. This prevented observers from talking about stimuli as they viewed them. The most recent study from our laboratory (Locher, Nodine, & Krupinski, manuscript submitted) overcame this limitation by using an eye-movement recording system that enabled us to simultaneously monitor observers' fixation patterns and their verbal reactions as they viewed artworks and evaluated them for pleasure. The art stimuli consisted of reproductions of visually right paintings by renowned artists such as Rembrandt, Bruegel, Matisse, and Giotto. Specifically, we examined the relationship across the time course of exploration among participants' verbal reactions to the paintings, characterized along a qualitative continuum of perceptual-cognitive processes (adapted from Locher, 2003, as described above), their fixation patterns, and the compositional organization of the artworks.

We (Locher et al., manuscript submitted) anticipated that observers would attend to a greater extent to major than to minor elements of the structural skeletons of the compositions. This necessitated that we identify for purposes of analyses the major compositional elements of each art stimulus employed. To do this, we asked individuals sophisticated in the visual arts to specify the five regions of each composition that made the greatest contribution to the perceptual and semantic meaning of the work. There was very strong agreement among the experts concerning the principal pictorial components of each work's structural skeleton. It was found that participants concentrated their gaze on these pictorial elements; other areas received little or no exploration. This was the case for the entire time course of exploration.

Analyses of participants' verbal responses revealed that their first reactions to the works did not reflect attention to single pictorial elements or to the compositions' beauty or realism, nor did they reflect personal taste. Rather, participants' initial reactions to a work, which occurred during the first 6 s of viewing, was to a group of elements perceived as a compositional unit, to the expressiveness of the whole composition, or to its style and form (20%, 41%, and 25%, respectively, of all reactions). This high occurrence of initial reactions based on information encoded from large areas of the pictorial field suggests that perception of the art stimuli began at a holistic or global level of analysis. Several participants were able to say almost immediately upon looking at a work that they had never seen it before. This type of response suggests that observers had early access to structural information from areas of the pictorial field which were not directly fixated. Following the initial scanning period, participants' verbal responses indicate that they continued to react to compositional units of each work, to its expressiveness, or to its style and form (28%, 26%, and 30%, respectively, of all reactions). Reactions to the expressiveness of the compositions were less frequent (26%) after the initial global response whereas such reactions accounted for 41% of participants' first impression of the composition. Finally, informal analysis of the data revealed a strong relationship between the pictorial field under scrutiny and the content of participants' verbal responses to the work.

Taken together, results of the studies described above demonstrate the salience of pictorial balance and its influence on the perception of paintings. The perceptual salience of balance has lead artists and philosophers interested in the art experience to speculate that the induced structure resulting from a balanced configuration of a painting hits the viewer's eye first, even before he or she becomes aware of its subject matter (e.g., Arnheim, 1974). This view suggests that vision is sensitive to the balanced configuration of elements in a pictorial field, and that viewers can detect a global percept of balance rapidly and effortlessly regardless of their background in the visual arts. The finding by Locher et al. (manuscript submitted) that observers' initial reactions to paintings reflected global or holistic properties of the compositions supports this assertion. Direct evidence that balance can be detected "at first glance" has been provided by a tachistoscopic study conducted by Locher and Nagy (1996). Their stimuli consisted of color and black-and-white reproductions of structurally balanced paintings and one or more reconstructed less-balanced versions of each artwork. Art-trained and untrained individuals rated the compositions for balance after presentation durations that permitted either a single glance at each image (100-ms tachistoscopic presentation) or multiple fixations directed to it for 5 s.

Locher and Nagy (1996) found that both naïve and sophisticated participants were able to reliably discriminate the less balanced from the more balanced versions of the pictures with a single glance at each. Participants' assessment of a composition's balance based on stimulus information encoded with one fixation did not significantly change when exposure duration permitted multiple fixations of that composition. These findings support the view that the visual processing of balance begins at a holistic or global level during which the overall pattern variation (i.e., balance) is detected automatically or preattentively. This suggests that the visual system is sensitive to balance at the neural level of processing and may be "hard-wired" to respond to balance.

A recent study by Vartanian and Goel (2004) provide some preliminary evidence to support this claim. They coupled the experimental manipulation of pictorial balance with the use of neuroimaging techniques to determine the neuroanatomical correlates of preference for paintings. The researchers created perturbed versions of 20 abstract and 20 representational paintings (along with a filtered version of each) using the same procedure as that employed by Locher et al. (1996) described above. The neural activation of adults was recorded using functional MRI as they rated each picture for preference on a 4-point scale. Of importance to the present discussion was Vartanian and Goel's finding of significant differential activation in the right lingual gyrus (BA 18) between trials involving the original compositions and those during which participants rated their less balanced altered versions. According to the researchers, activation in this area of the brain has been associated with processing pictures that vary in emotional valence and reward value. These findings suggest that the visual system is differentially sensitive to the structural organization of balanced paintings as contrasted with that of less-balanced versions of each. They conform to and support the widely held belief mentioned above that the induced structure resulting from the balanced configuration of a painting hits the viewer's eye first, even before he or she becomes aware of its subject matter.

In summary, the research findings presented above demonstrate the valuable contribution that the scientific study of balance perception has made to theoretical aesthetics in general and to notions of balance and art composition in particular. Clearly, the techniques described above have great potential to reveal the perceptual/cognitive processes that occur during an aesthetic episode with visual art.

REFERENCES

Arnheim, R. (1974). *Art and visual perception*. Berkeley, CA: University of California Press.

Arnheim, R. (1988). *The power of the center*. Berkeley, CA: University of California Press.

Bouleau, C. (1980). *The painter's secret geometry*. New York: Hacker Books.

Gordon, I., & Gardner, C. (1974). Responses to altered pictures. *British Journal of Psychology, 65*, 243-251.

Kandinsky, V. (1979). *Point and line to plane* (Dearstyne, H., Rebay, H., Trans.). New York: Dover (original work published in 1926).

Locher, P. (1996). The contribution of eye-movement research to an understanding of the nature of pictorial balance perception: A review of the literature. *Empirical Studies of the Arts, 14*, 143-163.

Locher, P. (2003). An empirical investigation of the visual rightness theory of picture perception. *Acta Psychologica, 114*, 147-164.

Locher, P., Gray, S., & Nodine, C. (1996). The structural framework of pictorial balance. *Perception, 25,* 1419-1436.

Locher, P., & Nagy, Y. (1996). Vision spontaneously establishes the percept of pictorial balance. *Empirical Studies of the Arts, 14,* 17-31.

Locher, P., Nodine, C., & Krupinski, E. (manuscript submitted). *Compositional design, visual scanning and observer reactions across the time course of an aesthetic episode with visual art.*

Locher, P., Overbeeke, C., & Stappers, P. (2005). Spatial balance of color triads in the abstract art of Piet Mondrian. *Perception, 34,* 169-189.

Locher, P., Stappers, P., & Overbeeke, C. (1999). The role of balance as an organizing principle underlying adults' compositional strategies for creating visual displays. *Acta Psychologica, 99,* 141-161.

McManus, I., Cheema, B., & Stoker, J. (1993). The aesthetics of composition: A study of Mondrian. *Empirical Studies of the Arts, 11,* 83-94.

Nodine, C. (1982). Compositional design as a perceptual determinant of aesthetic judgment. *Review of Research in Visual Arts Education, 15,* 43-54.

Nodine, C., Locher, P., & Krupinski, E. (1993). The role of formal art training on the perception and aesthetic evaluation of art compositions. *Leonardo, 26,* 219-227.

Nodine C., & McGinnis, J. (1983). Artistic style, compositional design, and visual scanning. *Visual Arts Research, 12,* 1-9.

Parsons, M. (1987). *How we understand art: A cognitive developmental account of aesthetic experience.* Cambridge: Cambridge University Press.

Stangos, N. (1994). *Concepts of modern art: From Fauvism to Postmodernism.* London: Thames & Hudson Ltd.

Taylor, J. (1964). *Design and expression in the visual arts.* New York: Dover.

Vartanian, O., & Goel, V. (2004). Neuroanatomical correlates of aesthetic preference for paintings. *Cognitive Neuroscience and Neuropsychology, 15,* 893-897.

CHAPTER 3

The Mere Exposure Effect and Aesthetic Preference

James E. Cutting

Canons contain the core works of many cultural pursuits—art, architecture, sculpture, theater, dance, poetry, literature, and film. These works have been the focus of what is taught, and they are among the most common objects of our aesthetic experience. To be sure, in the 1980s and particularly in the United States, canons were objects of intense controversy, and since then arts academics have generally moved toward more global and contemporary concerns. But courses on canonical Western art still thrive, and in art museums canonical images are seen by larger numbers of people than ever before. For these and many other reasons canons are worthy of considerable study. In this chapter I focus on the particular canon of French Impressionist art.

Why French Impressionism? First, it is modern. This has the useful consequence that documentation of its formation and maintenance are more available than for the canons of earlier periods. Classical Greek, Gothic, and even Renaissance and Baroque canons, for example, have very little documentation written at the time their works were wrought. Second, Impressionism is sufficiently old. By this I mean it is relatively crystallized, and that there is little change going on within it, at least in terms of the artworks' reproduction in texts. Virtually the entire Impressionist corpus is known and owned by museums or in private hands. Third, of all schools of art Impressionism may be the most popular. This fact may have started in reaction to some official scorn cast on it in the 1870s and beyond, and in the amplification of that apparent scorn in the retelling of the story of Impressionism by legions of twentieth century writers. It also seems likely that the general accessibility and color of Impressionist works have pleased many. The images appear easy to "understand." They portray the everyday. No heritage of iconography—classical or Biblical—seems necessary to enjoy them. Moreover, and perhaps for these reasons, French Impressionist paintings have commanded high sales prices at art auctions throughout the twentieth century, and they were the focus of many of the largest and best-attended art exhibitions in the 1980s and 1990s. All of this hoopla for Impressionism over the years has also brought it very close to popular culture, and made it generally known by the public. Finally, although undeniably French, Impressionism has a distinctively American cachet. Many of those with the largest collections of Impressionist works were American. Indeed, France and the Musée d'Orsay notwithstanding, there are more Impressionist paintings in museums in the United States than anywhere else. Impressionist works are embedded within contemporary American culture. They also forge strong ties with a Europe of the nineteenth century, where modernism began.

MERE EXPOSURE AND CULTURE

The central argument in this chapter is that the laboratory phenomenon *mere exposure* (Zajonc, 1968, 1980) can be generalized to our broader culture in important ways. I claim it part of the fabric of establishing and maintaining an artistic canon. Through repeated occurrences of objects and events in our lives, we acquire information and attitudes, and we do so nonconsciously. This process helps shape our preferences, even our aesthetic preferences. It is a biologically sensible mechanism and it works for many kinds of creatures. For example, by having an animal exposed to a home environment, it will grow to like it, feel comfortable in it, and generally prefer it to strange environments. Such a mechanism keeps toddlers and the young of many species nearby their caregivers. Moreover, as human beings grow up, they enlarge upon the familiarities of their domiciles to include the familiarities of the neighborhoods, and eventually for those of their culture, both broadly and narrowly defined.

Mere exposure is a phenomenon related to *implicit learning* (see Seamon et al., 1995). That is, we are unaware that it is happening, but the focus of this learning is deeply connected to affect. Consider pictures. From childhood through college and throughout adulthood, we are exposed to a myriad of images. Only a few of these concern art and most are representations of art, but occasionally as during a museum visit we may see the artwork itself. But whether the image is an artwork or not, we often do not remember it, much less where we saw it. We often do not even recognize it when we see it again. Nonetheless, its trace is left within us. It is easily demonstrated that our history with it can influence our future judgments. Such effects result from simply being in a culture populated with cultural artifacts (see Zajonc, 1970).

Laboratory evidence suggests that what we are exposed to, and then prefer, can be quite meaningless (see Bornstein, 1989)—line drawings, polygons, ideographs, nonsense words or syllables, sounds. But they can also be meaningful—photographs of objects or people, or even music (Szpunar, Schellenberg, & Pliner, 2004). What about paintings? Laboratory results have been mixed. Berlyne (1970) found mere exposure effects for abstract paintings, but then research and discussion was dragged in a different direction. Berlyne also found an interaction that complex paintings were preferred over simpler ones, which fit better with his theoretical views (Berlyne, 1971). Zajonc, Shaver, Tavris, and Van Kreveld (1972) found the reverse effect, and Brickman, Redfield, Harrison, and Crandall (1972) found both effects depending on initial responses, favorable or unfavorable. But as studies relying on laboratory exposure, these research efforts did not explore the everyday exposure of individuals to artwork. The purpose of this research was to assess effects of mere exposure measured as it might occur across many years.

I should also note that much of the more recent research on mere exposure has allied itself methodologically with subliminal perception. Stimuli are presented extremely briefly, but then masked such that observers cannot overtly report what they have seen, have been shown to prime other responses (e.g., Kunst-Wilson & Zajonc, 1980; Monahan, Murphy, & Zajonc, 2000; Moreland & Zajonc, 1977; Seamon, Brody, & Kauff, 1983). These results are interesting and important, but from my perspective subliminal perception is a laboratory phenomenon used to mimic other processes in real life—in particular, those of inattention and forgetting over the long haul. Thus, in this context then, I am less interested in alternative theories that may explain mere subliminal exposure (e.g., Bonanno & Stilling, 1986; Klinger & Greenwald, 1994; Smith, 1998; Winkielman, Zajonc, & Schwarz, 1997; Zajonc, 2001) than in the more general phenomenon.

THE IMAGES

Distel (1994) organized a celebration for the centennial of the death of Gustave Caillebotte (1848-1894), a minor Impressionist artist and a collector of his better-known colleagues works. In an appendix to her book Distel presented a large number of small, black-and-white images of those works. In part because Caillebotte had fascinated me for well over a decade, and because I had recognized many but not all of these images, I decided that they would form half the basis of my studies (Cutting, 2003). I used 66 of the images in his collection and bequest to the State of France as stimuli—2 Caillebottes, 5 Cézannes, 8 Degas, 4 Manets, 16 Monets, 14 Pissarros, 9 Renoirs, and 8 Sisleys. I then sought as many high-quality reproductions of these images as I could find, and digitized the best of them (51 in color). I then matched each of these images to another by the same artist, in generally the same style, from roughly the same period, and with the same general subject matter. These second 66 images were selected from the same general sources, screened for reproduction quality in the same way, and digitized. Color images were paired with colored images, and black-and-white with black-and-white. They were chosen generally without regard for their location, although a good many were in the Musée d'Orsay, as with the bulk of Caillebotte's collection. After selecting the images, a research assistant and I began to consult all the relevant books we could find in the Cornell University libraries. Our intent was to record every occurrence of each image in Cornell's more than seven million volumes. Carrying an electronic notebook with us, we created and then continually updated 132 separate databases.

Several constraints governed the tallies. Multiple copies of the same book were not considered, although a foreign language book and its English-language translation were counted separately, as well as different editions of the same book. In a given book occasionally there would be both a full image and a detail of it. Both were counted, with the idea that if the author felt it important enough to show the image twice, or more, it should be counted each time it or a part of it occurred. We searched over 6000 books in 20 months in at least 200 library visits. Totals were accumulated each month and compared with those of previous months. Correlations were always extremely high. Thus, however many books we missed while assembling our databases, the counts of images in them would not change the relative patterns. In all, we located over 4000 reproductions of the 132 images in nearly 1000 different books published between 1901 and 2002. The frequencies of occurrence across all images ranged from 2 to 278. The mean was 31.5, the median 16. Counts varied widely—7 images occurred more than 100 times, 41 fewer than 10 times, with the rest in between. Thus, across the 132 images there was a clear gradation from the core canon of Impressionism to its base corpus.

An important issue arises about the utility of these databases and image frequencies. How representative are the relative occurrences of these 132 images to what would be more broadly available in our culture? I approximated an answer in two ways. First, I searched the online catalog of the Cornell libraries for all occurrences of the last name of each 8 artists used by keyword, inspected the results for relevancy (e.g., excluding Russian texts with "monet" in the title; *monet* is the Russian word for money), and recorded the number. I did the same in the Bibliography of the History of Art, a professional online database of books and articles published since 1973. The correlation between the frequency of relevant titles at Cornell and in the BHA was very high (r = .97). Thus, the holdings at Cornell on these artists and the broader scholarly work done on them in the last third of the twentieth century are quite tightly related. But are the images in the books representative? Second, I created an index of obtained versus expected values for the images of each painter within the Cornell system. For each artist its numerator was the total number of books in which any of these images appeared. Its denominator was the total number of books that were accessed using the artist's name as a keyword plus those accessed using either the keywords "Impressionism" or "Impressionist." The logic of the index is that, if the artist's works among these stimuli were central to his *oeuvre*, one might reasonably expect that at least one of those in the sample would appear in every book on the painter and in every book on Impressionism generally. Thus, index values should be near 1.0. The fact that the mean indices for these seven artists were a bit higher (1.15), suggests that these stimuli formed a suitable and representative sample of the Impressionist canon.

A few statistics across the image set are important. First, images from the Caillebotte collection did not appear with any reliably different frequency than their matched pairs. Means were 33 and 30, respectively. Second, Musée d'Orsay images *did* appear more often than those elsewhere. Means were 43 and 18, respectively. This was not a surprise. The *Musées nationaux de France* have been thorough in promoting their art for a long time. Finally, paintings and pastels that reside in any museum—the Orsay or elsewhere—appeared reliably more often than those in private collections, 37 vs. 6, respectively. This was not a surprise either. Most artworks in private collections are seldom reproduced, and in another larger database I found the median to be zero.

MERE EXPOSURE AS A FUNCTION OF PUBLICATION FREQUENCY

Various pairs of these images were presented for a few seconds across several studies to undergraduates (n = 278), older adults (mean age = 46; n = 19), and children (ages 6 to 10; n = 66). Their order in sequence was different across studies and for each it was random with several constraints. Images by the same artist could not follow one another. They were balanced left and right across experiments by previous ownership (Caillebotte or not), and by location (Orsay or not). All viewers were asked which image, that presented on the left or right of each pair, they liked better. Undergraduates and older adults were also asked if they recognized either of the images in each pair while making the preference judgment. They also filled out a brief questionnaire indicating how often they went to museums each year, if they had ever been to the Musée d'Orsay, and for undergraduates whether they had taken an art history course or not. Only 17% had.

The results divide a number of ways. First consider claims of recognition. Undergraduate viewers recognized less than 3% of the images. The older adults did a bit better, recognizing 19%, but they saw a different and more frequently reproduced set. Multiple regression showed that the number of images viewers claimed to recognize was correlated with how often they went to museums, and if they had been to the Musée d'Orsay. However, once these were factored out for the undergraduates, there was no effect of how many art history courses they had taken. The Caillebotte images were not recognized with any reliably different frequency than their matched pair. In addition, those in the Musée d'Orsay were not recognized more often than those elsewhere. Finally, those images in museums *were* recognized a bit more often—3.3 vs. 1.5% for the undergraduates. All of the images presented to the older adults were from museums.

Notice, I make no assumption that observers' responses necessarily represent the true recognition of a particular painting or pastel. There would be no way to verify these claims, except perhaps for those who had taken art history courses. Nonetheless, there are some interesting trends. For example, against the mean backdrop recognition of less than 3%, the undergraduates claimed to recognize the seven images of Degas dancers at a mean rate of 9%. Such results, I would claim, are examples of generic recognition—evidence that an individual had seen some Degas-like dancers before. For a laboratory analog see Monahan et al. (2000). Given that Degas produced 600 pastels and paintings of dancers perhaps this is not entirely surprising.

Consider next the preferences. First, the undergraduates, the older adults, and the children expressed no preference for the Caillebotte images, choosing them 48, 51, and 50% of the time, respectively. Thus, there is nothing unusual in this context about the paintings and pastels in the Caillebotte collection. Second, as might be expected adults viewers did prefer somewhat the images in the Musée d'Orsay. Undergraduates and adults selected them 54 and 52% of the time, respectively, when one was paired against a non-Orsay image. Nonetheless, when frequency differences were factored out, there was not a reliable preference for Orsay images in either group. Thus, what distinguishes this selection of Orsay holdings is only that its images appear more often.

Most importantly, however, are the data for image preference by frequency of publication in my databases. Over all pairs, undergraduate and adult viewers preferred the more frequently occurring image of each pair on 59% of all trials. This highly reliable effect is about the size of many mere exposure effects in the literature (e.g., Seamon & Delgado, 1999). Indeed, for the undergraduates 43 more frequent images of 64 pairs were preferred (with 2 ties), and for adults 17 of 25 were preferred. Moreover, unlike the recognition results this effect was uniform across all types of observers. Among undergraduates, it occurred equally for those who never had an art history course, and those who had taken at least one such course. Among all viewers it occurred for those not visiting a museum in the past year, those visiting once, and those visiting more than once; and it occurred equally for those not visiting and visiting the Musée d'Orsay. Moreover, when differences in recognition rates are compared with preferences for each of the 66 images pairs, there is no reliable correlation.

As importantly, children showed no preference for the more frequent image of each pair—51 vs. 49%. Overall preferences for more frequent images were 49, 47, 53, and 56%, respectively, for the 6, 7, 8, and 9-year-olds—a tantalizing trend—but variance was large and this pattern of increase was not reliable. Moreover, the children's results for the images pairs were uncorrelated with those of the undergraduates and the adults. Thus, what governed the adult preferences is not operative in the preferences of children. These are important null results. Although elementary school children may have seen a few Impressionist paintings before, they lack the broad cultural exposure to Impressionist art that would systematically match them to what adults have experienced. What drives all of these preference results, at least statistically, would appear to be frequency of appearance. But consider some other possibilities.

COMPLEXITY AND PREFERENCE

Bornstein (1989) reviewed the literature on complexity and preference in laboratory experiments on mere exposure. He found that six of nine published studies found stronger mere exposure effects for complex than simple stimuli, but more relevant are those using art works as stimuli. As noted earlier the results of Berlyne (1970), Zajonc et al. (1972), and Brickman et al. (1972) were mixed. Thus, it seemed worthwhile to pursue the idea with these stimuli. Since complexity cannot be defined with rigor in most domains (Goodman, 1972), I let the observers define it for themselves. In a new study (Cutting, 2003), I asked 112 undergraduates to serve as viewers of a sequence of individually presented stimuli, all 132 in this set. Only 17% of the students had taken an art history course and 7% had been to the Musée d'Orsay. Viewers were asked to make a judgment about which image was more complex. Complexity judgments were not correlated with preferences or claims of recognition. Inspecting the judgments for each pair suggests that viewers were simply counting things, often people or trees, in the pictures. Thus, they thought that images with more elements were more complex—neither a surprising nor a particularly interesting result.

PROTOTYPICALITY AND PREFERENCE

One account for the preference results might be that viewers, when faced with making preference judgments, were comparing images on the basis of what they thought were the most representative (prototypical) Impressionist paintings. Indeed, this has been a hotly debated topic in the psychology and art literature (see Boselie, 1991, 1996; Farkas, 2002; Hekkert & Snelders, 1995; Martindale, 1996; Martindale, Moore, & West, 1988). Thus, another study was designed to address this issue (Cutting, 2003). Twenty-one undergraduates in a seminar on visual perception viewed a PowerPoint sequence of 138 images—all 132 used previously, plus 6 more by Gustave Caillebotte. These images were presented singly and viewers rated them on a 1-to-7 scale as to how representative each was of Impressionist paintings generally, with 7 being the most prototypical. Farkas (2002) called these *style-typical* judgments. Presentation order was again haphazard with the constraints that images by the same artist could not follow one another.

Perhaps surprisingly, prototypicality judgments were *not* correlated with experimental variables of previous interest—either the frequencies of the images or the recognition rates. The differences in prototypicality judgments within a pair were also not correlated with preferences or with complexity judgments. Moreover, all of this is true whether the correlations are calculated in a linear or nonlinear fashion (the latter would be suggested from the work of Berlyne, 1971; see also Martindale et al., 1988). Some have suggested that familiarity ought to be controlled for when assessing prototypicality (for example, Boselie, 1996). If recognition is used as a metric for familiarity then one might be able to factor out this effect using the differences in recognition for the images in each pair. However, once these differences are considered, the residual correlation of preference rates and the differences in proto-typicality across pairs is still not reliable. Given the methodology used here it is not clear how these results should be taken with respect to Martindale's preference-for-prototypes theory (e.g., Martindale, 1990, 1996; Martindale et al., 1988), but they are clearly not a ringing endorsement.

Nonetheless, there were some striking prototypicality effects by painter. Most prototypical were the 16 images by Sisley (mean rating = 5.3). This is interesting because he is clearly the least major of the seven "major" impressionists by any count of images that appear in Impressionist books. Clustered next and together were the 32 works of Monet (5.0), the 28 of Pissarro (4.9), and the 18 of Renoir (5.0), with the first two reliably different than Sisley. Clustered next, and reliably below these four, were the 16 works of Degas (4.6) and 10 of Cézanne (4.2). Finally, well below these were the 8 of Manet (2.8) and the 10 of Caillebotte (2.8). Interestingly, Cézanne and Manet are often described as not really being Impressionist painters. Cézanne's most important works are later than the period of the 1870s and 1880s—the heyday of Impressionism—and Manet's were earlier. In addition, at the time of the Impressionist exhibitions Caillebotte's work was often favorably reviewed when that of the others was not. Finally, Degas never painted outdoors, which certainly influenced the content of his works, and which then may have influenced judgments.

Other classifications of images also show some interesting differ-ences. Of this set of 138 images, 90 were landscapes, 44 were portraits (often of groups and often outside), and 4 were still lifes. Mean ratings for landscapes (5.0) was reliably higher than those for portraits (4.1) and still lifes (3.8). The latter two did not differ. It should be noted that, among these images and throughout their *oeuvres*, Sisley painted only landscapes, Pissarro mostly landscapes, Renoir mostly portraits, and Degas almost exclusively portraits.

OVERVIEW

Undergraduates and older adults viewers generally liked the images in each pair that were more frequently published across the twentieth century. Children, on the other hand, did not. Viewers recognized few of these Impressionist images—undergraduates less than 3%. Low recognition rates are requisite for laboratory demonstrations of mere exposure (Kunst-Wilson & Zajonc, 1980). Recognition rates were not related to any frequency counts. Moreover, they were not related preferences either, another requisite for laboratory demonstrations of mere exposure. This lack of relation shows, yet again, that our knowledge of what we overtly know, sometimes called explicit memory, is dissociable from our broader experience, which even against our knowledge affects our behavior, our preferences, and our desires.

Several conclusions can also be made about various collections. First, images from the Caillebotte collection were neither preferred more often nor recognized more often than those matched to them. It has often been said that Caillebotte had extraordinary taste in amassing his collection. This is no doubt true, but at least for contemporary viewers that taste did not outstrip that of the many collectors involved in amassing the collections from which the matched images were chosen. Second, the Musée d'Orsay holdings did occur more often in this sample. This is not a surprise. A systematic culling of images from the Orsay, which arguably owns one sixth of all Impressionist paintings publicly available, would form the bulk of the core of the canon. However, at least with respect to this corpus of images and these viewers, the Orsay's holdings are neither preferred more often nor recognized more often than other images matched to their frequencies of occurrence. Third, art in private collections is not in the Impressionist canon. These images occur less often in the literature; they are less frequently recognized; and, lacking exposure, they are preferred less.

Together, all of these trends support the idea that it is not where an image is, or who bought it, but how often it appears, that affects public appreciation. Any artwork in a prized location—such as in the Musée d'Orsay—has a great advantage over other artworks, but systematic promotion by other museums and authors can overcome this advantage.

QUALITY AND PREFERENCE

There is, of course, the thorny issue of quality. Perhaps the paintings that are reproduced more often are simply "better" paintings. Perhaps people simply respond to quality in art. This has been an idea popular since Immanuel Kant (1794/1952), and more recently both outside (Feynman, 1985; Pirsig, 1974) and within art history (Rosenberg, 1967; Woodford, 1983). But it is not likely to be true (see Bal & Bryson, 1991; Cheetham, 2002; Moxey, 1994). In yet another experiment (Cutting, 2003) I presented these images to students in my undergraduate course on perception, randomly interspersed in my PowerPoint presentations on various scientific topics such as the cochlear microphonic, stereopsis, and sensory substitution. I presented—as nonsequitors—102 of these images (all of those in color), about 12 per lecture, for a few seconds each and without comment. Across two dozen lectures I presented singly the images that were less frequent in the literature in each pair a total of four times. I presented the more frequent member only once. Still later I presented the images together in pairs, and found that I had reversed the students' preferences. That is, this group now liked slightly better the images that they had seen in class more often. Thus, what governs these judgments is not quality, but how often the images have been seen before.

MERE EXPOSURE AS A MEDIATOR OF CANON MAINTENANCE

How might mere exposure work within a culture for art? How might it affect an artistic canon, its reception, and its maintenance? All of us are members of a culture, and we all absorb what is around us. As visual beings, we digest images voraciously even without noticing. A very small proportion of the images we see are from the Impressionist corpus and canon. Nonetheless, we respond to their occurrences in our future interactions with Impressionism. We like the ones we've seen before, and particularly those we may have seen many times.

We find these images everywhere. Impressionist paintings are not only in galleries, but also in books and on textbook covers, calendars, posters, coasters, tee shirts, and towels, and one can find them readily on the Internet. Mere exposure dictates that every occurrence can matter, particularly when an image is otherwise rare. Museum curators ought to note this. Museums already do a reasonable job at promoting their collections, but placing images everywhere (and without cost to the public) will go a long way towards ramifying the importance of their collections as received by the broader public. But the competition is stiff; everyone seems to be doing it. Currently, the correlation of what's in the literature and what's on the Internet is not high. If this difference is maintained, the canons of the future could change in directions independent of goals and interests of art professionals.

CONCLUSION

Artistic canons are promoted and maintained by a diffuse but continual broadcast of images to the public by museums, authors, and publishers. The repeated presentation of images to the public without direct awareness or memory makes mere exposure a prime vehicle for canon maintenance. Tacitly and incrementally over time, it teaches the public to like the images, to prefer them, eventually to recognize them as part of the canon, and to want to see them again. In turn, it seems likely that this implicit education also reinforces the choices made by professionals in what they present to that public. The public's appreciation rewards museums, scholars, and the publishing industry by demonstrating an interested and responsive audience.

In this manner, mere exposure cyclically reinforces canons across generations of authors and curators on the one hand, and museum goers and book buyers on the other. Although it may be tacit, I do not think this is necessarily a subversive trend, nor one to be denigrated. I claim it is part of the same force that binds a culture. It is part of our human nature, built on an evolutionary substrate that makes very good sense. It helps ensure steadiness in culture more generally, and relative constancy in artistic canons more particularly.

REFERENCES

Bal, M., & Bryson, N. (1991). Semiotics and art history. *Art Bulletin, 73*, 174-208.

Berlyne, D. E. (1970). Novelty, complexity, and hedonic value. *Perception & Psychophysics, 8*, 279-286.

Berlyne, D. E. (1971). *Esthetics and psychobiology*. New York: Appleton-Century-Crofts.

Bonanno, G. A., & Stilling, N. A. (1986). Preference, familiarity, and recognition after repeated brief exposure to random geometric shapes. *American Journal of Psychology, 99*, 403-415.

Bornstein, R. (1989). Exposure and affect: Overview and meta-analysis of research, 1968-1987. *Psychological Bulletin, 106*, 265-289.

Boselie, F. (1991). Against prototypicality as a central concept in aesthetics. *Empirical Studies in the Arts, 9*, 65-73.

Boselie, F. (1996). Prototypicality revisited: A rejoinder to Hekkert and Snelders. *Empirical Studies of the Arts, 14*, 99-104.

Brickman, P., Redfield, J., Harrison, A. A., & Crandall, R. (1972). Drive and predisposition as factors in the attitudinal effects of mere exposure. *Journal of Experimental Social Psychology, 8*, 31-44.

Cheetham, M. A. (2002). *Kant, art, and art history*. Cambridge, UK: Cambridge University Press.

Cutting, J. E. (2003). Gustave Caillebotte, French Impressionism, and mere exposure. *Psychonomic Bulletin & Review, 10*, 319-343.

Distel, A., director (1994). *Gustave Caillebotte: 1848-1894*. Paris: Réunion des Musées Nationaux.

Farkas, A. (2002). Prototypicality-effect in Surrealist paintings. *Empirical Studies of the Arts, 20*, 127-136.

Feynman, R. (1985). *"Surely you're joking, Mr. Feynman:" Adventures of a curious character*. New York: Norton.

Goodman, N. (1972). *Problems and projects*. Indianapolis, IN: Bobbs-Merrill.

Hekkert, P., & Snelders, H. M. J. J. (1995). Prototypicality as an explanatory concept in aesthetics. *Empirical Studies in the Arts, 13,* 149-160.

Kant, I. (1794/1952). *Critique of aesthetic judgment.* (J. Meredith, trans.) Oxford, UK: Clarendon Press.

Klinger, M. R., & Greenwald, A. (1994). Preferences need no inferences? The cognitive basis of unconscious mere exposure effects. In P. M. Neidenthal & S. Kitayama (Eds.), *The heart's eye: Emotional influences in perception and attention* (pp. 67-85). San Diego: Academic Press.

Kunst-Wilson, W. R., & Zajonc, R. B. (1980). Affective discrimination of stimuli that cannot be recognized. *Science, 207,* 557-558.

Martindale, C. (1990). *The clockwork muse: The predictability of artistic change.* New York: Basic Books.

Martindale, C. (1996). A note on the relationship between prototypicality and preference. *Empirical Studies of the Arts, 14,* 109-113.

Martindale, C., Moore, K., & West, A. (1988). Relationship of preference judgments to typicality, novelty, and mere exposure. *Empirical Studies in the Arts, 6,* 79-96.

Monahan, J. L., Murphy, S. T., & Zajonc, R. B. (2000). Subliminal mere exposure: Specific, general, and diffuse effects. *Psychological Science, 11,* 462-466.

Moreland, R. L., & Zajonc, R. B. (1977). Is stimulus recognition a necessary condition for the occurrence of exposure effects? *Journal of Social and Personality Psychology, 35,* 191-199.

Moxey, K. (1994). *The practice of theory: Poststructuralism, cultural politics, and art history.* Ithaca, NY: Cornell University Press.

Pirsig, R. (1974). *Zen and the art of motorcycle maintenance.* New York: Morrow.

Rosenberg, J. (1967). *On quality in art: Criteria of excellence, past and present.* Princeton, NJ: Princeton University Press.

Seamon, J. G., Brody, N., & Kauff, D. M. (1983). Affective discrimination of stimuli that are not recognized: II. Effect of delay between study and test. *Bulletin of the Psychonomic Society, 21,* 544-555.

Seamon, J. G., & Delgado, M. R. (1999). Recognition memory and affective preference for depth-rotated solid objects: Part-based structural descriptions may underlie the mere exposure effect. *Visual Cognition, 6,* 145-164.

Seamon, J. G., Williams, P. C., Crowley, M. J., Kim, I. J., Langer, S. A., Orne, P. J., & Wishengrad, D. L. (1995). The mere exposure effect is based on implicit memory: Effects of stimulus type, encoding conditions, and number of exposures on recognition and affects judgments. *Journal of Experimental Psychology: Learning, Memory, and Cognition, 21,* 711-721.

Smith, E. E. (1998). Mental representation and memory. In D. T. Gilbert, S. T. Fiske, & G. Lindzey (Eds.), *The handbook of social psychology* (4th ed., pp. 391-445). Boston: McGraw-Hill.

Szpunar, K. K., Schellenberg, E. G., & Pliner, P. (2004). Liking and memory for musical stimuli as a function of exposure. *Journal of Experimental Psychology: Learning, Memory, and Cognition, 30,* 370-381.

Winkielman, P., Zajonc, R. B., & Schwarz, N. (1997). Subliminal affective priming resists attributional interventions. *Cognition and Emotion, 11,* 433-465.

Woodford, S. (1983). *Looking at pictures.* Cambridge, UK: Cambridge University Press.

Zajonc, R. B. (1968). Attitudinal effects of mere exposure. *Journal of Personality and Social Psychology, 9,* 1-27.

Zajonc, R. B. (1970, February). Brainwash: Familiarity breeds comfort. *Psychology Today,* pp. 33-35, 60-62.

Zajonc, R. B. (1980). Feeling and thinking: Preferences need no inferences. *American Psychologist, 35,* 151-175.

Zajonc, R. B. (2001). Mere exposure: A gateway to the subliminal. *Current Directions in Psychological Science, 10,* 224-228.

Zajonc, R. B., Shaver, P., Tavris, C., & Van Kreveld, D. (1972). Exposure, satiation, and stimulus discriminability. *Journal of Personality and Social Psychology, 21,* 270-280.

CHAPTER 4

The Nature and Growth of Aesthetic Fluency

Lisa F. Smith and Jeffrey K. Smith

> Flowers can be enjoyed without knowing about the interactions of soil, air, moisture, and the seeds of which they are the result. But they cannot be understood without taking just these interactions into account—and theory is a matter of understanding. (Dewey, 1958, p. 12)

Individuals who frequent art museums sometimes experience the pleasure of encountering an artist never seen before. This happened to us on a visit to the Whitney Museum of American Art where we encountered two works by Charles Sheeler. One, "River Rouge Plant," was particularly moving with the deep earth tones used to depict the Ford Motor assembly plant, giving it a warm and inviting feeling. Since the Whitney does not use interpretative labels, we were left to our own devices for making meaning out of the work. Our sense was one of an artist reconciling the impersonal dehumanizing effects of the Industrial Revolution with the sentiment that the plant worked for the people, producing not only Ford automobiles that the common person could own, but employing workers as well. This is a reasonable reaction and interpretation of the painting, but as any Charles Sheeler fan reading this chapter will immediately understand, not the least bit related to the artist who once said, "I find myself unable to believe in Progress—Change, yes. Greater refinements in the methods of destroying Life are the antithesis of Progress" (Sheeler, 1968, p. 71).

Several years later we encountered Sheeler again, this time at the Museum of Fine Arts in Boston. Seeing a new work by Sheeler brought the River Rouge Plant painting back to mind, but the new work was different, broadening and altering our conception of Sheeler. The new painting was also industrial in nature, but was stronger and somewhat harsher than the first work. This revision of our idea of Sheeler and his work was once again refined in looking up the artist on the Internet while doing the research for this chapter. "Precisionism" became a term in our art vocabulary, and aesthetic linkages were made among Sheeler, Demuth, Chase, and Duchamp. These linkages refined not only our understanding of Sheeler, but of the other artists as well. After an additional 20 or so works of art were viewed, this time on the Internet, the dimensions of Sheeler's art became more strongly established. Finally, reading an interview with Sheeler and his wife made him a real human being, bringing to us fascinating stories of their anecdotes with famous individuals such as Isadora Duncan and recollections of fond memories as well as some of the petty jealousies of life.

MODELS OF AESTHETIC UNDERSTANDING

What do these encounters with an artist, his life, and his work mean in the development of aesthetic understanding or appreciation? How does the knowledge acquired from these explorations affect how art is viewed in general, or Sheeler specifically? How are the experiences with works by the artist different afterward from before? Dewey (1958) differentiated the artistic (the production of a work of art) from the aesthetic (the experience of a work of art). Experiencing a work of art is inherently a psychological process, and has been the subject of discussion and theorizing among psychologists over a number of decades. Several theories of how people understand art have used the developmental stages framework pioneered by Piaget (1952) as their basis. Particularly notably among these theories are works by Parsons (1987) and Housen (1992). The purpose of these theories is to explain how individuals approach works of art in terms of the interpretation, understanding, and appreciation of them.

The theories of Parsons (1987) and Housen (1992) are fairly similar, each comprised of five stages that begin with views of art that begin in childhood and end with a stage that is acquired only by adults that have broad experience in the arts. A comparison of the stages is presented in Figure 1.

The reduction of the theories to a brief comparative chart is not fair to either theory; we encourage any reader intrigued by this work to read the original authors' explications of their ideas, which have been constructed over many years of data collection and careful thought. We did not include this chart to compare the two models, or to critique them so much as to use them as a point of departure. It can be seen even

	Parsons	Housen
Stage 1	Favoritism: This stage is associated with young children; paintings exist for pleasure.	Accountive: The viewer creates a narrative of the art. Evaluation is based on what the viewer likes.
Stage 2	Beauty and Realism: Paintings exist to represent things and should be attractive.	Constructive: Personal judgments of whether works of art look like they are supposed to.
Stage 3	Expressiveness: The expressiveness of the painting as it is personally understood is more important than beauty.	Classifying: Works described in art historical terms, using a school, genre, or period as a basis.
Stage 4	Style and Form: Medium, style, and form are important. The work of art exists in public and in an artistic tradition.	Interpretative: Personal feelings and meanings guide interpretation of the work.
Stage 5	Autonomy: The individual can transcend traditional and cultural limitations on interpretation of the work.	Re-Creative: Personal meaning combines with broader understandings and concerns.

Figure 1. Comparison of Parsons' and Housen's development models of art appreciation.

in this brief exposition that somewhere in the middle of the development of one's thinking about art, it becomes necessary to *know* something about art. Less sophisticated viewers rely primarily on their emotions or knowledge of other aspects of life; more sophisticated viewers place works of art in an art historical context. Sometimes that context is embraced for purposes of understanding and appreciating the work; other times it is questioned, or even rejected, but it must first be understood. As Dewey (1958) makes clear:

> The perceiver, as much as the creator, needs a rich and developed background which, whether it be painting in the field of poetry, or music, cannot be achieved except by consistent nurture of interest. (p. 266)

THE CONCEPT OF AESTHETIC FLUENCY

There is much to know about art. Art has a vocabulary, a history, a pantheon of great individuals, schools, genres, techniques, theories, movements, and millions upon millions of individual works of art. *The Dictionary of Art* (Turner, 1996) contains 34 volumes, each roughly 900 pages long. Universities have schools of art and departments of art history. They may have art libraries and art museums. Art, and art history, are *taught*. They are proper subjects of formal study. For our purposes, the concern is not with art as it is created, but with art as it is experienced, which Dewey (1958) calls the aesthetic. Does that make this knowledge base art history? Possibly, but that seems limiting, both in terms of history and in terms of art. Was realizing that Sheeler did not want to romanticize factories an historical understanding? Does learning the purpose of gesso make one a better art historian, or just make one have a broader understanding of what is involved in the creative process of oil painting? One of the problems in thinking about the idea of an aesthetic fluency is the question of fluency in what? What is the structure of knowledge in aesthetics, in particular in the fine arts? This is a nettlesome issue at best. Is the structure of knowledge of fine arts similar to the structure found in music? Or literature? Or history? Is aesthetic fluency the same thing as art history? Can the idea of aesthetic fluency be considered without first not only addressing, but answering this question? Our tentative answer is, we hope so, because we intend to do just that.

For now, we will offer a fairly simple definition of aesthetic fluency. Aesthetic fluency is the knowledge base concerning art that facilitates aesthetic experience in individuals. It can be acquired through direct instruction, but it can also be learned through experience. This experience occurs primarily in art museums, but it also occurs by reading books, visiting galleries, and on the Internet. Our experience in observing people look at art comes from art museums, but we cannot discount the importance of other venues. Roughly as many people enter the Metropolitan Museum of Art Website each day as enter the museum itself (and over 5 million people visit the Met in a typical year).

Our approach to trying to understand aesthetic fluency flows from our experience in watching it develop. We conduct research on how people behave in art museums. We have been systematically observing art museum visitors for almost 20 years. We watch them as they look at art, track their behavior, have them complete surveys, and engage them in experiments in lab settings and in museum settings. The ideas we argue for here are based in that experience, and are supported by some empirical findings we present later in the chapter.

Aesthetic fluency is the knowledge that a person has about art and aspects of life closely related to art. Importantly, aesthetic fluency is both verbal and visual. It is understanding what *chiaroscuro* means *and* being able to spot its use in a painting. It is the ability to explain the difference between Harnett and Haberle *and* the ability to say,

"That painting is more similar to Harnett than Haberle, but I don't think it is by either one of them," and be right. Aesthetic fluency is the base we stand upon in order to "get a better look" at the art we are contemplating. It is a semantic and perceptual web of related understandings, realizations, comprehensions, and insights that have accumulated over years of viewing art, talking about art, and reading about art, that is available to us when we encounter the next painting.

As museum researchers, this concept of aesthetic fluency fits with what we observe in watching people in museums (Smith & Smith, 2001; Smith & Wolf, 1996). We see people who look at dozens, sometimes hundreds of works in a single visit, who rarely spend more than 30 seconds on a work of art, and who are frequently as interested in the label that provides accompanying information to a work as the work itself. We see individuals who tell us that they are extremely moved by an exhibition, and then cannot tell us a specific work of art that was particularly moving, but that it was the exhibition as a whole. Indeed, we think it requires thinking about the museum visit as the appropriate unit of analysis that leads to a better understanding of what happens in museums, and the development of the concept of aesthetic fluency.

We liken aesthetic fluency to vocabulary, and the development of aesthetic fluency to the development of vocabulary. Graves (1986) estimated that schoolchildren increase their vocabularies by roughly 3000 words a year. Stahl (1991) argued that only 300 to 400 of those words could come from direct instruction in school. So where do the other 2600-2700 words (almost 8 per day, every day) come from? Stanovich (1986) posited that there is an interaction between reading and the development of vocabulary in that as students read more they increase their vocabulary and that as their vocabularies increase, they are able to increase the depth and breadth of their reading. Clark (1973) showed how children's understanding of words is often rough and incomplete, with just a rudimentary idea of what the word means and how to use it, and that this knowledge grows over time. This is known as the incremental conceptualization of vocabulary development. Vocabulary development is viewed by literacy researchers as growing incrementally with interaction with words, both written and spoken. Vocabulary knowledge does not increase in discrete word units, with words moving from unknown to known; instead the recognition, comprehension, and ability to use words grow incrementally with exposure to them. This process continues through adulthood. It is not hard to think of the following possibilities with regard to words:

- Words you have never seen before and didn't know were in the English language (there are not so many of these for mature and highly literate individuals, but there are some).
- Words you know are words but don't know their definitions.
- Words that you have a vague comprehension of.
- Words that you have a fairly good, but not precise definition of.
- Words that you understand, but do not use yourself.
- Words you use.

We propose that knowledge about art works in much the same way. There are artists or ideas in art that people do not know exist, others they are vaguely familiar with, and so on. This is true not only of artists and the ideas of art, but true about works of art as well. We argue that the ideas behind vocabulary development are also roughly true of one's vocabulary in understanding and appreciating art, or, to borrow Dewey's (1958) distinction between artistic and aesthetic, and combining it with a term from vocabulary research, one's "aesthetic fluency."

AN EMPIRICAL INVESTIGATION OF
AESTHETIC FLUENCY

Taking this idea, we have begun to explore what it might mean from an empirical perspective. We surveyed 400 individuals who were visiting the Metropolitan Museum of Art in June of 2003 to look at how they perceived knowledge of artists and ideas in art. As part of the survey, we asked individuals how much they knew about the following artists and art ideas:

- Mary Cassatt
- Isamu Noguchi
- John Singer Sargent
- Alessandro Boticelli
- Gian Lorenzo Bernini
- Fauvism
- Egyptian Funerary Stelae
- Impressionism
- Chinese Scrolls
- Abstract Expressionism

Visitors were asked to rate each of these concepts on the following 5-point scale:

0 – I have never heard of this artist or term
1 – I have heard of this but don't really know anything about it
2 – I have a vague idea of what this is
3 – I understand this artist or idea when it is discussed
4 – I can talk intelligently about this artist or idea in art

These questions were included in a survey that also asked individuals a number of demographic questions, questions about their museum visitation, and questions about their overall educational level, and training in art history.

RESULTS OF THE EMPIRICAL INVESTIGATION

We began the study by factor analyzing the 10 items. If our model that aesthetic fluency accrues incrementally through a wide and continued exposure to the arts is plausible, then the 10 items concerning art knowledge should come together fairly consistently as a single factor as opposed to a set of individual factors each relating to different sub areas of art. Table 1 provides the results of a principal components analysis of the 10 items with a varimax rotation. The first eigenvalue for the analysis was 5.27 and the second eigenvalue was 1.32, providing fairly strong evidence for a single factor solution, using a scree test as a criterion. It should be noted that if one retains two factors (using an eigenvalue greater than one criterion), that a second factor can be found which includes Egyptian funerary stelae and Chinese scrolls, the two

Table 1. Factor Analysis Results for 10 Item Aesthetic Fluency Scale

Item	Component 1	Component 2
Fauvism	.720	.305
Egyptian Funerary Stelae	.142	.809
Impressionism	.783	.049
Chinese Scrolls	.185	.812
Abstract Expressionism	.669	.281
Gian Lorenzo Bernini	.633	.496
Mary Cassatt	.839	.102
Alessandro Botticelli	.692	.341
Isamu Noguchi	.676	.376
John Singer Sargent	.841	.138

non-western areas of art. However, the argument is probably stronger for a single factor. We then calculated Cronbach's alpha on the scale to see what the reliability would be. Alpha equaled .90, an impressive result for a 10-item scale, further lending credence to the notion that there is one factor here.

The 10 items of the scale were selected to represent a range of knowledge levels with regard to various areas of art. Figure 2 is a plot of the mean knowledge levels of the artists and areas of art with a 95% confidence interval about the mean. We see that Impressionism is fairly widely known, whereas few visitors profess any knowledge about Chinese scrolls.

The next series of analyses were conducted to see how the scale was related to various characteristics of visitors to the museum. We hypothesized that if aesthetic fluency developed gradually through continued exposure to art, then age and frequency of museum visitation should be strongly related to the scale. We anticipated that training in art history would also be related to aesthetic fluency, but that formal education probably would only be marginally related, if at all. These expectations were investigated through a multiple regression analysis that looked at how training in art history, visits to art museums, age, and education related to aesthetic fluency. Results are presented in Table 2. The results show that frequency of museum visitation, age,

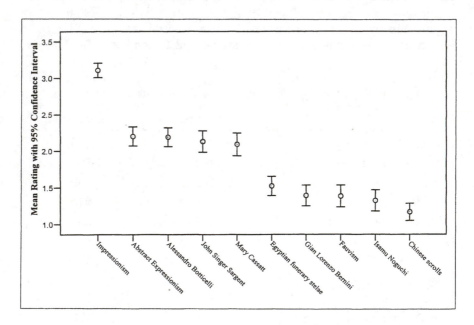

Figure 2. Ratings of knowledge of the 10 item aesthetic fluency scale.

Table 2. Regression of Aesthetic Fluency on Age, Training, and
Frequency of Museum Visitation

Variable	B	SE B	β	t
Age	.78	.24	.12	3.24*
How often do you visit art museums in general	3.88	.32	.48	12.23**
How much training do you have in art or art history	3.53	.35	.38	9.98**
Education	.65	.37	.07	1.75

Note: $p < .001$ for the model. R-square for the model = .544.
*$p = .001$.
**$p < .001$.

and training in art history are all related to aesthetic fluency, but that education is not. An examination of beta weights indicates that aesthetic fluency is most strongly influenced by museum visitation, followed by training in art history, and finally age. The analysis also indicates that these variables as a set are quite strongly related to aesthetic fluency, with an R-square estimated at .544.

Following the regression analyses, we looked at the relationship between individual variables and ratings of the 10 aesthetic fluency items. This was done for the four variables in the regression analysis; we present the results for age and art history training in Figures 3 and 4. These figures reveal two interesting findings. First, it is clear that both age and training in art history are related to aesthetic fluency. Secondly, it appears that training in art history leads to a more general understanding of art history (in that the differences in different levels of art history training are fairly constant over all of the terms), whereas age appears to be associated with stronger gains in particular areas (such as Mary Cassatt and Fauvism).

The final analysis looked at item response curves, which show the relationship between performance on an item and performance on the scale as a whole. Figure 5 presents an example of one of these item characteristic curves. What can be seen here is a regular increase in perceived knowledge on the item as overall aesthetic fluency increases. This type of result is quite consistent with item level research in vocabulary measures and lends support to the argument that aesthetic fluency develops in a fashion similar to vocabulary development.

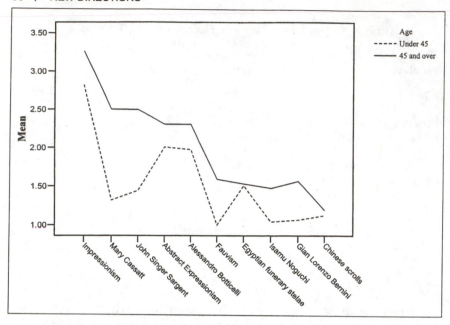

Figure 3. Relationship between age and aesthetic fluency items.

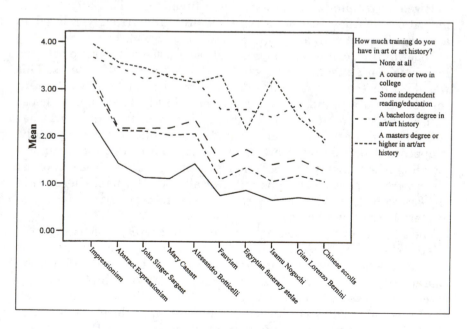

Figure 4. Relationship between training in art history
and aesthetic fluency items.

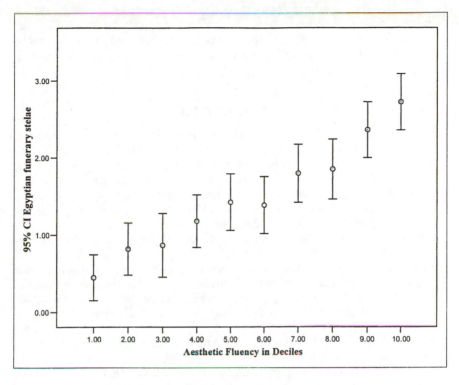

Figure 5. Item characteristic curve for Egyptian funerary stelae.

DISCUSSION

We are encouraged by the results of the empirical study and by the overall congruence between what we have observed over the years in museums, and the model for aesthetic fluency understanding and development that the work in vocabulary development provides. We think that this approach to thinking about the knowledge base that people bring to museums and that they use as they appreciate the works of art before them is useful to a better comprehension of what goes on in museums. At this point we are not ready to put it forward as a competing hypothesis to the developmental approaches of Parsons (1987) or Housen (1992). Our thinking at this time is that the two approaches might be better understood as complementary. The developmental level determines an overall approach and level of sophistication in looking and understanding or appreciating a work of art. The level of aesthetic fluency provides the cognitive and knowledge bases for engaging in the public or private discourse that facilitates understanding. Aesthetic fluency appears to accrete gradually and broadly across areas of art and is greatly influenced (in this sample at least) by frequency of visitation to museums and age, as well as training in art history.

REFERENCES

Clark, E. V. (1973). What's in a word? On the child's acquisition of semantics in his first language. In T. E. Moore (Ed.), *Cognitive development and the acquisition of language* (pp. 65-110). New York: Academic Press.

Dewey, J. (1958). *Art as experience*. New York: Capricorn Books.

Graves, M. E. (1986). Vocabulary learning and instruction. In E. Z. Rothkopf & L. C. Ehri (Eds.), *Review of research in education* (Vol. 13, pp. 49-89). Washington, DC: American Educational Research Association.

Housen, A. (1992). Validating a measure of aesthetic development for museums and schools. *ILVS Review, 2,* 213-237.

Parsons, M. J. (1989). *How we understand art. A cognitive developmental account of aesthetic experience*. Cambridge: Cambridge University Press.

Piaget, J. (1952). *The origins of intelligence in children*. New York: Macmillan.

Sheeler, C. (1968). *National collection of fine arts*. Washington, DC: Smithsonian Institution Press.

Smith, J. K., & Smith, L. F. (2001). Spending time on art. *Empirical Studies in the Arts, 19,* 229-236.

Smith, J. K., & Wolf, L. F. (1996). Museum visitor preferences and intentions in constructing aesthetic experience. *Poetics: Journal for Empirical Research in Literature, Media and the Arts, 24,* 219-238.

Stahl, S. A. (1991). Beyond the instrumental hypothesis: Some relationships between word meanings and comprehension. In P. J. Schwanenflugel (Ed.), *The psychology of word meanings* (pp. 157-185). Hillsdale, NJ: Lawrence Erlbaum Associates.

Stanovich, K. E. (1986). Mattew effects in reading: Some consequence of individual differences in the acquisition of literacy. *Reading Research Quarterly, 21,* 360-407.

Turner, J. (Ed.). (1996). *The dictionary of art*. New York: Grove's Dictionaries.

CHAPTER 5

Aesthetic Universals in Cultural Perception and Practice

Dorothy Washburn

In this chapter I will overview the diversity of perspectives in anthropology regarding the applicability of the Western concept—aesthetics—to non-Western cultural expressions. This chapter begins with the premise that a concept of beauty as a sensual response is universally held by all peoples (e.g., Maquet, 1986). Indeed, some biologists are now suggesting that what humans consider to be aesthetically beautiful may emanate from genetically predetermined processing rules about form centered in the central nervous system (see Rentschler, Harzberger, & Epstein, 1988; Zeki, 1999, but see debate in Goguen, 1999), thus making possible greater understanding of this universal aesthetic experience. However, here I will focus my remarks on aspects of the nature of the aesthetic that non-Western cultures find in activities and beliefs, and in the verbal and visual representations that support them, and suggest one feature that cross-cultural perception tests for preference could show to be an aesthetic universal.

The key to an anthropological study of aesthetic responses lies in discovery of features engendering these responses that represent the culture's, rather than the analyst's, ideas about beauty. Coote's (1992) call to consider how objects are *perceived* within the culture is such an emic approach that focuses on the cultural values behind the formal and ideational qualities considered beautiful. "The anthropology of aesthetics consists in the comparative study of valued perceptual experience in different societies" (p. 247). From this perspective it should be possible to link psychologists' preference tests with real world cultural studies.

As an example, I will suggest that if psychological preference tests for geometric pattern configurations are administered to members of a non-Western community, their preference for certain formal geometric relationships would replicate the social relationships and community values that knit the society together. I propose that analysis will find that these geometric configurations are used to configure designs on their textiles, ceramic vessels, and other decorated media. This cross-disciplinary approach should enable us to enhance our understanding about cross-cultural aesthetic universals.

ANTHROPOLOGICAL APPROACHES TO ART AND AESTHETICS

Although it is commonly stated that a *concept* of aesthetics did not develop until after the Renaissance when secular interests and market economies supported the commissioning and collecting of "art" for art's sake (cf. Eco, 1986; Pasztory, 1996; Shelton, 1992), in fact, the notion of *sensory perception* as aesthetic can be traced back to the Greek *aisthetikos*. Nevertheless, it was in the West in the 18th and 19th centuries that art historians honed aesthetic criteria for the narrower category of "fine art" as created in Europe and other Westernized nations. By the 20th century, perhaps beginning with Picasso's appreciation of the presence of pleasing combinations of form and line in African imagery, critics began applying this notion to religious articles and other functional objects made by non-Western peoples despite the fact that they do not share Western notions about the aesthetics of "art."

This categorization of tools and other primarily functional objects from non-Western cultures as "art" has always been problematic for anthropologists who focus on the contextual nexus of all objects and behaviors rather than on objects as aesthetic entities in themselves and claim to eschew the judgmental comparisons that such an "art" aesthetic demands. Indeed, for most non-Western cultures neither "art" nor "aesthetics" exist as categories of thought in the same sense that they are defined in the West. Nevertheless, there has arisen a movement for an Anthropology of Art as a sub-discipline for the study of certain forms of material culture, such as ceramics, sculpture, dance, or ceremonial paraphernalia (cf. Layton, 1981) as well as an Anthropology of Aesthetics for the study of aesthetics as a cross-cultural category (cf. Leuthold, 1998; Morphy, 1994).

Acceptance of these concepts and fields of study has not been seamless. The debate (see, for example, *Cambridge Archaeological Journal: Viewpoint 1994*; Ingold, 1996; Layton, 2003) over the applicability of aesthetics to all human activity, particularly to experiences of non-Western peoples, has been contentious. Some anthropologists assert that all humans are born with certain cognitive universals, one being sensory responses to objects and ideas (cf. Dissanayake, 1992). Others believe that because aesthetics is an evaluative scheme that is the product of Western thought and values it cannot be used to evaluate activities in cultures who do not make such judgments. But by narrowly focusing only the "evaluative" aspect of the Western concept of aesthetics, we miss, I believe, much of the fundamental intangible "felt" value of social action. For example, by arguing that "Melanesian aesthetics is about efficacy, the capacity to accomplish tasks, not [about] beauty" (p. 94). Gell (1998) is ironically illustrating the fact that many peoples, the Melanesian tool makers and users among them, see beauty in the *processes and practices of making and using* objects, not simply in the object's form. By focusing on form as the only entity that has aesthetic qualities, we lay bare our general ignorance about the *aesthetic component of social practice.*

Despite these differing positions, many anthropologists entertain the notion that cultures have a felt aesthetic concept that pervades many domains, although most characterize this aesthetic as unique to different domains and different cultures (cf. Coote, 1992; Forrest, 1988; Hardin, 1993; Morphy, 1992; Schevill, 1992; Shelton, 1992; Vogel, 1980; Warren & Andrews, 1977). Two examples exemplify these particularistic studies.

Coote (1992) studied the aesthetic sensibilities found in perceptions about cattle that are the central focus of some Nilotic speakers of the southern Sudan. A number of features make these animals especially desirable: pied hide coloring, glossy hide sheen, well-shaped horns, and large fat bodies. Well-fed and shaped cattle are considered beautiful not because they will bring a better price at market or will provide more food for a feast, but because they are a "feast for the eyes"; only secondarily are they thought of as a feast for the stomach. The pied markings of the cattle metaphorically replicate the overcast skies thought to represent the divinity Deng, who is associated with rain, thunder, and lightning so necessary for watering the grasses on which the cattle graze. These same kinds of aesthetically valued features are also manifest in ritual body decoration, clothing, and dance gestures.

Morphy (1991, 1992) studied the aesthetic system of the Yalngu, an aboriginal people living in northern Australia, finding that it centers around the sense of brilliance and light associated with ancestral power. Ritual paintings take on this power during their production. Images are first outlined on boards or bodies and in this state they are considered to be dull. It is only when the shapes are painstakingly

filled in by crosshatching do they gain a certain "shimmering brilliance," said to be the embodiment of ancestral power. Yalngu say
they feel an uplift in spirit when they view these hatched images that is
akin to the "flash of light" experienced by initiates after bloodletting.

While these studies illustrate how it is possible to identify certain
features that hold aesthetic value in specific cultures, I wish to go
further and suggest that beneath the observable variability in sensory
responses to different ideas and things are universal qualities that
also engender aesthetic responses. It would seem worth the effort
to refine perceptual tests that have been developed by experimental
psychologists in acultural laboratory settings to investigate the validity
of the concept of aesthetics as inclusive of the preference for perceived
universals with real world cross-cultural studies before discarding this
idea on principle. To illustrate this approach I explore here the nature
of the aesthetic response to the beauty that people find in a wide variety
of life-sustaining activities and beliefs as it is embedded in their perceptual preference for certain symmetrical arrangements of design.
Defining and understanding how this aesthetic is manifested in metaphor is the first step in the development of cross-cultural tests for this
perceptual universal.

Prior research (Sekaquaptewa & Washburn, 2004; Washburn, 1999)
has demonstrated that certain pattern configurations are visual
metaphors for valued social relationships. Within this perspective,
designs are beautiful because they display, and thus communicate
metaphorically in their geometrical format, these social relationships.
The aesthetic sensibilities in each domain, metaphorically "stated,"
complement and reinforce each other to create a wholeness in the
system of cultural beliefs and activities within a given culture. Importantly, we can measure the perception of the visual representation
of metaphor—that uniquely human mental process that creates
relationships between things from different domains. For this reason,
in order to study the aesthetic sensibilities that underpin cultures,
one must first discover the metaphorical manifestations of the cosmological system as they appear in tangible things and intangible
ideas that permeate daily and ritual life. Upon discovery of these
key metaphorical relationships and how they are expressed in the
geometry of pattern, we should then be able to develop preference tests
that take into account cultural differences in perception (cf. Kubovy
& Strother, 2004).

I have studied how the cosmological principles of life metaphorically
pervade the structure of design configurations on prehistoric and
historic ceramics and other media made by the Hopi, a Uto-Aztecan
speaking farming people living in northern Arizona, United States and,

specifically, how the aesthetic sensibilities of Hopi culture are carried in the domain of song with a study of the content of 20th century Hopi *katsina* song. Song is mentioned by Coote (1992) and Morphy (1991) as a vehicle for transmitting aesthetic notions. For example, Morphy explored the uplift listeners perceive from the "shimmering" aesthetic in Yalngu ritual song where the content is structured so as to progress from dark and dull to light and brilliant—the same sequence of transformations that occurred in the process of making bark and body paintings. The Hopi experience similar feelings of uplift when they listen to the words of *katsina* songs sung during dance performances that stimulate them to action. But further, I hope to explicate how the ideational content of song is metaphorically reproduced in ceramic design configurations in order to suggest how this one manifestation of the Hopi aesthetic is embedded in a perceptual universal that can be discovered with perceptual preference tests, thus enabling cross-disciplinary study of the issue of aesthetic universals.

THE HOPI AESTHETIC IN RITUAL SONG

The Hopi, who live in 12 farming villages in northern Arizona, like all other Native American groups in North America, traditionally transferred their cultural values and ideals through verbal, visual, and kinesthetic means. In contrast to other kinds of recording systems developed by peoples in Central and South America, such as Mayan glyphs and Inca *quipus*, no North American cultural group in the pre-contact period had a system of writing. Through ritual song, decorated material culture, and dance performances as well as within the practices of daily living, the Hopi live a life in which almost every act has an aesthetic component tied to their cosmology. Significantly, the meaning behind these ritual and daily activities are metaphorically embedded in certain perceptually measurable features such as the structure of ceramic design. It is from this source that we can begin not only to understand the Hopi aesthetic but also to test the validity of the idea that preference for pattern configuration in the role of ideational metaphor is a universal aesthetic feature.

The Hopi are known to the outside world principally through their religious ceremonies in which "masked dancers" called *katsinas* come to perform in the Hopi villages between February and July. At their homes in the Four Directions, these spirit beings observe the Hopi, judge the worthiness and sincerity of their prayers for rain, and, if deserving, "adorn" themselves with clouds, "arriving as rain," *yooya'öki,* in the Hopi villages. As rain, they embody the perfect, that is, the beautiful life where everyone lives a long life of fulfillment with good health and plenty of food. As rain, they are perfect beings because rain is, literally and metaphorically, the ultimate nourishment for the Hopi and their fields of corn. The structure of *katsina* song replicates this reciprocal relationship: if the Hopi do X [pray], the *katsinas* will respond with Y [rain].

Thus, to define the Hopi aesthetic is to understand how this fundamental reciprocity pervades all aspects of Hopi life and how it is expressed in the verbal and visual metaphors that describe and drive this lifeway. Beauty lies in a perfect life of health and happiness achieved through adherence to the proper ritual practices and communal obligations and responsibilities fundamental to the continual well-being of the Hopi community. For example, the striving to properly participate in this Hopi life is metaphorically encapsulated in the process of growing. Growing in beauty means growing in perfection in the way one's life is lived. This idea is metaphorically embodied in the different stages of corn growth. More precisely, it is not enough for the corn to grow, it must grow right and have ears that reach full maturity. Perfect corn is full of kernels that are both food for the present generation and seeds for the next generation. The gift of perfect ears of corn to new babies is a prayer for them to grow, be healthy, and have a long fulfilling life.

Many of these instructional metaphors for living a perfect life of fulfillment and happiness—the crux of the Hopi aesthetic—are expressed in the songs that *katsinas* sing at public ceremonials. These verbalized sentiments about the beauty of right action that is reciprocally rewarded with life-giving rain are couched in creative phrases that are themselves beautifully evocative of the past perfect life to which the Hopi aspire. When sung in performance, they are designed, in the eloquence of their expression, not only to catch the attention of Hopi listeners and bring them "felt" pleasure, but also, in so doing, to inspire and renew their dedication to the Hopi way of life.

Distinctive to Hopi song are special compound words and phrases that creatively combine words in order to build metaphors that bring to mind associated things and ideas that highlight the ideal beautiful life. For example, the idea of making perfection on earth visibly manifest is emphasized with use of the word "display" when referring to the earth. Thus, the Hopi visualize their land as an altar [*pongya*] that displays beauty: *tuwapongyava*. [earth, display place]. Likewise, life properly lived is said to *display* beauty. There are countless combinations of words that reference the beauty of this perfect life. *Lomaqatsi*, is a good life; *lomatunatya*, are good intentions done with sincerity of purpose; *lomawuwanta* refers to individuals that are having good thoughts; *loma'unangewa*, references an individual who has a good heart, that is one that is focused solely on the good of the community; and *loma'omaw* references a beautiful rain cloud, that is, one that is full of rain. In fact, Whiteley (1992) has noted that personal names often begin with adverbial or adjectival forms, such as *Loma*- (beautiful) or *Kuwa*- (brightly colored), that signal an individual's perception of the beauty of a clan totem or a social relationship.

Song metaphors give beauty to and enhance the effective presentation of Hopi concepts of life. I exemplify below how the Hopi aesthetic principles about living a good, that is a beautiful life, are metaphorically packaged in several 20th century *katsina* songs. I begin by describing some of the key Hopi metaphors of life as voiced by the *Tsa'kwayna Katsinas* in an early 20th century song (# 13): *katsinas* are clouds; rain is cornmeal; and toads are grateful Hopi farmers.

> *Omawkiinawita, Tukwunangwmamantu*
> Throughout the dwelling places of the clouds, the Cumulus Cloud Maidens
> *Paayoy'nguman'iniy angqw pew na'sasa'yyungwa.*
> have their rain as corn flour prepared for here.
> *Yang puma umuu'uyiy put ang yoknayaniqe'e,*
> Because they are going to make that as rain along your planted fields.
> *Yan'i yani uma'a naawakinaya.*
> For this you have been praying.
> *Oovi, umuu'uyiy anga'a yooyokvaqö'ö*
> So, when it rains along your fields
> *Ang paatalawvaqö'ö*
> and when they shimmer and sparkle with rainwater,
> *Tuvevakwatu, Mösivakwatu*
> Different kinds of toads, the food-laden toads,
> *Ang puma'a töötökimakyangw sosonkiwyani'i.*
> As they move along there with their calls, they will make pleasing sounds.

The first section of the song is concerned with activities of the Cumulus Cloud Maidens who are preparing rain in their clouds as if they are Hopi girls grinding corn for food. Thus, the ground corn flour on their trays readied for the preparation of food is likened to rain drops contained in the clouds ready to fall as rain. Both are seen as food that insures the survival of the Hopi: rain nourishes the fields of corn just as corn flour nourishes the Hopi. The second section is concerned with the beautiful consequences of rain. Toads emerge in the puddles and sing constantly, metaphorically referencing not only the happiness and gladness the Hopi feel upon seeing their fields covered with water, but also the renewal of life that comes with rain.

The beauty of new life and life renewed that is voiced in this song is reiterated in many other Hopi metaphors that relate Hopi life to life in the natural world. For example, song #95 metaphorically likens the leaves of the corn plants to young girls, described in this song as corn plant maidens, who will dance in the breeze and sparkle in the sun with the dewy drops of rain. Rain, like new life, is one of the most beautiful results of prayerful activity and proper living. In this song the *Owaqöl* maidens take on the likeness of butterflies, beautiful beings that flit among flowering plants, and in this way are metaphors for the process of fertilization and thus the beginning of new life. The process of corn growth is metaphorically likened to a child's maturation. In this song corncobs are described as "wrapped children" in their husks—a metaphor for the new brides as they appear at *Nimantiqueve* enveloped in their white wedding robes symbolizing the beginning of their new life stage as mothers.

Nuu vii nu'hookonmaanatuuy nuu vii nu'siikyaavooliwmanaatuu,
I, monarch butterfly maiden; I, yellow butterfly maiden
Nu'yep tuwaati, Owaqölmanaa iqatsiivongyaayuy epe'e
For my part here as an *Owaqöl* maiden according to my way of living,
Soosok hiita qatsii'uunangwata kuwan'ewniniiqat naatwaantaa'qö'ö
If I practice all things that show the will to live a life that will be beautiful
Putaakw namuur qaavoo haqam yang
With that, hopefully, sometime tomorrow
Paavaasnawiit yang sakwaatalaawvataa'a
Along the cultivated fields after they brighten in green
Nalöönatsve'e timookimuuy naatukwsiinaayaani.
The corn plants will grow their wrapped children in four ears, one above the other.
Paypu namuur tuuwatii.
For your part, let it be so.
"Iiyoo iiyoo," kitootani paavönmanaatuu'u
"It is raining," This is what they will say, the young corn plant maidens.
Haqamii tuwaat paavaasnawiit yang paayoysimaasay puyayaataani.
For their part, along the cultivated fields here, [young corn plant maidens] will be flapping their watered wings sparkling with rain.

In this way, corn in all its stages is likened to growing children and to women who, upon maturing, gain the potential to produce new generations. Thus, when Hopi comment that young girls are blossoming in beauty, they are referring to their growing capabilities to reproduce, rather than to improvements in their outward physical appearance. For example, the word *osuwa'yta* that describes the appearance of new growth at the tips of plants is often used to metaphorically describe girls who are reaching puberty. In the song (# 12) below the leaves of the corn plants are metaphors for maturing Hopi girls whose growth is seen to be as beautiful as unfolding butterfly wings. Indeed, we often refer to the period of growing up as "flapping one's wings."

> *Pas hapi uma nuy no'aya paavönmanatu.*
> Truly you delight me you young corn plant maidens
> *Kur uma yeephaqam umuumasay kuwantimaakyangw*
> *puyaayaatotal'angwnaawiita*
> You unfold your wings resplendent in color here throughout the summer.

Although the Hopi certainly enjoy the visible beauty of life, as expressed in these songs about the patterning on butterflies and the colorful flowering plants in the fields, as well as iridescent colors on rain soaked plant leaves sparkling in the sun, they also see this visible beauty as a metaphorical manifestation of the Hopi adherence to their most valued principles of life.

In sum, the Hopi aesthetic is focused on the concept of living the perfect life agreed to at their Emergence into this the Fourth World—rather than simply on the visual appearance of things and practices. Specifically, this aesthetic is metaphorically manifested in the goodness and nurturing qualities of corn and rain. Rain is beautiful because it brings life; it is never considered as inclement weather. From this perspective, even heavy rainstorms that may wash away some plants are desirable because such rains also bring new soils to rejuvenate the fields. However, massive, totally destructive floods are understood to be warning signs that the Hopi have deviated too far from living the perfect life.

Beauty is, above all, rooted in the processes and practices of living that serve the welfare and continuity of the Hopi community. Prayers for rain are not effective unless *everyone's* prayers are made with humble sincerity. Thus, beauty is found not only in the rain itself, the ultimate object of the Hopis' prayers, but also in the *process* of everyone collectively preparing heartfelt prayers for that rain by smoking, making prayer feathers, and having pure thoughts. Each Hopi person must constantly strive to do his or her share in support of their chosen life based on hand cultivated corn agriculture. Thus, beauty lies in the humility of participating in work for the communal good. In all work one finds beauty. The beauty of hearing the girls sing grinding songs as they grind the hard corn kernels into flour alludes to the beauty that comes from this work—the new life that is so fundamental to Hopi continuity.

In the West, art critics dictate aesthetic criteria. But among people in societies such as the Hopi, everyone knows the principles and practices that lead to a perfect life and strives to live by them because the well being of the community depends on *everyone's* participation.

Uma yeepe'e lolmat qatsiit wuuwanmaaqam
  You here that are thinking of the good life for all
Uma yeepe'e nanaa'vangwaqw'ö
  When you here help one another
Naanan'ivaqw pew yooyaa ökiini.
  The rains will arrive from every direction
Yan uma nawaakinaya.
  In this way you should be praying

THE HOPI AESTHETIC IN OTHER DOMAINS

The beautiful essences of a proper life that are well defined in song are also brought to mind in image. The same ideals verbalized in the metaphorical song phrases appear metaphorically in representational images on murals and metaphorically in the structure of pattern on other forms of material culture (ceramics, textiles, basketry). For example, in a 15th century kiva mural from the prehistoric Hopi site of *Kawaika'a* (Figure 1), perfect ears of corn appear to be "growing" directly from the earth. This, obviously, is not an accurate picture of what a growing corn plant actually looks like, but rather, bundled in the single cob "planted" on a line is the metaphorical message that Mother Earth provides when the Hopi do their part by living properly. The single corncob is a visual metaphor for a field of corn. In its multicolored and completely kernelled state, it is also a metaphor for the beauty of a perfect Hopi life. In this way, the Hopi concept of beauty is embodied in the visual projection of values shared and collectively practiced.

These reciprocal concepts, deeply seated within a culture's cosmology, can be traced in their metaphorical counterparts in imagery and pattern to other culturally affiliated groups as well as back into the past. For example, if we compare Hopi cosmology to that of other Uto-Aztecan

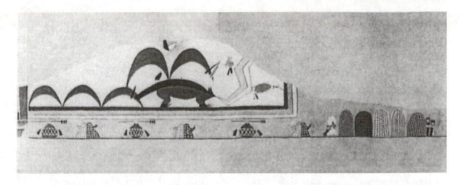

Figure 1. Kiva mural, *Kawaika'a,* Room 6. From Smith, 1952, Fig. 62.

speaking groups in Mexico, we find that the Huichol aesthetic (Shelton, 1992) is very similar. Since both peoples are Uto-Aztecan speakers and since archaeology and oral tradition indicate that some ancestors of the Hopi migrated north from northwestern Mexico where the Huichol now live, it is not surprising that even today these two groups retain fragments of belief and practice in common. For example, the Huichol communicate with their deities via prayers sent on feathered sticks conceived as arrows similar in form and metaphorical conception to Hopi prayer sticks. Huichol prayers are sent to the rain mothers who raise themselves from the four cardinal regions, transform themselves into clouds, and fall as rain serpents. Similarly, Hopi petition the *katsinas,* spirit beings, with prayers and they in turn come from the four cardinal directions as clouds and fall as rain, nourishing the earth. Both the Huichol and Hopi cycle of production and reproduction results only when the deities are approached with humility and appropriate offerings—a reciprocal relationship between the world of the deities and people that is metaphorically replicated in almost every social and ritual practice.

I suggest that these deeply seated principles of living are metaphorically projected in the structure of pattern and that it should be possible to access and reconfirm such a deeply seated behavioral aesthetic using simple preference tests for symmetrical pattern configurations being developed in perceptual psychology (studies for the detection of symmetry reviewed in Wagemans, 1995; studies for the preference of symmetry found in Humphrey, 1997 and Washburn & Humphrey, 2002). For example, the reciprocal connection between Huichol practices of living right and the deities coming as rain is depicted in designs woven into their shoulder bags. The rain is depicted generally as geometric shapes that replicate the patterns on the backs of snakes, each of which contains a flower motif, a symbol of the perfect world of the ancients to which every Huichol should aspire. Thus, embedded in this geometric pattern (Figure 2) is the metaphorical relationship between the deities and the Huichol that is considered to be as aesthetically beautiful as it is ritually fulfilling.

Likewise, the Hopi aesthetic of the perfect life embedded in the reciprocal agreement between the Hopi and *katsinas* that is verbalized in the ritual songs should be metaphorically manifested in the same reciprocal relationship in geometric design, here illustrated by ceramic designs organized by bifold rotation. That is, in Figure 3 two equivalent units are interlocked in a rotating position such that the superposition of one on the other is a metaphorical statement of the interlocking, reciprocal roles and obligations between the *katsinas* and Hopi people. Because this is a prescribed and thus preferred cultural relationship, it should occur on the majority of patterns. Indeed, the graph in Figure 4 shows that designs on the late prehistoric Hopi ceramic types of Jeddito B/Y and Awatovi B/Y are predominantly structured by this interlocked

Figure 2. Shoulder bag, Huichol. Cat. No. 472-56. California Academy of Sciences, San Francisco. Photograph by Christopher Thomas.

Figure 3. *C2 Sityatki* polychrome ceramic design.
From Fewkes, 1898, Plate CXL.

configuration that is described geometrically as bifold rotation. That is, these designs can be characterized as *C2* finite designs in which the two interlocking parts are superimposed by bifold rotation.

If we refine the process whereby we show a series of pictures of ceramic designs based on this symmetry as well as others to contemporary Hopi individuals and record their preference for pattern configuration, we should find, just as we did on prehistoric Hopi ceramics (Figure 4) that the prevailing preference is for *C2*. Importantly, it is not that the *C2* configuration itself is seen as beautiful, but that the *C2* configuration is metaphorical of a particular reciprocal relationship in Hopi culture that is believed to be beautiful—the interlocking and interdependent roles and responsibilities of the *katsinas* and Hopi people. In this way preference tests would be another way to confirm these aesthetic principles.

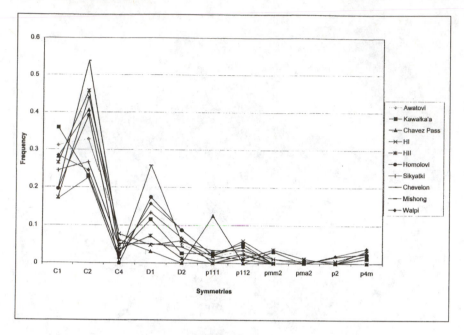

Figure 4. Percentage frequency of finite and one-dimensional symmetries on Jeddito B/Y and Awatovi B/Y ceramic designs from 10 Hopi sites. Note high frequency of *C2* symmetry.

CONCLUSION

I have explored culturally mediated perceptions and conceptions of beauty and found that non-Western peoples not only see beauty in the visible appearance of objects, but also in beliefs and practices permeating daily living linked to the cosmological principles that define them as a people. We should not limit this view of a behavioral aesthetic to non-Western cultures. Even in our Western societies where the concept of aesthetics is generally restricted to the beauty of line and form in a fine oil painting, there are those who see beauty in everyday activities (cf. Forrest, 1988). During my studies of the process of horse-drawn agriculture that typified farming in pre-industrial America, I have found that farmers talk about the beauty in a well-plowed field where the furrows are uniformly deep and straight and the sod is completely turned over so that no weeds are showing (Washburn, nd.). Indeed, the wood frames of fodder choppers—utilitarian guillotine-like devices used to chop corn stalks for animal feed and bedding display finely stenciled with colorful floral designs and script by craftsmen at the turn of the century as a way to honor this most basic enterprise—growing food. Vestiges of this farming aesthetic that concern the processes and practices of farming still remain and resonate within some farming communities today.

From this perspective, aesthetics is a lived entity that permeates all domains of a community's life. Beauty lies not only in the visible form of created objects, but also in many processes and practices associated with them. We should bring the perspectives of perceptual psychology to bear on this new entrant in the anthropological stream through studies that confirm the existence of preferences for certain universal features that are used to metaphorically state intangible aesthetic principles that reflect the beliefs and practices of life seen as beautiful.

ACKNOWLEDGMENTS

This research is based on the transcription and translation of 125 *katsina* songs with Emory Sekaquaptewa, a native Hopi speaker and life long participant in Hopi culture. Washburn was funded with a Research Fellowship from the National Endowment for the Humanities. The song numbers correspond to the songs in the database studied archived at the Bureau of Applied Research in Anthropology, University of Arizona.

REFERENCES

Cambridge Archaeological Journal (1994). Viewpoint: Is there a place for aesthetics in Anthropology? *Cambridge Archaeological Journal, 4,* 249-269.

Coote, J. (1992). Marvels of everyday vision: The anthropology of aesthetics and the cattle-keeping Nilotes. In J. Coote & A. Shelton (Eds.), *Anthropology art and aesthetics* (pp. 245-273). Oxford: Clarendon Press.

Dissanayake, E. (1992). *Homo aestheticus.* New York: The Free Press.

Eco, U. (1986). *Art and beauty in the Middle Ages.* New Haven: Yale University Press.

Fewkes, J. W. (1898). *Archaeological expedition to Arizona in 1895.* Seventeenth Annual Report, Bureau of American Ethnology, 1895-96. Washington, DC.

Forrest, J. (1988). *Lord I'm coming home: Everyday aesthetics in Tidewater North Carolina.* Ithaca: Cornell University Press.

Gell, A. (1998). *Art and agency: An anthropological theory.* Oxford: Oxford University Press.

Goguen, J. (Ed.). (1999). Special feature on 'Art and the brain.' *Journal of Consciousness Studies, 6.*

Hardin, K. (1993). *The aesthetics of action: Continuity and change in a West African town.* Washington, DC: Smithsonian Institution Press.

Humphrey, D. (1997). Preferences in symmetries and symmetries in drawings: asymmetries between ages and sexes. *Empirical Studies of the Arts, 43,* 265-182.

Ingold, T. (Ed.). (1996). *Key debates in anthropology.* 1993 Debate: Aesthetics is a Cross-Cultural Category. London: Routledge.

Kubovy, M., & Strother, L. (2004). The perception of band patterns: Going beyond geometry. In D. Washburn (Ed.), *Embedded symmetries, natural and cultural* (pp. 19-26). Albuquerque: University of New Mexico Press.

Layton, R. (1981). *The anthropology of art.* New York: Columbia University Press.

Layton, R. (2003). Art and agency: A reassessment. *The Journal of the Royal Anthropological Institute, 9,* 447-464.

Leuthold, S. (1998). *Indigenous aesthetics.* Austin: University of Texas Press.

Maquet, J. (1986). *The aesthetic experience.* New Haven: Yale University Press.

Morphy, H. (1991). *Ancestral connections: Art and an aboriginal system of knowledge.* Chicago: University of Chicago Press.

Morphy, H. (1992). From dull to brilliant: The aesthetics of spiritual power among the Yalngu. In J. Coote & A. Shelton (Eds.), *Anthropology art and aesthetics* (pp. 181-208). Oxford: Clarendon Press.

Morphy, H. (1994). Aesthetics across time and place: An anthropological perspective. In viewpoint: Is there a place for aesthetics in archaeology? *Cambridge Archaeological Journal, 4,* 257-260.

Pasztory, E. (1996). Aesthetics and pre-Columbian art. *RES,* 29/30, 318-325.

Rentschler, I., Harzberger, B., & Epstein, D. (Eds.). (1988). *Beauty and the brain: Biological aspects of aesthetics.* Basel: Brikhauser Verlag.

Schevill, M. (1992). Lila Morris O'Neale: Ethnoaesthetics and the Yurok-Karok basket weavers of northwestern California. In J. Berlo (Ed.), *The early years of Native American art history* (pp. 162-190). Seattle: The University of Washington Press.

Sekaquaptewa, E., & Washburn, D. (2004). They go along singing: Reconstructing the Hopi past from ritual metaphors in song and image. *American Antiquity, 69*(3), 457-486.

Shelton, A. (1992). Predicates of aesthetic judgment: Ontology and value in Huichol material representation. In J. Coote & A. Shelton (Eds.), *Anthropology art and aesthetics* (pp. 209-244). Oxford: Clarendon Press.

Smith, W. (1952) *Kiva mural decorations at Awatovi and Kawaika'a.* Papers of the Peabody Museum of Archaeology and Ethnology 37. Cambridge: Harvard University.

Vogel, S. (1980). *Beauty in the eyes of the Baule: Aesthetics and cultural values.* Working Papers in the Traditional Arts 6. Philadelphia: Institute for the Study of Human Issues.

Wagemans, J. (1995). Detection of visual symmetries. *Spatial Vision, 9,* 9-32.

Warren, D. M., & Andrews, J. K. (1977). *An ethnoscientific approach to Akan arts and aesthetics.* Working Papers in the Traditional Arts 3. Philadelphia: Institute for the Study of Human Issues.

Washburn, D. (nd.) *Unpublished oral histories*. Howell Living History Farm, Titusville, New Jersey.

Washburn, D. (1999). Perceptual anthropology: The cultural salience of symmetry. *American Anthropologist, 101*, 547-562.

Washburn, D., & Humphrey, D. (2002). Symmetries in the mind: Production, perception and preference for seven one-dimensional patterns. *Visual Arts Research, 27*, 57-68.

Whiteley, P. (1992). *Hopitutungwni*: Hopi names as literature. In B. Swann (Ed.), *On the translation of Native American literature* (pp. 208-227). Washington, DC: Smithsonian Institution Press.

Zeki, S. (1999). *Inner vision: An exploration of art and the brain*. Oxford: Oxford University Press.

PART II

NEW DIRECTION IN CREATIVITY

CHAPTER 6

Stalking the Elusive Creativity Quark: Toward a Comprehensive Theory of Creativity

Robert J. Sternberg

A quarter-century ago, I wrote and had published an article entitled "Stalking the IQ Quark" (Sternberg, 1979). At the time, the title seemed appropriate because the nature of intelligence seemed so elusive. After studying both intelligence and creativity for a number of years, I have come to realize how much more elusive creativity is than intelligence. Several years ago, I edited handbooks of both creativity (Sternberg, 1999a) and intelligence (Sternberg, 2000). It became clear to me, in working on the volumes, that although there were many disagreements in both fields, there was *much* more agreement about intelligence than about creativity. In our own work, we have tried to view creativity from a multi-faceted point of view in order to try to understand the nature of creativity, how to develop it, and how to measure it, recognizing that the disagreements that exist in the field will not disappear solely on account of our own work!

In this chapter, I review the work my collaborators and I have done in our efforts toward the development of a comprehensive theory of creativity. We are far from that point. But, over the years, we at least have been moving in that direction.

Todd Lubart and I (Sternberg & Lubart, 1995, 1996) have identified several distinct approaches to the study of creativity, of which the psychometric approach is only one.

Mystical approaches attempt to understand creativity in terms of some kind of spiritual or other extra-scientific force (see Ghiselin, 1985, for a description of how great creators have attributed their creative abilities to mystical forces). Such approaches are not useful scientifically precisely because they eschew and reject science as a basis for understanding creativity. Pragmatic approaches (e.g., DeBono, 1985, 1992) are primarily oriented at developing methods of training that can be used in corporate or other settings. They are largely commercial in nature and typically have either not been tested or have been tested only weakly. This is not to say they do not work, only that they have not been adequately tested. Psychodynamic approaches (e.g., Freud, 1908/1959) seek to understand creativity in terms of largely unconscious forces, most of which are assumed to have taken root in childhood. Psychometric approaches, preferred by Guilford (1950, 1957) and Torrance (e.g., Torrance, 1974, 1988), attempt to measure creativity and to assign scores to creative work for qualities such as novelty and quality of responses to various kinds of stimuli. Cognitive-psychological approaches seek to understand creativity in terms of underlying mental representations and processes (e.g., Finke, Ward, & Smith, 1992; Weisberg, 1999). Social-psychological approaches (e.g., Amabile, 1983, 1996) attempt to understand the social forces that contribute to or impede creativity. Finally, systems or confluence approaches attempt to combine some of the approaches described above (e.g., Csikszentmihalyi, 1996; Gardner, 1993; Sternberg & Lubart, 1995). Our own preference has been to use a systems approach as a basis for our investment theory of creativity.

THE INVESTMENT THEORY OF CREATIVITY

Our *investment theory of creativity* (Sternberg & Lubart, 1991, 1995) is a confluence theory. According to this theory, creative people are the ones who are willing and able to "buy low and sell high" in the realm of ideas (see also Rubenson & Runco, 1992, for use of concepts from economic theory). Buying low means pursuing ideas that are unknown or out of favor but that have growth potential. Often, when these ideas are first presented, they encounter resistance. The creative individual persists in the face of this resistance, and eventually sells high, moving on to the next new, or unpopular idea.

Aspects of the Investment Theory

According to the investment theory, creativity requires a confluence of six distinct but interrelated resources: intellectual abilities, knowledge, styles of thinking, personality, motivation, and environment. Although levels of these resources are sources of individual differences, often the decision to use a resource is a more important source of individual differences. Below I discuss the resources and the role of decision making in each.

Intellectual Skills

Three intellectual skills are particularly important (Sternberg, 1985): (a) the synthetic skill to see problems in new ways and to escape the bounds of conventional thinking; (b) the analytic skill to recognize which of one's ideas are worth pursuing and which are not; and (c) the practical-contextual skill to know how to persuade others of—to sell other people on—the value of one's ideas. The confluence of these three skills is also important. Analytic skills used in the absence of the other two skills results in powerful critical, but not creative thinking. Synthetic skill used in the absence of the other two skills results in new ideas that are not subjected to the scrutiny required to improve them and make them work. And practical-contextual skill in the absence of the other two skills may result in societal acceptance of ideas not because the ideas are good, but rather, because the ideas have been well and powerfully presented.

We have tested the role of creative intelligence in creativity in several studies. In one study, we presented 80 individuals with novel kinds of reasoning problems that had a single best answer. For example, they might be told that some objects are green and others blue; but still other objects might be grue, meaning green until the year 2000 and blue thereafter, or bleen, meaning blue until the year 2000 and green thereafter. Or they might be told of four kinds of people on the planet Kyron, blens, who are born young and die young; kwefs, who are born old and die old; balts, who are born young and die old; and prosses, who are born old and die young (Sternberg, 1982; Tetewsky & Sternberg, 1986). Their task was to predict future states from past states, given incomplete information. In another set of studies, 60 people were given more conventional kinds of inductive reasoning problems, such as analogies, series completions, and classifications, but were told to solve them. But the problems had premises preceding them that were either conventional (dancers wear shoes) or novel (dancers eat shoes). The participants had to solve the problems as though the counterfactuals were true (Sternberg & Gastel, 1989a, 1989b).

In these studies, we found that correlations with conventional kinds of tests depended on how novel or nonentrenched the conventional tests were. The more novel the items, the higher the correlations of our tests with scores on successively more novel conventional tests. Thus, the components isolated for relatively novel items would tend to correlate more highly with more unusual tests of fluid abilities (e.g., that of Cattell & Cattell, 1973) than with tests of crystallized abilities. We also found that when response times on the relatively novel problems were componentially analyzed, some components better measured the creative aspect of intelligence than did others. For example, in the "grue-bleen" task mentioned above, the information-processing component requiring people to switch from conventional green-blue thinking to grue-bleen thinking and then back to green-blue thinking again was a particularly good measure of the ability to cope with novelty.

Knowledge

On the one hand, one needs to know enough about a field to move it forward. One can't move beyond where a field is if one doesn't know where it is. On the other hand, knowledge about a field can result in a closed and entrenched perspective, resulting in a person's not moving beyond the way in which he or she has seen problems in the past. Knowledge thus can help or it can hinder creativity.

In a study of expert and novice bridge players, for example (Frensch & Sternberg, 1989), we found that experts outperformed novices under regular circumstances. When a superficial change was made in the surface structure of the game, the experts and novices were both hurt slightly in their playing, but quickly recovered. When a profound, deep-structural change was made in the structure of the game, the experts initially were hurt more than the novices, although the experts later recovered. The reason, presumably, is that experts make more and deeper use of the existing structure, and hence have to reformulate their thinking more than do novices when there is a deep-structural change in the rules of the game.

Thus, one needs to decide to use one's past knowledge, but also *decide* not to let the knowledge become a hindrance rather than a help. Everyone has a knowledge base. How they choose to use it is a decision they must make.

Thinking Styles

Thinking styles are preferred ways of using one's skills. In essence, they are *decisions* about how to deploy the skills available to one. With regard to thinking styles, a legislative style is particularly important for creativity (Sternberg, 1988, 1997), that is, a preference for thinking and a decision to think in new ways. This preference needs to be distinguished from the ability to think creatively: Someone may like to think along new lines, but not think well, or vice versa. It also helps, to become a major creative thinker, if one is able to think globally as well as locally, distinguishing the forest from the trees and thereby recognizing which questions are important and which ones are not.

In our research (Sternberg & Grigorenko, 1995), we found that legislative individuals tend to be better students than less legislative students, if the schools in which they study value creativity. If the schools do not value or devalue creativity, they tend to be worse students. Students were also found to receive higher grades from teachers whose own styles of thinking match their own.

Personality

Numerous research investigations (summarized in Lubart, 1994, and Sternberg & Lubart, 1991, 1995) have supported the importance of certain personality attributes for creative functioning. These attributes include, but are not limited to, willingness to overcome obstacles, willingness to take sensible risks, willingness to tolerate ambiguity, and self-efficacy. In particular, buying low and selling high typically means defying the crowd, so that one has to be willing to stand up to conventions if one wants to think and act in creative ways (Sternberg, 2003; Sternberg & Lubart, 1995). Often, creative people seek opposition, in that they decide to think in ways that countervail how others think. Note that none of the attributes of creative thinking is fixed. One can *decide* to overcome obstacles, take sensible risks, and so forth.

In one study (Lubart & Sternberg, 1995), we found that greater risk-taking propensity was associated with creativity for artwork but not for essays. When we investigated why this was so, we found that some evaluators tended to mark down essays that took unpopular positions. We learned, therefore, that one of the risks people face when they are creative, even in an experiment on risk-taking, is that the evaluators will not appreciate the risks if they go against their own beliefs!

Motivation

Intrinsic, task-focused motivation is also essential to creativity. The research of Amabile (1983) and others has shown the importance of such motivation for creative work, and has suggested that people rarely do truly creative work in an area unless they really love what they are doing and focus on the work rather than the potential rewards. Motivation is not something inherent in a person: One *decides* to be motivated by one thing or another. Often, people who need to work in a certain area that does not particularly interest them will decide that, given the need to work in that area, they had better find a way to make it interest them. They will then look for some angle on the work they need to do that makes this work appeal to rather than bore them.

Environment

Finally, one needs an environment that is supportive and rewarding of creative ideas. One could have all of the internal resources needed in order to think creatively, but without some environmental support (such as a forum for proposing those ideas), the creativity that a person has within him or her might never be displayed.

Environments typically are not fully supportive of the use of one's creativity. The obstacles in a given environment may be minor, as when an individual receives negative feedback on his or her creative thinking, or major, as when one's well-being or even life are threatened if one thinks in a manner that defies convention. The individual therefore must *decide* how to respond in the face of the pretty close to omnipresent environmental challenges that exist. Some people let unfavorable forces in the environment block their creative output; others do not.

Confluence

Concerning the confluence of these six components, creativity is hypothesized to involve more than a simple sum of a person's level on each component. First, there may be thresholds for some components (e.g., knowledge) below which creativity is not possible regardless of the levels on other components. Second, partial compensation may occur in which a strength on one component (e.g., motivation) counteracts a weakness on another component (e.g., environment). Third, interactions may also occur between components, such as intelligence and motivation, in which high levels on both components could multiplicatively enhance creativity.

Creative ideas are both novel and valuable. But they are often rejected when the creative innovator stands up to vested interests and defies the crowd (cf. Csikszentmihalyi, 1988). The crowd does not maliciously or willfully reject creative notions. Rather, it does not realize, and often does not want to realize, that the proposed idea represents a valid and advanced way of thinking. Society often perceives opposition to the status quo as annoying, offensive, and reason enough to ignore innovative ideas.

Evidence abounds that creative ideas are often rejected (Sternberg & Lubart, 1995). Initial reviews of major works of literature and art are often negative. Toni Morrison's *Tar Baby* received negative reviews when it was first published, as did Sylvia Plath's *The Bell Jar*. The first exhibition in Munich of the work of Norwegian painter Edvard Munch opened and closed the same day because of the strong negative response from the critics. Some of the greatest scientific papers have been rejected not just by one, but by several journals before being published. For example, John Garcia, a distinguished biopsychologist, was immediately denounced when he first proposed that a form of learning called classical conditioning could be produced in a single trial of learning (Garcia & Koelling, 1966).

From the investment view, then, the creative person buys low by presenting an idea that initially is not valued and then attempting to convince other people of its value. After convincing others that the idea is valuable, which increases the perceived value of the investment, the creative person sells high by leaving the idea to others and moving on to another idea. People typically want others to love their ideas, but immediate universal applause for an idea often indicates that it is not particularly creative.

CREATIVITY AS A DECISION

Creativity, according to the investment theory, is in large part a decision. The view of creativity as a decision suggests that creativity can be developed. Simply requesting students to be more creative can render them more creative, if they believe that the decision to be creative will be rewarded rather than punished (O'Hara & Sternberg, 2000-2001).

To be creative, one must first *decide* to generate new ideas, analyze these ideas, and sell the ideas to others. In other words, a person may have synthetic, analytical, or practical skills, but not apply them to problems that potentially involve creativity. For example, one may decide to follow other people's ideas rather than synthesize one's own; or not to subject one's ideas to a careful evaluation; or to expect other people to listen to one's ideas and therefore decide not to try to persuade other people of the value of these ideas. The skill is not enough: One first needs to make the decision to use the skill.

For example, ability to switch between conventional and unconventional modes of thinking is important to creativity. One aspect of switching between conventional and unconventional thinking is the decision that one is willing and able to think in unconventional ways—that one is willing to accept thinking in terms different from those to which one is accustomed and with which one feels comfortable. People show reliable individual differences in willingness to do so (Dweck, 1999). Some people (what Dweck calls "entity theorists") prefer to operate primarily or even exclusively in domains that are relatively familiar to them. Other people (what Dweck calls "incremental theorists") seeks out new challenges and new conceptual domains within which to work.

We have proposed a number of different decisions by which one can develop one's own creativity as a decision (Sternberg, 2001; Sternberg & Lubart, 1995; Sternberg & Williams, 1996).

Redefine Problems

Redefining a problem means taking a problem and turning it on its head. Many times in life individuals have a problem and they just don't see how to solve it. They are stuck in a box. Redefining a problem essentially means extricating oneself from the box. It is an aspect of problem finding, as opposed merely to problem solving. This process is the divergent part of creative thinking.

Question and Analyze Assumptions

Creative people question assumptions and eventually lead others to do the same. Questioning assumptions is part of the analytical thinking involved in creativity. Society tends to make a pedagogical mistake by emphasizing the answering and not the asking of questions. The good student is perceived as the one who rapidly furnishes the right answers. The expert in a field thus becomes the extension of the expert student— the one who knows and can recite a lot of information. As John Dewey (1933) recognized, how one thinks is often more important than what one thinks. Schools need to teach children how to ask the right questions (questions that are good, thought-provoking, and interesting) and lessen the emphasis on rote learning.

Do Not Assume That Creative Ideas
Sell Themselves: Sell Them

As Galileo, Edvard Munch, Toni Morrison, Sylvia Plath, and millions of others have discovered, creative ideas do not sell themselves. On the contrary, creative ideas are usually viewed with suspicion and distrust. Moreover, those who propose such ideas may be viewed with suspicion and distrust as well. Because people are comfortable with the ways they already think, and because they probably have a vested interest in their existing way of thinking, it can be extremely difficult to dislodge them from their current way of thinking.

Encourage Idea Generation

As mentioned earlier, creative people demonstrate a "legislative" style of thinking: They like to generate ideas (Sternberg, 1997). The environment for generating ideas can be constructively critical, but it must not be harshly or destructively critical.

Recognize That Knowledge is a Double-Edged Sword and Act Accordingly

On the one hand, one cannot be creative without knowledge. Quite simply, one cannot go beyond the existing state of knowledge if one does not know what that state is. Many children have ideas that are creative with respect to themselves, but not with respect to the field because others have had the same ideas before. Those with a greater knowledge base can be creative in ways that those who are still learning about the basics of the field cannot be.

Identify and Surmount Obstacles

Buying low and selling high means defying the crowd. And people who defy the crowd—people who think creatively—almost inevitably encounter resistance. The question is not whether one will encounter obstacles; one will. When one buys low, one defies the crowd, and generally engenders in others a reaction of, at best, puzzlement, and, at worst, hostility. The question is whether the creative thinker has the fortitude to persevere. I have often wondered why so many people start off their careers doing creative work and then vanish from the radar screen. I think I know at least one reason why: Sooner or later, they decide that being creative is not worth the resistance and punishment. The truly creative thinkers pay the short-term price because they recognize that they can make a difference in the long term. But often it is a long while before the value of creative ideas is recognized and appreciated.

Sensible Risk-Taking

When creative people defy the crowd by buying low and selling high, they take risks in much the same way as do people who invest. Some such investments simply may not pan out. The person may generate an idea that is unpopular when it first is generated, and that stays unpopular over the long term. Moreover, defying the crowd means risking the crowd's disdain for "buying" into the wrong idea, or even wrath for disagreeing with others. But there are levels of sensibility to keep in mind when defying the crowd.

Creative people take sensible risks and produce ideas that others ultimately admire and respect as trend-setting. In taking these risks, creative people sometimes make mistakes, fail, and fall flat on their faces.

Nearly every major discovery or invention entailed some risk. When a movie theater was the only place to see a movie, someone created the idea of the home video machine. Skeptics questioned if anyone would want to see videos on a small screen. Another initially risky idea was the home computer. Many wondered if anyone would have enough use for a home computer to justify the cost. These ideas were once risks that are now ingrained in our society.

Few children are willing to take risks in school, because they learn that taking risks can be costly. Perfect test scores and papers receive praise and open up future possibilities. Failure to attain a certain academic standard is perceived as deriving from a lack of ability and motivation and may lead to scorn and lessened opportunities. Why risk taking hard courses or saying things that teachers may not like when that may lead to low grades or even failure? Teachers may inadvertently advocate children only learning to "play it safe" when they give assignments without choices and allow only particular answers to questions. Thus, we need not only to encourage sensible risk-taking, but also to reward it.

Encourage Tolerance of Ambiguity

People often like things to be in black and white. People like to think that a country is good or bad (ally or enemy) or that a given idea in education works or does not work. The problem is that there are a lot of grays in creative work, just as there are when one invests in a stock whose value may or may not go up. Many stocks are low-valued. The ambiguities arise as to which will go up, when they will go up, and, even, for some individuals, what they can do to make them go up. Artists working on new paintings and writers working on new books often report feeling scattered and unsure in their thoughts. They often need to figure out whether they are even on the right track. Scientists often are not sure whether the theory they have developed is exactly correct. These creative thinkers need to tolerate the ambiguity and uncertainty until they get the idea just right.

A creative idea tends to come in bits and pieces and develops over time. However, the period in which the idea is developing tends to be uncomfortable. Without time or the ability to tolerate ambiguity, many may jump to a less than optimal solution.

Self-Efficacy

Bandura (1996) has pointed out the importance of self-efficacy in many forms of achievement. When doing creative work, there come times when people seem to cease believing in what one is doing. Without self-efficacy, one may find oneself lacking the will to go on.

Find What One Loves to Do

The most creative people are intrinsically motivated in their work (Amabile, 1996). Less creative people often pick a career for the money or prestige and are bored with or loathe their careers. Most often, these people do not do work that makes a difference in their field.

Delay Gratification

Part of being creative means being able to work on a project or task for a long time without immediate or interim rewards, just as in investing one often must wait quite a while for the value of a stock to rise. People must learn that rewards are not always immediate and that there are benefits to delaying gratification. The fact of the matter is that, in the short term, people are often ignored when they do creative work or even punished for doing it.

Many people believe that they should reward children immediately for good performance, and that children should expect rewards. This style of teaching and parenting emphasizes the here and now and often comes at the expense of what is best in the long term.

The short-term focus of most school assignments does little to teach children the value of delaying gratification. Projects are clearly superior in meeting this goal, but it is difficult for teachers to assign home projects if they are not confident of parental involvement and support. By working on a task for many weeks or months, children learn the value of making incremental efforts for long-term gains.

Role-Model Creativity

There are many ways teachers and parents can provide an environment that fosters creativity (Sternberg & Williams, 1996). The most powerful way for teachers to develop creativity in children is to *role model creativity*. Children develop creativity not when they are told to, but when they are shown how.

The teachers most people probably remember from their school days are not those who crammed the most content into their lectures. The teachers most people remember are those teachers whose thoughts and actions served as a role model. Most likely they balanced teaching content with teaching children how to think with and about that content. The Nobel laureates, before they received their prizes, made excellent role models in large part because they were outstanding examples of creativity in action that students could emulate (Zuckerman, 1977, 1983).

Cross-Fertilize Ideas

Teachers also can stimulate creativity by helping children *to cross-fertilize in their thinking* to think across subjects and disciplines. The traditional school environment often has separate classrooms and classmates for different subjects and seems to influence children into thinking that learning occurs in discrete boxes—the math box, the social studies box, and the science box. However, creative ideas and insights often result from integrating material across subject areas, not from memorizing and reciting material.

Teaching children to cross-fertilize draws on their skills, interests, and abilities, regardless of the subject. If children are having trouble understanding math, teachers might ask them to draft test questions related to their special interests. For example, teachers might ask the baseball fan to devise geometry problems based on a game. The context may spur creative ideas because the student finds the topic (baseball) enjoyable and it may counteract some of the anxiety caused by geometry. Cross-fertilization motivates children who aren't interested in subjects taught in the abstract.

Take Time for Creative Thinking

Often, creativity requires time for incubation (Wallas, 1926). Many societies today are societies in a hurry. People eat fast food, rush from one place to another, and value quickness. Indeed, one way to say someone is smart is to say that the person is *quick* (Sternberg, 1985), a clear indication of an emphasis on time. This is also indicated by the format of many of the standardized tests used—lots of multiple-choice problems squeezed into a brief time slot.

Most creative insights do not happen in a rush (Gruber & Davis, 1988). People need time to understand a problem and to toss it around. If children are asked to think creatively, they need time to do it well. If teachers stuff questions into their tests or give their children more homework than they can complete, they are not allowing them time to think creatively.

Reward Creativity

We also need *to reward creativity*. They may choose differentially to reward the different kinds of creative contributions, depending on the circumstances and the students. For example, if teachers ask students to be bold in their thinking, the teachers may choose less to reward conceptual replications than bolder redirections (at levels of innovation characteristic of students, of course). Thus, teachers may choose not to limit their rewards to "crowd-defying creativity," but may choose to allocate rewards, depending upon circumstances and expectations for particular students. It is not enough to talk about the value of creativity. Children are used to authority figures who say one thing and do another. They are exquisitely sensitive to what teachers value when it comes to the bottom line—namely, the grade or evaluation.

Allow Mistakes

Teachers also need *to allow mistakes*. Buying low and selling high carries a risk. Many ideas are unpopular simply because they are not good. People often think a certain way because that way works better than other ways. But once in a while, a great thinker comes along—a Freud, a Piaget, a Chomsky, or an Einstein—and shows us a new way to think. These thinkers made contributions because they allowed themselves and their collaborators to take risks and make mistakes.

Although being successful often involves making mistakes along the way, schools are often unforgiving of mistakes. Errors on schoolwork are often marked with a large and pronounced X. When a student responds to a question with an incorrect answer, some teachers pounce on the student for not having read or understood the material, which results in classmates snickering. In hundreds of ways and in thousands of instances over the course of a school career, children learn that it is not all right to make mistakes. The result is that they become afraid to risk the independent and the sometimes-flawed thinking that leads to creativity.

When children make mistakes, teachers should ask them to analyze and discuss these mistakes. Often, mistakes or weak ideas contain the germ of correct answers or good ideas. In Japan, teachers spend entire class periods asking children to analyze the mistakes in their mathematical thinking. For the teacher who wants to make a difference, exploring mistakes can be an opportunity for learning and growing.

Take Responsibility for Both Successes and Failures

Another aspect of teaching children to be creative is teaching them *to take responsibility for both successes and failures*. Teaching children how to take responsibility means teaching children to (1) understand their creative process, (2) criticize themselves, and (3) take pride in their best creative work. Unfortunately, many teachers and parents look for—or allow children to look for—an outside enemy responsible for failures.

Encourage Creative Collaboration

Teachers also can work *to encourage creative collaboration* (Chadwick & De Courtivron, 1996; John-Steiner, 2000). Creative performance often is viewed as a solitary occupation. We may picture the writer writing alone in a studio, the artist painting in a solitary loft, or the musician practicing endlessly in a small music room. In reality, people often work in groups. Collaboration can spur creativity. Teachers can encourage children to learn by example by collaborating with creative people.

Imagine Things from Others' Points of View

Children also need to learn how *to imagine things from other viewpoints*. An essential aspect of working with other people and getting the most out of collaborative creative activity is to imagine oneself in other people's shoes. Individuals can broaden their perspective by learning to see the world from different points of view. Teachers and parents should encourage their children to see the importance of understanding, respecting, and responding to other people's points of view. This is important, as many bright and potentially creative children never achieve success because they do not develop practical intelligence (Sternberg, 1985, 1997). They may do well in school and on tests, but they may never learn how to get along with others or to see things and themselves as others see them.

Maximize Person-Environment Fit

Teachers also need to help children recognize person-environment fit. What is judged as creative is an interaction between a person and the environment (Csikszentmihalyi, 1988, 1996; Gardner, 1993; Sternberg & Lubart, 1995). The very same product that is rewarded as creative in one time or place may be scorned in another.

EVIDENCE REGARDING THE THEORY OF CREATIVITY

Two kinds of evidence regarding our thinking about creativity are relevant: assessment and instruction.

Assessment of Creativity

Research within the investment framework has yielded support for this model (Lubart & Sternberg, 1995). This research has used tasks such as (a) writing short stories using unusual titles (e.g., the octopus' sneakers), (b) drawing pictures with unusual themes (e.g., the earth from an insect's point of view), (c) devising creative advertisements for boring products (e.g., cufflinks), and (d) solving unusual scientific problems (e.g., how we could tell if someone had been on the moon within the past month?). This research showed creative performance to be moderately domain-specific, and to be predicted by a combination of certain resources, as described below. The exact blend of resources and the success with which these resources are blended may vary from one culture to another. For example, Niu and Sternberg (2001) found that both American and Chinese evaluators rated two distinct artistic products (collages and science-fiction characters) of American college students to be more creative than products of Chinese college students roughly matched for conventional intelligence (Niu & Sternberg, 2001).

In a recent study, creativity was measured using open-ended performance-based measures (Sternberg & the Rainbow Project Collaborators, 2005) to assess creativity. These performance tasks were expected to tap an important part of creativity that might not be measured using multiple-choice items alone, because open-ended measures require more spontaneous and free-form responses.

For each of the tasks, participants were given a choice of topic or stimuli on which to base their creative stories or cartoon captions. Although these different topics or stimuli varied in terms of their difficulty for inventing creative stories and captions, these differences are accounted for in the derivation of IRT ability estimates.

Each of the creativity performance tasks were rated on criteria that were determined *a priori* as indicators of creativity.

Cartoons

Participants were given five cartoons purchased from the archives of *The New Yorker*, but with the captions removed. The participants' task was to choose three cartoons, and to provide a caption for each cartoon. Two trained judges rated all the cartoons for cleverness, humor, originality, and task appropriateness on 5-point scales.

A combined creativity score was formed by summing the individual ratings on each dimension except task appropriateness, which theoretically is not a measure of creativity *per se*.

Written Stories

Participants were asked to write two stories, spending about 15 minutes on each, choosing from the following titles: "A Fifth Chance," "2983," "Beyond the Edge," "The Octopus's Sneakers," "It's Moving Backwards," and "Not Enough Time" (Lubart & Sternberg, 1995; Sternberg & Lubart, 1995). A team of six judges was trained to rate the stories. Each of six judges rated the stories for originality, complexity, emotional evocativeness, and descriptiveness on 5-point scales.

Oral Stories

Participants were presented with five sheets of paper, each containing a set of 11 to 13 images linked by a common theme (keys, money, travel, animals playing music, and humans playing music). There were no restrictions on the minimum or maximum number of images that needed to be incorporated into the stories. After choosing one of the pages, the participant was given 15 minutes to formulate a short story and dictate it into a cassette recorder, which was timed by the proctor for the paper assessments and by the internal computer clock for the computer assessments. As with the written stories, each judge rated the stories for originality, complexity, emotional evocativeness, and descriptiveness on 5-point scales.

In a sample of 793 first-year college students from around the United States, in colleges ranging from not selective at all to very selective, we found that adding these creative measures to analytical as well as practical measures roughly doubled the predictive value of the SAT for our sample in predicting grades for first-year college students (Sternberg & the Rainbow Collaborators, 2005). The measures also served to *decrease* ethnic differences between groups.

Evidence Regarding the Investment Theory: Instruction

One can teach students to think more creatively (Sternberg & Williams, 1996; Williams, Markle, Brigockas, & Sternberg, 2001). However, the emphasis in our research has been on evaluating our ideas about creativity in the classroom for instruction of conventional subject matter.

In a first set of studies, we explored the question of whether conventional education in school systematically discriminates against children with creative and practical strengths (Sternberg & Grigorenko, 2000; Sternberg, Grigorenko, Ferrari, & Clinkenbeard, 1999; Sternberg & Spear-Swerling, 1996). Motivating this work was the belief that the systems in most schools strongly tend to favor children with strengths in memory and analytical abilities. However, schools can be unbalanced in other directions as well. One school we visited in Russia in 2000 placed a heavy emphasis upon the development of creative abilities—much more so than on the development of analytical and practical abilities. While on this trip, we were told of yet another school—catering to the children of Russian businessman—that strongly emphasized practical abilities, and in which children who were not practically oriented were told that, eventually, they would be working for their classmates who were practically oriented.

To validate our ideas, we have carried out a number of instructional studies. In one study, we used the Sternberg Triarchic Abilities Test (Sternberg, 1993). The test was administered to 326 children around the United States and in some other countries who were identified by their schools as gifted by any standard whatsoever. Children were selected for a summer program in (college-level) psychology if they fell into one of five ability groupings: high analytical, high creative, high practical, high balanced (high in all three abilities), or low balanced (low in all three abilities). Students who came to Yale were then divided into four instructional groups. Students in all four instructional groups used the same introductory-psychology textbook (a preliminary version of Sternberg [1995]) and listened to the same psychology lectures. What differed among them was the type of afternoon discussion section to which they were assigned. They were assigned to an instructional condition that emphasized either memory, analytical, creative, or practical instruction. For example, in the memory condition, they might be asked to describe the main tenets of a major theory of depression. In the analytical condition, they might be asked to compare and contrast two theories of depression. In the creative condition, they might be asked to formulate their own theory of depression. In the practical condition, they might be asked how they could use what they had learned about depression to help a friend who was depressed.

Students in all four instructional conditions were evaluated in terms of their performance on homework, a midterm exam, a final exam, and an independent project. Each type of work was evaluated for memory, analytical, creative, and practical quality. Thus, all students were evaluated in exactly the same way. What did we find?

First, we observed when the students arrived at Yale that the students in the high creative and high practical groups were much more diverse in terms of racial, ethnic, socioeconomic, and educational backgrounds than were the students in the high-analytical group, suggesting that correlations of measured intelligence with status variables such as these may be reduced by using a broader conception of intelligence. Thus, the kinds of students identified as strong differed in terms of populations from which they were drawn in comparison with students identified as strong solely by analytical measures. More importantly, just by expanding the range of abilities measured, we discovered intellectual strengths that might not have been apparent through a conventional test.

Second, we found that all three ability tests—analytical, creative, and practical—significantly predicted course performance. When multiple-regression analysis was used, at least two of these ability measures contributed significantly to the prediction of each of the measures of achievement. Perhaps as a reflection of the difficulty of deemphasizing the analytical way of teaching, one of the significant predictors was always the analytical score.

Third and most importantly, there was an aptitude-treatment interaction whereby students who were placed in instructional conditions that better matched their pattern of abilities outperformed students who were mismatched. In other words, when students are taught in a way that fits how they think, they do better in school. Children with creative or practical abilities, who are almost never taught or assessed in a way that matches their pattern of abilities, may be at a disadvantage in course after course, year after year.

A follow-up study (Sternberg, Torff, & Grigorenko, 1998a, 1998b) examined learning of social studies and science by third-graders and eighth-graders. The 225 third-graders were students in a very low-income neighborhood in Raleigh, North Carolina. The 142 eighth-graders were students who were largely middle to upper-middle class studying in Baltimore, Maryland, and Fresno, California. In this study, students were assigned to one of three instructional conditions. In the first condition, they were taught the course that basically they would have learned had there been no intervention. The emphasis in the course was on memory. In a second condition, students were taught in a way that emphasized critical (analytical) thinking. In the third condition, they were taught in a way that emphasized analytical, creative, and practical thinking. All students' performance was assessed for memory learning (through multiple-choice assessments) as well as for analytical, creative, and practical learning (through performance assessments).

As expected, students in the analytical, creative, practical combined condition outperformed the other students in terms of the performance assessments. One could argue that this result merely reflected the way they were taught. Nevertheless, the result suggested that teaching for these kinds of thinking succeeded. More important, however, was the result that children in the successful-intelligence condition outperformed the other children even on the multiple-choice memory tests. In other words, to the extent that one's goal is just to maximize children's memory for information, teaching for creative as well as analytical and practical thinking is still superior. It enables children to capitalize on their strengths and to correct or to compensate for their weaknesses, and it allows children to encode material in a variety of interesting ways.

We have extended these results to reading curricula at the middle-school and the high-school level. In a study of 871 middle-school students and 432 high school students, we taught reading either creatively, analytically, and practically or through the regular curriculum. At the middle-school level, reading was taught explicitly. At the high school level, reading was infused into instruction in mathematics, physical sciences, social sciences, English, history, foreign languages, and the arts. In all settings, students who were taught using our expanded model substantially outperformed students who were taught in standard ways (Grigorenko, Jarvin, & Sternberg, 2002).

Thus the results of three sets of studies suggest that teaching for creative thinking, as well as for analytical and practical thinking, is worthwhile. Some kinds of students do not maximally profit from conventional instruction, but may profit from the kinds of expanded instruction we can offer.

When we speak of teaching for creativity, we may think of creativity as being of a single piece. It is not: There are different *kinds* of creative contributions.

KINDS OF CREATIVE CONTRIBUTIONS

Creative contributors make different *decisions* regarding *how* to express their creativity. We have proposed a propulsion theory of creative contributions (Sternberg, 1999b; Sternberg, Kaufman, & Pretz, 2002) that addresses this issue of how people decide to invest their creative resources. The basic idea is that creativity can be of different kinds, depending on how it propels existing ideas forward. When developing creativity, we can develop different kinds of creativity, ranging from minor replications to major redirections in their thinking.

Creative contributions differ not only in their amounts but also in the kinds of creativity they represent. For example, both Sigmund Freud and Anna Freud were highly creative psychologists, but the nature of their contributions seems in some way or ways to have been different. Sigmund Freud proposed a radically new theory of human thought and motivation and Anna Freud largely elaborated on and modified Sigmund Freud's theory. How do creative contributions differ in quality and not just in quantity of creativity?

The type of creativity exhibited in a creator's works can have at least as much of an effect on judgments about that person and his or her work as does the amount of creativity exhibited. In many instances, it may have more of an effect on these judgments. For example, a contemporary artist might have thought processes, personality, motivation, and even background variables similar to those of Monet, but that artist, painting today in the style of Monet, probably would not be judged to be creative in the way Monet was. He or she was born too late. Artists, including Monet, have experimented with impressionism, and unless the contemporary artist introduced some new twist, he or she might be viewed as imitative rather than creative.

The importance of context is illustrated by the difference, in general, between creative discovery and rediscovery. For example, BACON and related programs of Langley, Simon, Bradshaw, and Zytkow (1987) rediscover important scientific theorems that were judged to be creative discoveries in their time. The processes by which these discoveries are made via computer simulation are presumably not identical to those by which the original discoverers made their discoveries. One difference derives from the fact that contemporary programmers can provide, in their programming of information into computer simulations, representations and particular organizations of data that may not have been available to the original creators. Moreover, the programs solve problems, but do not define them. But putting aside the question of whether the processes are the same, a rediscovery might be judged to be creative with respect to the rediscoverer, but would not be judged to be creative with respect to the field at the time the rediscovery is made.

Given the importance of purpose, creative contributions must always be defined in some context. If the creativity of an individual is always judged in a context, then it will help to understand how the context interacts with how people are judged. In particular, what are the types of creative contributions a person can make within a given context? Most theories of creativity concentrate on attributes of the individual (see Sternberg, 1999b). But to the extent that creativity is in the interaction of person with context, we would need as well to concentrate on the attributes of the individual and the individual's work relative to the environmental context.

A taxonomy of creative contributions needs to deal with the question not just of in what domain a contribution is creative, but of what the type of creative contribution is. What makes one work in biology more creative or creative in a different way from another work in biology, or what makes its creative contribution different from that of a work in art? Thus, a taxonomy of domains of work is insufficient to elucidate the nature of creative contributions. A field needs a basis for scaling how creative contributions differ quantitatively and, possibly, qualitatively.

A creative contribution represents an attempt to propel a field from wherever it is to wherever the field is to wherever the creator believes the field should go. Thus, creativity is by its nature *propulsion*. It moves a field from some point to another. It also always represents a decision to exercise leadership. The creator tries to bring others to a particular point in the multidimensional creative space. The attempt may or may not succeed. There are different kinds of creative leadership that the creator may attempt to exercise, depending on how he or she decides to be creative.

The propulsion model suggests eight types of contributions that can be made to a field of endeavor at a given time. Although the eight types of contributions may differ in the extent of creative contribution they make, the scale of eight types presented here is intended as closer to a nominal one than to an ordinal one. There is no fixed a priori way of evaluating *amount* of creativity on the basis of the *type* of creativity. Certain types of creative contributions probably tend, on average, to be greater in amounts of novelty than are others. But creativity also involves quality of work, and the type of creativity does not make any predictions regarding quality of work.

The eight types of creative contributions are divided into three major categories, contributions that accept and contributions that reject current paradigms, and paradigms that attempt to integrate multiple current paradigms. There are also subcategories within each of these two categories: paradigm-preserving contributions that leave the field where it is (Types 1 and 2), paradigm-preserving contributions that move the field forward in the direction it already is going (Types 3 and 4), paradigm-rejecting contributions that move the field in a new direction from an existing or pre-existing starting point (Types 5 and 6), paradigm-rejecting contributions that move the field in a new direction from a new starting point (Type 7), and paradigm-integrating contributions that combine approaches (Type 8).

Thus, Type 1, the limiting case, is not crowd-defying at all (unless the results come out the wrong way!). Type 2 may or may not be crowd-defying, if the redefinition goes against the field. Type 3 typically leads the crowd. Type 4 goes beyond where the crowd is ready to go, so may well be crowd-defying. And Types 5-8 typically are crowd-defying in at least some degree. Obviously, there often is no "crowd" out there just waiting to attack. Rather, there is a field representing people with shared views regarding what is and is not acceptable, and if those views are shaken, the people may not react well.

Types of Creativity that Accept Current Paradigms and Attempt to Extend Them

1. *Replication.* The contribution is an attempt to show that the field is in the right place. The propulsion keeps the field where it is rather than moving it. This type of creativity is represented by stationary motion, as of a wheel that is moving but staying in place.

2. *Redefinition.* The contribution is an attempt to redefine where the field is. The current status of the field thus is seen from different points of view. The propulsion leads to circular motion, such that the creative work leads back to where the field is, but as viewed in a different way.

3. *Forward Incrementation.* The contribution is an attempt to move the field forward in the direction it already is going. The propulsion leads to forward motion.

4. *Advance Forward Incrementation.* The contribution is an attempt to move the field forward in the direction it is already going, but by moving beyond where others are ready for it to go. The propulsion leads to forward motion that is accelerated beyond the expected rate of forward progression.

Types of Creativity that Reject Current Paradigms and Attempt to Replace Them

5. *Redirection.* The contribution is an attempt to redirect the field from where it is toward a different direction. The propulsion thus leads to motion in a direction that diverges from the way the field is currently moving.

6. *Reconstruction/Redirection.* The contribution is an attempt to move the field back to where it once was (a reconstruction of the past) so that it may move onward from that point, but in a direction different from the one it took from that point onward. The propulsion thus leads to motion that is backward and then redirective.

7. *Reinitiation.* The contribution is an attempt to move the field to a different as yet unreached starting point and then to move from that point. The propulsion is thus from a new starting point

in a direction that is different from that the field previously has pursued.

8. *Integration*. The contribution is an attempt to integrate two formerly diverse ways of thinking about phenomena into a single way of thinking about a phenomenon. The propulsion thus is a combination of two different approaches that are linked together.

The eight types of creative contributions described above are largely qualitatively distinct. Within each type, however, there can be quantitative differences. For example, a forward incrementation can represent a fairly small step forward or a substantial leap. A reinitiation can restart a subfield (e.g., the work of Leon Festinger on cognitive dissonance) or an entire field (e.g., the work of Einstein on relativity theory). Thus, the theory distinguishes contributions both qualitatively and quantitatively.

CONCLUSION

In this chapter, I have reviewed some of the theory and research my collaborators and I have developed in our efforts to understand the nature of creativity—to stalk the creativity quark. We have not dealt with every question that a complete theory of creativity must answer—far from it. But we have tried to consider at least a sampling of its aspects. Our fundamental premise is that creativity is in large part a decision that anyone can make but that few people actually do make because they find the costs to be too high. Society can play a role in the development of creativity by increasing the rewards and decreasing the costs.

ACKNOWLEDGMENTS

Preparation of this chapter was supported by Grant REC-9979843 from the National Science Foundation and by a grant under the Javits Act Program (Grant No. R206R000001) as administered by the Institute of Education Sciences, U.S. Department of Education. Grantees undertaking such projects are encouraged to express freely their professional judgment. This chapter, therefore, does not necessarily represent the position or policies of the National Science Foundation, Office of Educational Research and Improvement or the U.S. Department of Education, and no official endorsement should be inferred.

REFERENCES

Amabile, T. M. (1983). *The social psychology of creativity.* New York: Springer.

Amabile, T. M. (1996). *Creativity in context.* Boulder, CO: Westview.

Bandura, A. (1996). *Self-efficacy: The exercise of control.* New York: Freeman.

Cattell, R. B., & Cattell, H. (1973). *Measuring intelligence with the Culture Fair Tests.* Champaign, IL: Institute for Personality and Ability Testing.

Chadwick, W., & De Courtivron, I. (Eds.). (1996). *Significant others: creativity & intimate partnership.* New York: Thames & Hudson.

Csikszentmihalyi, M. (1988). Society, culture, and person: A systems view of creativity. In R. J. Sternberg (Ed.), *The nature of creativity* (pp. 325-339). New York: Cambridge University Press.

Csikszentmihalyi, M. (1996). *Creativity: Flow and the psychology of discovery and invention.* New York: HarperCollins.

De Bono, E. (1985). *Six thinking hats.* Boston: Little, Brown.

De Bono, E. (1992). *Serious creativity: Using the power of lateral thinking to create new ideas.* New York: HarperCollins.

Dewey, J. (1933). *How we think.* Boston: Heath.

Dweck, C. S. (1999). *Self-theories: Their role in motivation, personality, and development.* Philadelphia: Psychology Press/Taylor & Francis.

Finke, R. A., Ward T. B., & Smith, S. M. (1992). *Creative cognition: Theory, research, and applications.* Cambridge, MA: MIT Press.

Frensch, P. A., & Sternberg, R. J. (1989). Expertise and intelligent thinking: When is it worse to know better? In R. J. Sternberg (Ed.), *Advances in the psychology of human intelligence* (Vol. 5, pp. 157–188). Hillsdale, NJ: Lawrence Erlbaum Associates.

Freud, S. (1908/1959). The relation of the poet to day-dreaming. In *Collected papers* (Vol. 4, pp. 173-183). London: Hogarth Press.

Garcia, J., & Koelling, R. A. (1966). The relation of cue to consequence in avoidance learning. *Psychonomic Science, 4,* 123–124.

Gardner, H. (1993). *Multiple intelligences: The theory in practice.* New York: Basic Books.

Ghiselin, B. (Ed.). (1985). *The creative process: A symposium.* Berkeley, CA: University of California Press.

Grigorenko, E. L., Jarvin, L., & Sternberg, R. J. (2002). School-based tests of the triarchic theory of intelligence: Three settings, three samples, three syllabi. *Contemporary Educational Psychology, 27,* 167-208.

Gruber, H. E., & Davis, S. N. (1988). Inching our way up Mount Olympus: The evolving-systems approach to creative thinking. In R. J. Sternberg (Ed.), *The nature of creativity* (pp. 243-270). New York: Cambridge University Press.

Guilford, J. P. (1950). Creativity. *American Psychologist, 5,* 444-454.

Guilford, J. P. (1957). *A revised structure of intellect* (Reprint No. 19). Los Angeles: University of Southern California, Psychological Laboratory.

John-Steiner, V. (2000). *Creative collaboration.* New York: Oxford University Press.

Langley, P., Simon, H. A., Bradshaw, G. L., & Zytkow, J. M. (1987). *Scientific discovery: Computational explorations of the creative processes.* Cambridge, MA: MIT Press.

Lubart, T. I. (1994). Creativity. In R. J. Sternberg (Ed.), *Thinking and problem solving* (pp. 290-332). San Diego: Academic Press.

Lubart, T. I., & Sternberg, R. J. (1995). An investment approach to creativity: Theory and data. In S. M. Smith, T. B. Ward, & R. A. Finke (Eds.), *The creative cognition approach.* Cambridge, MA: MIT Press.

Niu, W., & Sternberg, R. J. (2001). Cultural influences on artistic creativity and its evaluation. *International Journal of Psychology, 36*(4), 225–241.

O'Hara, L. A., & Sternberg, R. J. (2000–2001). It doesn't hurt to ask: Effects of instructions to be creative, practical, or analytical on essay–writing performance and their interaction with students' thinking styles. *Creativity Research Journal, 13*(2), 197–210.

Rubenson, D. L., & Runco, M. A. (1992). The psychoeconomic approach to creativity. *New Ideas in Psychology, 10,* 131-147.

Sternberg, R. J. (1979, September). Stalking the I.Q. quark. *Psychology Today, 13,* 42–54.

Sternberg, R. J. (1982). Natural, unnatural, and supernatural concepts. *Cognitive Psychology, 14,* 451-488.

Sternberg, R. J. (1985). *Beyond IQ: A triarchic theory of human intelligence.* New York: Cambridge University Press.

Sternberg, R. J. (1988). Mental self-government: A theory of intellectual styles and their development. *Human Development, 31,* 197-224.

Sternberg, R. J. (1993). *Triarchic abilities test.* Unpublished test.

Sternberg, R. J. (1995). *In search of the human mind.* Orlando, FL: Harcourt Brace Jovanovich.

Sternberg, R. J. (1997). *Successful intelligence.* New York: Plume.

Sternberg, R. J. (Ed.). (1999a). *Handbook of creativity.* New York: Cambridge University Press.

Sternberg, R. J. (1999b). A propulsion model of creative contributions. *Review of General Psychology, 3,* 83-100.

Sternberg, R. J. (Ed.). (2000). *Handbook of intelligence.* New York: Cambridge University Press.

Sternberg, R. J. (2001). Teaching psychology students that creativity is a decision. *The General Psychologist, 36*(1), 8–11.

Sternberg, R. J. (Ed.). (2003). *Psychologists defying the crowd: Stories of those who battled the establishment and won.* Washington, DC: American Psychological Association.

Sternberg, R. J., & Grigorenko, E. L. (2000). *Teaching for successful intelligence.* Arlington Heights, IL: Skylight.

Sternberg, R. J., Grigorenko, E. L., Ferrari, M., & Clinkenbeard, P. (1999). A triarchic analysis of an aptitude-treatment interaction. *European Journal of Psychological Assessment, 15*(1), 1-11.

Sternberg, R. J., & Gastel, J. (1989a). Coping with novelty in human intelligence: An empirical investigation. *Intelligence, 13,* 187-197.

Sternberg, R. J., & Gastel, J. (1989b). If dancers ate their shoes: Inductive reasoning with factual and counterfactual premises. *Memory and Cognition, 17,* 1-10.

Sternberg, R. J., & Grigorenko, E. L. (1995). Styles of thinking in school. *European Journal for High Ability, 6*(2), 201–219.

Sternberg, R. J., Kaufman, J. C., & Pretz, J. E. (2002). *The creativity conundrum: A propulsion model of kinds of creative contributions.* New York: Psychology Press.

Sternberg, R. J., & Lubart, T. I. (1991). An investment theory of creativity and its development. *Human Development, 34*(1), 1-31.

Sternberg, R. J., & Lubart, T. I. (1995). *Defying the crowd: Cultivating creativity in a culture of conformity.* New York: Free Press.

Sternberg, R. J., & Lubart, T. I. (1996). Investing in creativity. *American Psychologist, 51*(7), 677-688.

Sternberg, R. J., & Spear-Swerling, L. (1996). *Teaching for thinking.* Washington, DC: American Psychological Association.

Sternberg & The Rainbow Project Collaborators. (2005). Augmenting the SAT through assessments of analytical, practical, and creative skills. In W. Camara & E. Kimmel (Eds.), *Choosing students: Higher education admission tools for the 21st century* (pp. 159-176). Mahwah, NJ: Erlbaum.

Sternberg, R. J., Torff, B., & Grigorenko, E. L. (1998a). Teaching for successful intelligence raises school achievement. *Phi Delta Kappan, 79,* 667-669.

Sternberg, R. J., Torff, B., & Grigorenko, E. L. (1998b). Teaching triarchically improves school achievement. *Journal of Educational Psychology, 90,* 374-384.

Sternberg, R. J., & Williams, W. M. (1996). *How to develop student creativity.* Alexandria, VA: Association for Supervision and Curriculum Development.

Tetewsky, S. J., & Sternberg, R. J. (1986). Conceptual and lexical determinants of nonentrenched thinking. *Journal of Memory and Language, 25,* 202-225.

Torrance, E. P. (1974). *Torrance tests of creative thinking.* Lexington, MA: Personnel Press.

Torrance, E. P. (1988). The nature of creativity as manifest in its testing. In R. J. Sternberg (Ed.), *The nature of creativity* (pp. 43-75). New York: Cambridge University Press.

Wallas, G. (1926). *The art of thought.* New York: Harcourt, Brace.

Weisberg, R. W. (1999). Creativity and knowledge: A challenge to theories. In R. J. Sternberg (Ed.), *Handbook of creativity* (pp. 226-250). New York: Cambridge University Press.

Williams, W. M., Markle, F., Brigockas, M., & Sternberg, R. J. (2001). *Creative intelligence for school (CIFS): 21 lessons to enhance creativity in middle and high school students.* Needham Heights, MA: Allyn & Bacon.

Zuckerman, H. (1977). *Scientific elite: Nobel laureates in the United States.* New York: Free Press.

Zuckerman, H. (1983). The scientific elite: Nobel Laureates' mutual influences. In R. S. Albert (Ed.), *Genius and eminence: The social psychology of creativity and exceptional achievement* (Vol. 5, pp. 241-252). New York: Pergamon Press.

CHAPTER 7

A Medaindividual Model
of Creativity

Leonid Dorfman

Some researchers have put forward a systems view of creativity (e.g., Csikszentmihalyi, 1999; Gruber, 1999; Rathunde, 1999). Most systems perspectives have been expanded to include personality research (e.g., Magnusson, 2001; Mayer, 1998; Pervin, 2001). It would seem that a systems perspective can underlay both personality and creativity research. What is known about personality and creativity (e.g., Amabile, 1996; Barron & Harrington, 1981; Eysenck, 1993, 1995; Martindale, 1989; Martindale & Dailey, 1996; Vartanian, Martindale, & Kingery, 2002; Vartanian, Poroshina, & Dorfman, 2002) can be incorporated into systems models that treat personality and creativity in a cohesive fashion.

Is it possible to integrate within a unitary framework a systems perspective for personality research and a systems perspective for creativity research? This question posses a great challenge for the future. Presently, systems research gives rise to two different strategies. One examines personality from a creativity systems perspective and the second examines creativity from a personality (individuality) systems perspective. The latter strategy is a starting point for a meta-individual model of creativity developed in this chapter.

THE METAINDIVIDUAL WORLD THEORY

Systems ideas are valuable because they give rise not only to an understanding of how people function in a coherent fashion but they also provide some directions for empirical research. Eminent Russian psychologist Volf Merlin (1986) elaborated the "integral study of individuality" from the hierarchical multi-level systems perspective. He treated individuality as self-regulated, hierarchical levels structured and arranged in a complex (integrated) system. Merlin's theory incorporates a systems perspective and the findings of empirical studies into one another.

The metaindividual world theory (Dorfman, 1993, 1995, 1997) is derived from the Merlinian theory. The crucial question to be debated is how does the integral individuality, being a complex system and operating for its own sake, respond and incorporate at the same time social rules, demands and expectations. A perspective raised in metaindividual world theory is the nature of the relationships between the integral individuality and the social environment from a multisystems perspective.

The focal concepts of the integral individuality theory upon which the metaindividual world theory was developed are intraindividuality, metaindividuality, and the social environment.

Intraindividuality is the integral individuality system itself. It is conceptualized as a set of individual enduring traits. They are arranged on subsystems that are conceived of as hierarchically structured levels. They are biochemical, somatic, and nervous subsystems/levels (individual bodily traits), temperamental and personality subsystems/levels (individual mental traits), individual aspects of social roles in groups, and social strata as subsystems/levels (individual socio-psychological traits). Polymorphous (many-to-many) links emerge between traits that refer to different subsystems/levels. Additionally, the integral individuality maintains relations with the outside world in many ways. One of them is depicted by the concept of metaindividuality. Metaindividual traits are conceived of as how individuals are seen (evaluated) by other people or a group. The latter attributes and imparts some of its own features to the individuals. They in turn can make "personal contributions" by investing themselves in other people or by changing them more or less at their own desires, intentions, or will. The corresponding changes in the target are metaindividual features, as well. *Social environment* is composed, in particular, of people, groups, social rules, demands, expectation, and so on.

In the metaindividual world theory, the concepts of metaindividuality and social environment were further developed from a multisystems perspective. The concept of social environment was revised and treated as a *social-cultural system* (SCs) in which individuals dwell. The SCs has been understood not as a monolithic entity but as interrelated social fields and cultural domains, in the vein of Csikszentmihalyi (1999). The term "*system*" meant the SCs as a self-organized and self-regulated entity. It would operate mainly for its own sake—from a viewpoint the individual perceives, feels, or experiences it or reacts to its rules, demands, and/or expectations. The metaindividuality was thus depicted as being shaped, regulated and controlled by the SCs and was treated therefore as its *subsystem*.

However the metaindividuality is able to invest him- or herself in social-cultural events and the target can be not only people but also objects material or immaterial in nature. In this case, social-cultural events can not be treated as a system in which the metaindividuality is included as its subsystem. Rather, social-cultural events are guided by and under regulation of the individual. This is an opposite way to look at the SCs and the metaindividuality as its subsystem. That is, the integral individuality operates here as a system but functions not only for its own sake (the intraindividuality) but it also extends to social-cultural events. When the metaindividuality is woven into social-cultural events it would seem as a subsystem of the intra-individuality system (IIs).

BASIC SUGGESTIONS

The integral individuality taken in the social-cultural context would be seen as the intersection of personal and social-cultural life. This broad scope was called the *"metaindividual world."* The view is similar to Sullivan's (1953) definition of personality as "the relatively enduring pattern of recurrent interpersonal situations which characterize a human life" (pp. 110–111) but from Merlin's (1986) integral individuality theory. Investigation of individual differences in the metaindividual world is potentially important for personality and social psychology, as well as environmental psychology, art studies, creativity, and so on.

The metaindividual world can differ and reveal substantial variability in the extent to which individuals' behavior is contingent upon either socio-cultural constraints and opportunities, that is, to the SCs or the integral individuality itself, the IIs. The metaindividual world can also differ and reveal variability if individuals occupy the metaindividual position regarding either the SCs or/and the IIs.

We come to understand, then, that intraindividuality and social-cultural events would seem as systems which function basically for their own sake. Yet, the metaindividuality subsystem (i.e., the SCs) and social-cultural events as the metaindividuality subsystem (i.e., the IIs) would become parts of larger systems. The terms "system" and "subsystem" are used here to mean that a feedback loop emerges between the metaindividuality subsystem and the SCs or the IIs.

Regions and Regulation

Of particular importance for this perspective is the notion of *regions*. This notion was used to emphasize functionally different units of the metaindividual world if it falls into systems and their subsystems. Second, it was introduced to address functionalist concerns conceptualized in a structuralist framework. Third, the notion of regions was used to emphasize the collection of properties rather than single variables. Fourth, a regulation criterion can provide a way the metaindividual world would seem differentiated. Given this, the metaindividual world may be divided into four broad regions.

The first major region appears to be contingent upon *internal or internally restricted self-regulation*. This is an area of the IIs. Hypothetically, there would be a wide set of events, and although different, they are derived from common internal self-regulation. To cite but a few examples, I pay attention to the I or the self-as-knower, a sense of personal identity and a sameness through time (James, 1890/1902) or the self as actor (Martindale, 1980), or the self as author (Hermans, 1996), internal locus of control (Rotter, 1990), internal perceived locus of causality and autonomy orientation (Ryan & Deci, 2000), the causal agent (Snyder & Higgins, 1997), and autonomy and independence as key components of the personalities of creative individuals (Feist, 1999). This region is commonly termed the *"Authorship."*

The second major region appears to be due to *internal* but *extended self-regulation*. This is an area of the social-cultural events as a metaindividuality subsystem of the IIs. This region would include a wide set of events, and though different, they are derived from common internal extended self-regulation. Hypothetically, they would be the assimilation of reality to the mind (Piaget, 1975/1985), "mine and property" that attaches people to objects (Furby, 1991; James, 1890/1902), psychological ownership (Pierce, Kostova, & Dirks, 2003), dominance (Wiggins, 1995), extraversion as a major dimension of personality (Eysenck, 1970), and "image-guided" orientation of artists (Cupchik, 1999). This region is commonly termed the *"Possession."*

The third major region appears due to *external "other-regulation"* and is based on other-acceptance. This is an area of the SCs or its parts to which the individual moves to comprehend, accept and/or apply them (but this does not mean that he or she refers them to him- or herself). Hypothetically, this region would include a wide set of various events relying on generalized other (Mead, 1934), external locus of control (Rotter, 1990), external perceived locus of causality (Deci & Ryan, 1985), external criteria for evaluation as a subscale of extrinsic motivation (Harter, 1981), and evaluation of other people, as well as experts' evaluations and aesthetic appraisals according to professional criteria (Csikszentmihalyi, 1999). This region is commonly termed the *"Other-acceptance."*

The fourth major region appears due to *internal or relational to* "other-regulation." This is an area of the metaindividuality subsystem of the SCs or its parts. This region would include a wide set of events, and though different, they are derived from common internal or relational other-regulation. There would be a wide set of events though even different but relaying on the internal or relational other-regulation. To cite but a few examples, I would point out the Me or self-as-known (James, 1890/1902; Mead, 1934) or self-concept (Martindale, 1980) or the Me as a complex, narratively structured self (Hermans, 1996), experience of pressure and tension, just as being controlled by external events or response on the promise of a reward (Deci & Ryan, 1985), submission (Wiggins, 1995), relatedness to others (Hodgins, Koestner, & Duncan, 1996), and "rule-guided" orientation of artists (Cupchik, 1999). This region is commonly termed the *"Relatedness."*

Relativity and Complementarity

One can easily find obvious conceptual contradictions between the IIs (including the metaindividuality subsystem extended to social-cultural events) and the SCs (including its metaindividuality subsystem in the individuality) because they are mutually exclusive. Derived from Aristotelian logic a single referent cannot be both "A" and "not A." Although the subject is to deal with the collection of variables (regions) rather than with single variables the Possession and the Other-acceptance regions functionally contradict each other being taken together. The Possession and the Relatedness regions look functionally as nonsense taken together. However the uncertainty that appears can have a resolution from relativity and complementarity principles rooted in systems theories (e.g., Blauberg & Sadovsky, 1977).

The metaindividual world can be captured by adopting the diversity of perspectives (world views). The IIs is one's "own" perspective; the SCs is "other" perspective. However there are no privileged positions from which the metaindividual world can be examined. This view posits the *relativity* principle similarly arrived at by Einstein's relativity theory and philosophical "objective relativism," according to which knowledge is more "objective" if a thing is viewed from many standpoints; then its multiplicity is discovered, yet synthesized into a coherent unity (Lovejoy, 1955).

In the metaindividual world, the Authorship and the Possession regions highlight one's own perspective, and vice versa the Other-acceptance and the Relatedness regions capture "other" perspective. Besides, in one aspect, the metaindividuality looks as relational to the SCs (the Relatedness region). In another aspect, the metaindividuality dwells in social-cultural events but looks as relational to the IIs (the Possession region). To comprehend the metaindividual world it should be thought of as a multi-aspect construct. The IIs (and its subsystem) and the SCs (and its subsystem) would complement each other. The *complementarity* principle as it is used here is concerned with an area the properties of which can be regulated and predicted either by the IIs or the SCs, or by the both.

The complementarity principle includes the two systems (and their subsystems) as major dimensions of the metaindividual world. These dimensions are major because along each of them the collection of many properties appears. Besides, dependent or endogenous variables can be treated as a point related to both dimensions. How one endogenous variable can be in two places is like the puzzle of how one identical point can be on two lines. As James pointed out "it can, if it be situated at their intersection" (1904/1976, p. 8).

The metaindividual world would thus be organized as the plural heterogeneous multidimensional multisystems entity. It involves a number of structured units and elements which can exist on many scales, as well as the interactions of systems and subsystems within or between the systems (see: Figure 1). These go through processes that are not describable by a single rule nor are they reducible to only one level of explanation.

Predictions and Explanations

Although the metaindividual world theory is derived from Merlin's (1986) theory of integral individuality the former can be considered as kinds of confluence theories. Likewise, Sternberg and Lubart (1996) developed the investment theory of creativity. As for the metaindividual world theory itself, the regulation as a functional criterion and the region as a structural criterion are those based on the sets of theories which can be clustered, yet treated as interrelated in some way. A challenge arises here in that the profile of regulations and regions come to be considered as latent factors underlying and intersecting variables that produce different theories. The strategy of predictions and explanations requires one to focus on something *beyond* particular events rather than searching for their *inner* gist. This way of "research thinking" involves generalization instead of specification. However, this

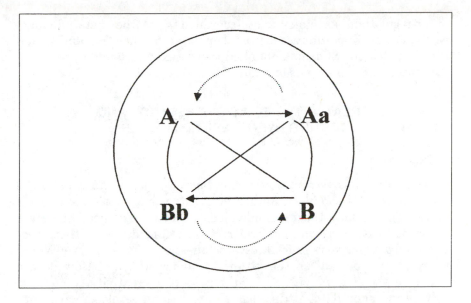

Figure 1. The metaindividual world principal outline.

A – the intraindividuality system (the Authorship region), Aa – social-cultural
events as the metaindividuality subsystem of the intraindividuality system
(the Possession region), B – the social-cultural system (the Other-acceptance
region), Bb – the metaindividuality subsystem of the social-cultural system
(the Relatedness region).

does not mean that any variable and any particular theory can be
incorporated into the metaindividual world theory. In what follows
though is another basis to make predictions and explanations.

First is a common latent factor for several variables which may be
predicted if each of them is under the same kind of regulation and refers
to the same region. If several variables are under different kinds of
regulation and refer to different regions then several appropriate latent
factors may be predicted. Yet, if a variable which refers to a region can
produce some effect on a dependent variable then another variable
referred to the same region can produce a similar effect on the same
dependent variable. Certainly predictions are not specific just to the
metaindividual world. To do that, theoretical discourse and empirical
support need to anticipate the predictions regarding the proper metaindividual world.

Second is the scope of explanations. Data obtained may be explained
and generalized in terms of the IIs (the self-regulation) or the SCs (the

other-regulation) as major axes (coordinates) of the metaindividual world, or how they interact or complement each other. Yet and within the IIs and/or the SCs, data obtained may be explained and generalized in terms of different kinds of regulation and regions.

CREATIVITY: LEVELS OF RESEARCH AND TESTING HYPOTHESIZED MODELS

A Background

Creativity is a construct that cannot be referred to as a region of the metaindividual world itself. Rather, creativity would be seen as a result or function of how the metaindividual world is arranged. Moreover different kinds of regulation and regions would differ in their contribution to creativity. Crucial research questions that arise are: Where is creativity "located" in the metaindividual world, and How do the regions of the metaindividual world contribute to creativity.

It seems helpful to distinguish at least three levels of creativity research in the metaindividual world. Specifically, three kinds of hypothesized models should be specified and tested. The first does not deal directly with creativity; it deals with variables that relate to different regions of the metaindividual world. The subject of hypothesized models here is which variables would present regions of the metaindividual world as latent factors. The second model addresses the issue of whether creativity can be treated as rooted "within" the metaindividual world and guided by its compounds. If so, exogenous factors should be distinguished from endogenous factors. The subject of hypothesized models here is which variables referred to different regions (exogenous factors) can reveal and predict the substantial variability of creativity (endogenous factors). The third types of models deal with mediating factors. The subject of hypothesized models here is assessing variables referred to one region (an exogenous factor) but mediating the relationships between variables referred to another region (an exogenous factor) and creativity (an endogenous factor). That is, regions of the metaindividual world would be considered as a unitary chain regulating creativity. However, endogenous factors (for instance, intelligence) which can mediate links between variables referred to several regions (exogenous factors) and creativity (an endogenous factor) would be hypothesized.

Next, I will illustrate this approach applying to recent studies conducted by Dorfman and Liakhova (2004), Dorfman and Ogorodnikova (2004), Dorfman and Gasimova (2004), and Gasimova (2004). There were 100 (sample 1 recruited from Perm high schools), 154 (sample 2 recruited from Perm State Teachers Training University), and 211 (samples 3 and 4 recruited from Perm high schools) participants, respectively.

I will address these studies several times in different contexts. Because of space limitation and to avoid repetitions I will describe measures and questionnaires used here. Dorfman and Liakhova (2004) examined dominance and nurturance measured by Interpersonal Adjective Scales (Wiggins, 1995) and extraversion and social desirability measured by the Eysenck Personality Questionnaire (EPQ-R Adult) (Eysenck & Eysenck, 1994). Creative thinking (standardized scores of fluency, flexibility, and originality) was measured using paper-and-pencil tasks in the Unusual Uses Test (Guilford, 1967; Wallach & Kogan, 1965). Dorfman and Ogorodnikova (2004) examined the personality domain using the adjective checklist developed by Gough and Heilbrun (1983) and three sets of scales–autonomy and aggression, achievement and affiliation, succorance and abasement, as well as a creative personality scale. Dorfman and Gasimova (2004) examined extraversion and social desirability measured by the Eysenck Personality Questionnaire (Eysenck & Eysenck, 1994), sensation seeking measured by the Sensation Seeking Scale (Zuckerman, 1979), dimensions of temperament such as object-related and people-related ergicity, object-related and people-related plasticity, object-related and people-related temp measured by the Rusalov temperamental questionnaire (Rusalov, 1997). Creative thinking (standardized scores of fluency, flexibility, and originality) was measured using paper-and-pencil tasks in the Unusual Uses Test (Wallach & Kogan, 1965; Guilford, 1967). In addition, Gasimova (2004) examined verbal intelligence using the German Intelligence Structure Test (IST-70) developed by Amthauer (1973). Verbal subtests were General Knowledge, Word-Grouping, Word Analogies, Word-Pairing, and Memory.

Variables Related and Latent Factors

A set of hypothesized models to be tested is that variables would relate one to another if they are contingent upon the same kind of regulation underlying each region. Dorfman and Liakhova (2004) found that the positive correlation between the scores of dominance and extraversion was .63 ($p < .001$). In Dorfman and Gasimova's (2004) study the score of extraversion correlated positively with the score of sensation seeking ($r = .35$, $p < .001$), dimensions of temperament such as people-related ergicity ($r = .59$, $p < .001$), people-related plasticity ($r = .37$, $p < .001$), people-related temp ($r = .31$, $p < .001$), object-related plasticity ($r = .25$, $p < .001$), and object-related temp

$(r = .49, p < .001)$. Similar correlations were found between the score of sensation seeking and dimensions of temperament. In addition, Dorfman and Liakhova (2004) found that the positive correlation between the scores of nurturance and social desirability was .34 $(p < .001)$. In Dorfman and Gasimova's study the correlation between the scores of social desirability and object-related ergicity was .25 $(p < .001)$.

Of course, this does not mean that variables hypothetically related to different kinds of regulation underlying various regions would not intercorrelate as well. However, this would mean that variables related to various regions would be guided by different latent factors.

In Dorfman and Ogorodnikova's (2004) study the hypothesis tested was that three sets of scales—autonomy and aggression, achievement and affiliation, succorance and abasement—would appear as different latent factors. Correlations were not only significant within mentioned pairs (p < .001) but also between some of their members (ps < .01 to .001). Nonetheless, when an exploratory factor analysis with Varimax normalized rotation was performed on these data three factors appeared which had eigenvalues greater than 1. Together they accounted for 88.70 % of the total variance associated with all variables. On Factor 1 (43.02%) the loadings of achievement and affiliation measures were significant. This factor was called "The Possession." On Factor 2 (27.38%) the loadings of autonomy and aggression measures were significant. This component was called "The Authorship." On Factor 3 (18.30%) the loadings of succorance and abasement measures were significant. This factor was called "The Relatedness."

In Dorfman and Gasimova's (2004) study an exploratory factor analysis with Varimax normalized rotation was done on the scores of extraversion and social desirability, sensation seeking, and dimensions of temperament. Two factors appeared which had eigenvalues greater than 1. Collectively, they accounted for 53.59% of the total variance of the variables. In particular, on Factor 1 (36.24%) the loadings of extraversion, sensation seeking, and people-related ergicity were highest and significant. On Factor 2 (17.35%) the loadings of social desirability and object-related ergicity were highest and significant. On both factors the loadings of people-related plasticity, object-related plasticity, and object-related temp were significant. These variables were removed from consideration. Factor 1 was called "The Possession" and Factor 2 was called "The Relatedness."

Data obtained support our suggestion that dominance, extraversion, sensation seeking, dimensions of temperament such as people-related ergicity would depart from the common source of regulation hypothetically underlying the Possession region. In turn, nurturance, social desirability, and object-related ergicity would depart from the common source of regulation hypothetically underlying the Relatedness region.

The Authorship and the Possession as Exogenous Factors and Creativity as an Endogenous Factor

Dorfman and Ogorodnikova's (2004) study tested the hypothesized model according to which creative personality is contingent on autonomy and aggression (the Authorship region), achievement and affiliation (the Possession region), and succorance and abasement (the Relatedness region). In structural equation modeling initial parameters were the Authorship exogenous factor and autonomy and aggression as its manifest variables, the Possession exogenous factor and achievement and affiliation as its manifest variables, the Relatedness exogenous factor and succorance and abasement as its manifest variables. The exogenous factors were included in the model as correlated. Creative personality scale was the endogenous variable. A correlation matrix for manifest variables was submitted to structural equation modeling using SEPATH in Statistica (Steiger, 1995). The method of discrepancy function estimation used was Generalized Least Squares. The line search method used was Golden section. Five indexes were used to assess model fit. They included the chi-square statistic, Steiger and Lind's root mean square error of approximation ($RMSEA$), the goodness-of-fit index (GFI), and the adjusted goodness-of-fit index ($AGFI$). The hypothesized model fit the data when the Authorship exogenous factor (and its manifest variables) and the Possession exogenous factor (and its manifest variables) correlated and were included in the model. The model summary was that the Possession exogenous factor included both achievement and affiliation manifest variables. The Authorship exogenous factor included autonomy and aggression manifest variable. Exogenous factors correlated. Paths passed from each exogenous factor to the creative personality endogenous factor, each path was positive ($p < .01 \pm .05$).

These data demonstrated that creative personality can be predicted and guided by either achievement and affiliation (the Possession) or autonomy and aggression (the Authorship). Findings revealed that the Authorship (the internal self-regulation) and the Possession (the internal but extended self-regulation) complement each other in their impact on creative personality. Additionally, because the Authorship and the Possession exogenous factors correlated, it may be suggested that the IIs and self-regulation are beyond the Authorship and the Possession.

Dorfman and Gasimova (2004) hypothesized the existence of a path to the creative thinking endogenous factor from the Possession exogenous factor (extraversion, sensation seeking, and people-related ergicity were its manifest variables) but not from the Relatedness exogenous factor (social desirability and object-related ergicity were its manifest variables). The correlation matrix for manifest variables was submitted to structural equation modeling using SEPATH in Statistica (Steiger, 1995). The model summary shows that the Possession exogenous factor included extraversion, sensation seeking, and people-related ergicity as its manifest variables. The Relatedness exogenous factor included social desirability and object-related ergicity. Exogenous factors correlated. The creative thinking endogenous factor included flexibility and originality as its manifest variables. The path passed to the creative thinking endogenous factor from the Possession exogenous factor ($p < .001$) but was nonsignificant from the Relatedness exogenous factor. These findings are consistent with results obtained by Martindale and Dailey (1996) for extraversion and by Vartanian, Martindale, and Kingery (2002) for Cloninger's (1987) novelty seeking dimension and cognitive disinhibition. The Possession contribution to creative thinking is consistent with results obtained by Amabile (1996) for intrinsic motivation, as well.

A more general task would be to search for other variables referred to the Authorship and the Possession regions as exogenous factors from which paths pass to creativity.

Mediating Factors (Variables)

Two kinds of hypothesized models were tested. The first assessed variables referred to one region (exogenous factors) which would mediate the relationships between variables referred to other regions (exogenous factors) and creativity (an endogenous factor). The second assessed endogenous mediating factors.

The Possession as a Mediating Factor

Dorfman and Liakhova (2004) tested an hypothesized model according to which creative thinking is contingent on both extraversion and dominance (the Possession region) in opposition to social desirability and nurturance (the Relatedness region). They found that the measure of extraversion correlated with the measures of fluency ($r = .21, p < .05$) and flexibility ($r = .21$, $p < .05$) and the measure of dominance correlated with the measures of fluency ($r = .25, p < .01$) and flexibility ($r = .26, p < .01$). The correlations between the measures of fluency, flexibility and social desirability, nurturance were nonsignificant.

The correlations between the measures of originality and extraversion, dominance, social desirability, and nurturance were nonsignificant. In structural equation modeling initial parameters were the Possession exogenous factor and extraversion and dominance as its manifest variables, the Relatedness exogenous factor and social desirability and nurturance as its manifest variables. The exogenous factors were included in the model as correlated. The endogenous factor was creative thinking and fluency and flexibility as its manifest variables. The method of discrepancy function estimation used was Generalized Least Squares. The line search method used was Golden section.

Indexes to assess model fit and other procedures were the same as those used by Dorfman and Ogorodnikova (2004). The hypothesized model fitted the data in such a way that most indexes were significant and some very close to being significant. The model summary indicated that the Possession exogenous factor included extraversion and dominance as its manifest variables. The Relatedness exogenous factor included social desirability and nurturance as its manifest variables. Exogenous factors correlated ($p < .01$). Given this, the path passed from the Possession exogenous factor to the creative thinking endogenous factor ($p < .01$). The path from the Relatedness exogenous factor to the creative thinking endogenous factor was nonsignificant. Data obtained evidenced that the Possession region (achievement and affiliation) can mediate the path from the Relatedness (succorance and abasement) to creative thinking. The Relatedness region (succorance and abasement) can enable creative thinking but inversely. A more general task would be in search for regions and their variables as exogenous factors from which paths pass to variables of the Possession region (a mediating factor) to creative thinking. These findings are consistent with results obtained by Martindale and Dailey (1996) on extraversion.

Intelligence as a Mediating Factor

It is well known that intelligence and creativity are related but not identical constructs (Sternberg, 1999). Dudorova and Dorfman (2002) found that verbal intelligence relates indirectly to subselves as mental representations of the Possession and the Relatedness regions. Based on findings obtained by Dudorova and Dorfman (2002), Dorfman and Gasimova (2004) constructed an hypothesized model to be tested by structural equation modeling. Extraversion, sensation seeking, and people-related ergicity were manifest variables of the Possession exogenous factor. Social desirability and object-related ergicity were manifest variables of the Relatedness exogenous factor. Verbal subtests were manifest variables of the verbal intelligence mediating factor. Fluency, flexibility, and originality were manifest variables of the creative thinking endogenous factor. The method of discrepancy function estimation used was Generalized Least Squares. The line search method used was Cubic interpolation. The hypothesized model fit the data in such a way that most indexes were significant and some very close to be significant.

The model summary indicated that the Possession exogenous factor included extraversion, sensation seeking, and people-related ergicity as its manifest variables. The Relatedness exogenous factor included social desirability and object-related ergicity as its manifest variable. The verbal intelligence mediating factor included General Knowledge, Word-Grouping, and Word Analogies as its manifest variables. The Creative thinking endogenous factor included originality only as its manifest variable. The paths passed from the Relatedness and the Possession exogenous factors to the verbal intelligence mediating factor ($p_1 < .02$; $p_2 < .02$) to the creative thinking endogenous factor ($p < .001$).

Data obtained evidenced that verbal intelligence (General Knowledge, Word-Grouping, and Word Analogies variables) can mediate links between the Possession region (extraversion, sensation seeking, and people-related ergicity) and the Relatedness region (social desirability and object-related ergicity) of metaindividual world and creative thinking (originality). A more general task would be to search for other regional variables as exogenous factors from which paths pass to other variables as mediating factors to creative thinking.

CONCLUSION

A metaindividual model of creativity was developed. Instead of looking at personality (individuality) from a creativity systems perspective, creativity was examined from a personality (individuality) systems perspective. The metaindividual world theory was considered as confluence theories. The regulation as a functional criterion and the region as a structural criterion were those based on which sets of theories were clustered, yet they are treated as interrelated in some way. The metaindividual world was divided into four broad regions. The first is the "Authorship," the second is the "Possession," the third is the "Other-acceptance," and the fourth is the "Relatedness."

Creativity (creative personality and creative thinking) was seen as a result or function of how the metaindividual world is arranged. Three levels of creativity research were described. The first did not deal with creativity directly but to variables which relate to different regions of the metaindividual world. In the second, creativity was treated as rooted in the metaindividual world and guided by its compounds. The focus of hypothesized models was upon variables referred to different regions (exogenous factors) revealing and predicting the substantial variability of creativity (endogenous factor). The third was concerned with mediating factors. A set of empirical findings supported a metaindividual model of creativity on each mentioned level of research.

REFERENCES

Amabile, T. M. (1996). *Creativity in context*. Boulder, CO: Westview.

Amthauer, R. (1973). *Intelligenz-Struktur-Test L S. T. 70. Handanweisung fur die Durchfahrung und Auswertung*. Gottingen: Verlag far Psychologie.

Barron, F., & Harrington, D. M. (1981). Creativity, intelligence, and personality. *Annual Review of Psychology, 32,* 439–476.

Blauberg, I. V., & Sadovsky, V. N. (1977). *Systems theory: Philosophy and methodological problems*. Moscow: Progress. (In Russian).

Csikszentmihalyi, M. (1999). Implications of a systems perspective for the study of creativity. In R. J. Sternberg (Ed.), *Handbook of creativity* (pp. 313–335). Cambridge: Cambridge University Press.

Cupchik, G. C. (1999). The thinking-I and the being-I in psychology of the arts. *Creativity Research Journal, 12*(3), 165–173.

Deci, E. L., & Ryan, R. M. (1985). The general causality orientations scale: Self-determination in personality. *Journal of Research in Personality, 19,* 109–134.

Dorfman, L. Ya. (1993). *Metaindividual world: Methodological and theoretical issues*. Moscow: Smysl. (In Russian, English Summary).

Dorfman, L. Ya. (1995). Metaindividual world. *Studia Psychologica, 37*(4), 279–286.

Dorfman, L. Ya. (1997). *Emotion in art: Theoretical and empirical considerations*. Moscow: Smysl. (In Russian, English Summary).

Dorfman, L. Ya., & Gasimova, V. A. (2004). Metaindividual world and creative thinking: Intelligence as a mediator. In L. Ya. Dorfman, Eu. A. Malianov, & E. M. Berezina (Eds.), *Metaindividual world and the plural self: Creativity, the arts, and ethnos* (pp. 40–51). Perm: Perm State Institute of Art and Culture. (In Russian).

Dorfman, L. Ya., & Liakhova, N. A. (2004). Regions of the metaindividual world and creative thinking. In L. Ya. Dorfman, Eu. A. Malianov, & E. M. Berezina (Eds.), *Metaindividual world and the plural self: Creativity, the arts, and ethnos* (pp. 9–18). Perm: Perm State Institute of Art and Culture. (In Russian).

Dorfman, L. Ya., & Ogorodnikova, A. V. (2004). Regions of the metaindividual world and personality creative potential. In L. Ya. Dorfman, Eu. A. Malianov, & E. M. Berezina (Eds.), *Metaindividual world and the plural self: Creativity, the arts, and ethnos* (pp. 19–29). Perm: Perm State Institute of Art and Culture. (In Russian).

Dudorova, C., & Dorfman, L. (2002). Plural self, intelligence, and cultural potentials. In E. A. Malianov, N. N. Zakharov, E. M. Berezina, L. Ya. Dorfman, V. M. Petrov, & C. Martindale (Eds.), *Personality, creativity, and art* (pp. 227–237). Perm: Perm State Institute of Art and Culture, Prikamsky Social Institute.

Eysenck, H. J. (1970). *The structure of human personality*. London, GB: Methuen.

Eysenck, H. J. (1993). Creativity and personality: Suggestions for a theory. *Psychological Inquiry, 4,* 147–178.

Eysenck, H. J. (1995). *Genius: The natural history of creativity*. Cambridge: Cambridge University Press.

Eysenck, H. J., & Eysenck, S. B. G. (1994). Manual of the Eysenck Personality Questionnaire (EPQ-R Adult) comprising the EPQ-Revised (EPQ-R) & EPQ-R Short Scale. San Diego, CA: EdITS.

Feist, G. J. (1999). Autonomy and independence. In M. A. Runco & S. R. Pritzker (Eds.), *Encyclopedia of creativity* (Vol. 1, pp. 157–163). San Diego: Academic Press.

Furby, L. (1991). Understanding the psychology of possession and ownership: A personal memoir and an appraisal of our progress. *Journal of Social Behavior and Personality, 6,* 457–463.

Gasimova, V. A. (2004). Factor structures of creative thinking, intelligence, personality and temperamental dimensions. In L. Ya. Dorfman, Eu. A. Malianov, & E. M. Berezina (Eds.), *Metaindividual world and the plural self: Creativity, the arts, and ethnos* (pp. 30–39). Perm: Perm State Institute of Art and Culture. (In Russian).

Gough, H. G., & Heilbrun, A. B. Jr. (1983). *The adjective check list (ACL): Manual*. Palo Alto, CA: Consulting Psychologists Press.

Gruber, H. E. (1999). Evolving systems approach. In M. A. Runco & S. R. Pritzker (Eds.), *Encyclopedia of creativity* (Vol. 1, pp. 689–693). San Diego: Academic Press.

Guilford, J. P. (1967). *The nature of human intelligence*. New York: McGraw-Hill.

Harter, S. (1981). A new self-report scale of intrinsic versus extrinsic orientation in the classroom: Motivational and informational components. *Developmental Psychology, 17,* 300–312.

Hermans, H. J. M. (1996). Voicing the Self: From information processing to dialogical interchange. *Psychological Bulletin, 119*(1), 31–50.

Hodgins, H. S., Koestner, R., & Duncan, N. (1996). On the compatibility of autonomy and relatedness. *Journal of Personality and Social Psychology Bulletin, 22*(3), 227–237.

James, W. (1890/1902). *The principles of psychology* (Vol. 1). London: Macmillan.

James, W. (1904/1976). Does consciousness exist? In *Essays in radical empiricism* (pp. 3–19). Cambridge, MA: Harvard University Press.

Lovejoy, A. (1955). *The revolt against dualism: An inquiry concerning the existence of ideas*. La Salle, IL: Open Court.

Magnusson, D. (2001). The holistic–interactionistic paradigm: Some directions for empirical developmental research. *European Psychologist, 6*(3), 153–162.

Martindale, C. (1980). Subselves. The internal representation of situational and personal dispositions. In L. Wheeler (Ed.), *Review of personality and social psychology* (Vol. 1, pp. 193–218). Beverly Hills: Sage.

Martindale, C. (1989). Personality, situation, and creativity. In J. A. Glover, R. R. Ronning, & C. R. Reynolds (Eds.), *Handbook of creativity* (pp. 211-232). New York: Plenum.

Martindale, C., & Dailey, A. (1996). Creativity, primary process cognition and personality. *Personality and Individual Differences, 20*(4), 409–414.

Mayer, J. D. (1998). A systems framework for the field of personality. *Psychological Inquiry, 9,* 118–144.

Mead, G. H. (1934). *Mind, self, and society.* Chicago: University of Chicago Press.

Merlin, V. S. (1986). *Essay on the integral study of the individuality.* Moscow: Pedagogika. (In Russian).

Pervin, L. A. (2001). A dynamic systems approach to personality. *European Psychologist, 6*(3), 172–176.

Piaget, J. (1975/1985). *The equilibration of cognitive structures.* Chicago: University of Chicago Press.

Pierce, J. L., Kostova, T., & Dirks, K. T. (2003). The state of psychological ownership: Integrating and extending a century of research. *Review of General Psychology, 7*(1), 84–107.

Rathunde, K. (1999). Systems approach. In M. A. Runco & S. R. Pritzker (Eds.), *Encyclopedia of creativity* (Vol. 2, pp. 605–609). San Diego: Academic Press.

Rotter, J. B. (1990). Internal versus external control of reinforcement: A case history of a variable. *American Psychologist, 45*(4), 489–493.

Rusalov, V. M. (1997). *A questionnaire of temperamental traits of the individuality (OFDSI).* Moscow: Russian Academy of Sciences Institute for Psychology (In Russian).

Ryan, R. M., & Deci, E. L. (2000). Self-determination theory and the facilitation of intrinsic motivation, social development, and well-being. *American Psychologist, 55*(1), 68–78.

Snyder, C. R., & Higgins, R. L. (1997) Reality negotiation: Governing one's self and being governed by others. *Review of General Psychology, 1*(4), 336–350.

Steiger, J. H. (1995). *Structural equation modeling in Statistica* (Version 5) [Computer software]. Tulsa, OK: Statsoft.

Sternberg, R. (1999). Intelligence. In M. A. Runco & S. R. Pritzker (Eds.), *Encyclopedia of creativity* (Vol. 2, pp. 81–88). San Diego: Academic Press.

Sternberg, R. J., & Lubart, T. I. (1996). Investing in creativity. *American Psychologist, 51,* 677–688.

Sullivan, H. S. (1953). *The interpersonal theory of psychiatry.* New York: Norton.

Vartanian, O., Poroshina, T., & Dorfman, L. (2002). Psychoticism and creativity among students and teachers of art and music in Russia. In L. Dorfman,

V. Petrov, & E. Grigorenko (Eds.), *Bulletin of Psychology and the Arts,* *3*(1), 30-33.

Vartanian, O., Martindale, C., & Kingery, L. (2002). Creativity and disinhibition. In E. A. Malianov, N. N. Zakharov, E. M. Berezina, L. Ya. Dorfman, V. M. Petrov, & C. Martindale (Eds.), *Personality, creativity, and art* (pp. 204–215). Perm: Perm State Institute of Art and Culture, Prikamsky Social Institute.

Wallach, M. A., & Kogan, N. (1965). *Modes of thinking in young children. A study of the creativity-intelligence distinction.* New York: Holt, Rinehart, and Winston, Inc.

Wiggins, J. S. (1995). *IAS: Interpersonal adjective scales.* Professional manual. PAR.

Zuckerman, M. (1979). *Sensation seeking: Beyond the optimal level of arousal.* Hillsdale, NJ: Erlbaum.

CHAPTER 8

Cinematic Creativity and Aesthetics: Empirical Analyses of Movie Awards

Dean Keith Simonton

Although Rudolf Arnheim initiated the psychological analysis of film as an art form back in the early 1930s (see Arnheim, 1957), empirical studies of cinematic creativity and aesthetics are noticeably less common than investigations of other forms of artistic expression, such as literature, music, and painting. Indeed, much of the empirical work on film concentrates on the medium as an expression of popular culture and societal norms. For instance, films have been frequently content analyzed to discern contemporary sexist stereotypes and gender roles (e.g., Bazzini, McIntosh, Smith, Cook, & Harris, 1997). Another set of empirical studies examine film from a more economic perspective, focusing on box office profits (e.g., Dodds & Holbrook, 1988; Litman, 1983; Sedgwick & Pokorny, 1999). Yet the money-making features of a motion picture may have minimal aesthetic merit (Holbrook, 1999). So the fact remains that relatively few investigations concentrate on cinema as a creative art form (but see Zickar & Slaughter, 1999).

There are probably several reasons for this neglect. One possible cause is that film has always had a somewhat ambiguous status as an artistic medium. Beginning in nickelodeons as a lucrative venture in popular entertainment, the transformation into a serious art form was a slow and precarious process that depended heavily on the emergence of film critics and film scholars who could discuss the medium independent of marketing and box office (see, e.g., Baumann, 2001). Even then, its claims to the position of genuine art continue to be threatened by the recurrent motivation on the part of many studios and independents to produce the "Hollywood blockbuster," an achievement too often devoid of aesthetic merit or creative expression.

Another feature of film renders it even more resistant to empirical inquiry: Its sheer complexity as a collaborative art form (Simonton, 2002, in 2004c). Most typically, a great painting is created by a single painter, a notable poem by an individual poet, a musical masterpiece by a lone composer. Indeed, collaborative artistic creations are extremely rare, and almost invariably represent inferior work in comparison to that produced by the same creators working alone (Jackson & Padgett, 1982). Prior to the advent of film the art form that may have come closest to representing a collective product was opera, given that this form often required the collaboration of the dramatist who wrote the libretto and the composer who wrote the music. Yet even in this case it has been shown that the composer's contribution so far outweighs that of the librettist as to render the latter's involvement almost trivial (Simonton, 2000). Although great operas exist that feature a mediocre libretto set to great music—as illustrated in Giuseppe Verdi's *Il Trovatore*—no counterexample exists of a great opera in which an outstanding libretto is set to pedestrian music. In striking contrast, film is an inherently collaborative work consisting of the collective efforts of screenwriters, directors, actors, set designers, cinematographers, editors, composers, and numerous other participants. An inferior contribution by any one of these collaborators can often undermine the entire enterprise, whether the culprit be ridiculous dialogue, implausible plot twists, inconsistent direction, over- or under-acting, murky cinematography, incoherent editing, laughable set design, costume or makeup, implausible special effects, over-the-top and distracting musical score, or poor sound quality.

This collaborative complexity renders film not very amenable to the methods that provide the basis for experimental aesthetics. There appear to be far too many parameters, sometimes interacting with each other in intricate ways. Rendering the medium even more inaccessible is the fact that the contributions of the various cinematic components unfold over a considerable period of time—usually close to two hours. Hence, to study a reasonable sample size of films would require that each participant devote hundreds of hours of effort. In contrast, a comparable number of poems, paintings, or compositions might be easily examined in a single experimental session. In any case, it should be evident that the study of cinematic creativity and aesthetics introduces obstacles that amply exceed what is encountered in most empirical studies of the arts. This inescapable reality suggests that this artistic medium might be more fruitfully investigated by some other methodology.

In this chapter I plan to illustrate an analytical strategy that enables the investigator to examine hundreds, even thousands of films. Besides studying feature-length films in their entirety, the approach permits the simultaneous examination of all the major contributions to a film's cinematic success. To be specific, the methodological approach takes advantage of the rich amount of raw data already available in archival sources, whether paper or electronic (e.g., *Corel All-Movie Guide 2 CD-ROM*, 1996; Internet Movie Database, n.d.). The illustrations will entail four published investigations: (a) film awards and critical acclaim (Simonton, 2004b), (b) creative clusters in cinematic art (Simonton, 2004c), (c) budget, box office, and aesthetic success (Simonton, 2005), and (d) gender differences in acting contributions (Simonton, 2005). Because these four studies do not answer all of the questions that might be entertained regarding cinematic creativity and aesthetics, I end this chapter with a brief discussion of other questions that can be addressed using the suggested research strategy.

FILM AWARDS AND CRITICAL ACCLAIM

A major event in the recognition of film as an art form was the founding of the Academy of Motion Picture Arts and Sciences in 1927. Although the Academy engaged in a diversity of activities, certainly the best known is the series of annual award ceremonies begun in 1929. The explicit purpose of these awards—which soon became known as the Oscars—was to honor the best contributions to filmmaking each year. At first, the main honors were bestowed for achievements in just a handful of categories, namely picture, director, male and female lead, screenplay (original and adapted), cinematography, art direction, and "engineering" effects. Over time, however, the number of categories expanded with the addition of male and female supporting roles, film editing, costume design, makeup, sound, sound effects editing, visual effects, musical score, and song. In addition, the voting membership of the Academy grew from a few dozen to several thousand, which enhanced the prima facie validity of the awards.

To be sure, not everyone concurs with the decisions made by the Academy voters, many critics arguing that the judgments are often swayed by factors unrelated to the true merit of the contribution (e.g., Peary, 1993). As a consequence, alternative award ceremonies eventually emerged. For instance, the New York Film Critics Circle awards were begun in 1935 precisely as an antidote to the Academy Awards, which the New York City critics thought were excessively swayed by Hollywood local tastes and studio politics. Because these rival honors are seldom granted to the exact same recipients, it is easy to infer that no consensus exists on the most outstanding accomplishments in film-making in a given year. Moreover, because these competing awards often seem to award contributions that fail to receive Oscar recognition, one might think that the Academy Awards are highly fallible indicators of the best creative and aesthetic accomplishments. Yet a recent empirical investigation showed that these conclusions are completely invalid (Simonton, 2004b). Not only does a substantial consensus exist on the comparative value of various cinematic contributions, but also the Academy Awards, for all their apparent faults, remain the best overall representatives of that overall agreement.

The study began with a sample of 1,132 films released between 1975 and 2002. In particular, the sample consisted of English-language feature-length narrative films that had received at least one award or award nomination in a major achievement category from one or more of the following seven distinct sources: (a) the Academy of Motion Picture Arts and Sciences; (b) the British Academy of Film and Television Arts (or "BAFTA"); (c) the Hollywood Foreign Press Association (which bestows the "Golden Globes"); (d) the National Board of Review; (e) the National Society of Film Critics; (f) the Los Angeles Film Critics Association; and (g) the New York Film Critics Circle.

These seven organizations were picked because (a) they all have been in existence for at least a quarter century, (b) they have consistently granted annual awards in most of the principal cinematic categories, and (c) they focus on widely-distributed, English-language motion pictures that are most likely to be included in movie/video guides (unlike movies honored at film festivals, such as Cannes, Venice, Berlin, or Sundance).

To the extent possible, the awards and nominations bestowed by these organizations were then used to define a series of measures for the following categories: picture, screenplay, direction, male and female leads, male and female supporting actors, cinematography, art direction, costume design, makeup, score, song, film editing, visual effects, and sound (omitting sound effects editing because only the Academy honors achievements in that area). In each case two points was allotted for an award, one point for a nomination, and zero points for neither an award nor a nomination. In addition, using the same scaling procedure, an alternative set of measures was created based on the awards granted by more specialized organizations, namely, the Directors Guild of America (direction), the Writers Guild of America (screenplay), the Screen Actors Guild (male and female lead and supporting acting), the American Society of Cinematographers (cinematography), the Grammy Awards (score and song), the Art Directors Guild (art direction), the Costume Designers Guild (costume design), and the American Cinema

Editors (film editing). Finally, an index of a film's cinematic success was devised using a highly reliable composite measure of five distinct movie guide ratings (see Simonton, 2002).

Detailed psychometric and correlational analyses yielded some very striking results. The following four findings deserve special attention.

First, almost all award categories exhibited a conspicuous consensus, as indicated by high internal consistency (Cronbach alpha) reliability coefficients. Furthermore, the Oscars provided the best single indicator of that overall agreement across almost all categories. This distinctive status was revealed by the finding that the deletion of the Academy award measures usually lowered the reliability coefficient by a greater increment than the deletion of any of the alternative honors.

Second, actual receipt of the Oscar provided meaningful information about cinematic creativity and achievement beyond that provided by merely being nominated for an Oscar. This was determined by correlating the Oscar measures with composites consisting of the remaining six award measures. It was found that the correlations were uniformly reduced if no extra points were provided for actually receiving the award. Hence, the correspondence revealed in the preceding paragraph cannot be ascribed to the Academy nominating the right achievements but awarding the wrong nominees.

Third, awards bestowed by the seven major organizations corresponded with more specialized awards granted by guilds and societies, with the Oscars usually providing the best correspondence. In particular, the awards offered by the seven organizations were directly correlated with comparable awards offered by the Directors Guild of America, the Writers Guild of America, the Screen Actors Guild, the American Association of Cinematographers, the Art Directors Guild, the Costume Designers Guild, and the Grammys. The correlations for the Academy awards were usually as high as or higher than any of the six alternative award measures. In fact, the various critic awards generally performed worse by this criterion.

Fourth and last, awards correlated positively with later movie guide ratings, the correlations being especially large in the categories of picture, direction, screenplay, and acting. Once more the Oscars generally outperformed the six alternative measures. In addition, the predictive validity of the honors bestowed by the critics was poor in comparison. This inferiority is surprising because the movie guide ratings actually represent critical evaluations.

To sum up, contrary to what is often assumed, the various honors offered by the seven distinct award ceremonies exhibit a strong consensus. Despite disagreements, their agreement compares favorably with standard psychometric instruments. Furthermore, of the seven sets of awards, the Academy awards enjoy the highest predictive validity as well as the strongest association with the overall consensus.

CREATIVE CLUSTERS IN CINEMATIC ART

The preceding study showed that the various awards offered by professional and critical organizations display a respectable agreement on the differential merits of various contributions to filmmaking. The next investigation took advantage of this consensus to compile measures of the various cinematic components (Simonton, 2004c). In particular, composite indicators were generated for picture, screenplay, direction, male and female leads, male and female supporting actors, cinematography, art direction, costume design, makeup, score, song, film editing, visual effects, sound effects editing, and sound. These composites were based on the awards conferred by the Academy of Motion Picture Arts and Sciences, the British Academy of Film and Television Arts, the Hollywood Foreign Press Association, the National Board of Review, the National Society of Film Critics, the Los Angeles Film Critics Association, and the New York Film Critics Circle. As before, two points were assigned for an award, one point for nomination, and zero points for neither award nor nomination. In addition, an index of a film's cinematic success was again defined by a composite measure of movie guide ratings. Finally, several control variables were introduced, namely, each film's release date, timing in minutes, genre (drama, comedy, romance, and musical), and the viewer rating provided by the Motion Picture Association of America (G, PG, PG-13, R, and NC-17). All this information was gathered for 1,327 English-language, narrative feature films released between 1968 and 1999.

The first step in the analysis of these data was to determine whether the various components of filmmaking formed what were termed *creative clusters*. This end was attained by subjecting the following award composites to a factor analysis: screenplay, direction, male and female leads, male and female supporting actors, cinematography, art direction, costume design, makeup, score, song, film editing, visual effects, sound effects editing, and sound. The factor analysis indicated that the 16 components could be consolidated into just four clusters. These were the *dramatic* (direction, screenplay, all four acting categories, and film editing), the *visual* (art direction, costume design, makeup, and cinematography), the *technical* (visual effects, sound effects editing, and sound), and the *musical* (score and song). Based on these results four composite variables were generated representing the four creative clusters.

The next step was to determine the relative importance of these four clusters in predicting a film's cinematic success. The latter criterion variable was assessed two ways, namely, the 7-item composite of best picture honors and the 5-item composite of movie guide ratings. Best picture honors correlated positively with all four clusters, namely dramatic, visual, technical, and musical, whereas movie guide ratings correlated positively with dramatic, visual, and technical, but not with musical. Significantly, the relative contributions of the four creative clusters agree across both criteria of cinematic success. The dramatic cluster is by far the most important, followed by the visual, technical, and musical, in that order. However, these zero-order correlations are misleading in that they represent bivariate associations without statistical controls and without tests for interaction effects between and among the creative clusters. Accordingly, two regression analyses were run, one for each criterion. The equations included the four creative clusters and all possible interaction terms (two-way through four-way) plus the control variables.

In the case of best picture honors, the resulting equation accounted for 75% of the variance and identified two simple or "main" effects, two two-way interaction effects, and one four-way interaction effect. With respect to the simple effects, this criterion was a positive function of just the dramatic and visual clusters. In other words, movies that score highest on dramatic and visual qualities have the best chance of earning best picture awards. Of the two factors, however, it is the dramatic cluster that is by far the most central, its effect size being about 10 times larger. On the other hand, contributions from the technical and musical clusters have no impact on best picture honors, at least not as main effects. However, the latter qualification is important because the technical and musical clusters do participate in interaction effects, specifically, Dramatic × Technical, Dramatic × Technical × Musical and Dramatic × Visual × Technical × Musical interactions. The only remaining interaction effect involves the Visual cluster, namely the Dramatic × Visual interaction. Although these effects vary in sign and order, they share one key feature in common: All include the dramatic cluster. Hence, the latter cinematic component can be viewed as a moderator variable, a moderator that determines the impact of the other three clusters. Nevertheless, too much should not be made of these interaction effects because the increment to the explained variance is only around 1%. As a result, it is possible to delete the multiplicative terms without losing much explanatory power. When the interactions are deleted, the musical cluster emerges as a positive main effect, joining the dramatic and visual clusters, while the null influence of the technical cluster remains.

The results for the criterion of movie guide ratings were somewhat different. All four creative clusters exhibited statistically significant main effects, joined by a pair of two-way interaction effects. The final regression equation accounted for 37% of the variance in the movie guide ratings. More specifically, cinematic success by this criterion was a positive function of dramatic, visual, and technical contributions, but a negative function of the musical contributions. These main effects were complicated by Dramatic × Visual and Dramatic × Technical interactions. Even so, the increment to the explained variance was again only a little more than 1%. Consequently, the interaction terms can be dropped with minimal loss in explanatory power. After the deletion is carried out, the movie guide ratings remain a positive function of dramatic, visual, and technical clusters, and a negative function of the musical cluster.

Although the outcomes were not identical for the two criteria of cinematic success, certain key findings replicated across both regression analyses. To begin with, two creative clusters emerged as significant predictors by both criteria, namely the dramatic and the visual. Of these two it is the dramatic cluster that is by far the most central to a film's impact. In the case of best picture honors, the dramatic cluster has 10 times the predictive power as does the visual cluster, whereas in the case of movie guide ratings the former has almost 6 times the predictive power as the latter. Furthermore, although interaction effects accounted for relatively little variance in both criteria, these interaction effects invariably involved the dramatic cluster as one of the components. In other words, the dramatic qualities of the film can moderate the influence of the other creative clusters. Hence, cinematic success depends primarily on the excellence of the direction, screenplay, acting, and film editing. In contrast, the visual contributions—art direction, costume design, makeup, and cinematography—play a very secondary role. Finally, even though the technical and musical clusters emerged as predictors in the case of the movie guide ratings, these effects were even smaller than that of the visual cluster. In concrete terms, visual effects, sound effects editing, sound, score, and song play a very minimal role in how a film is rated in movie guides. Consequently, the principal determinants of a film's cinematic success are the same across both criteria.

The differential impact of the three film clusters is illustrated by *Gone With the Wind*. Although not in this particular research sample, this film is often placed among the best ever made. In fact, it receives a perfect score—the equivalent of "five stars"—in every single movie guide used in this investigation. This film also receives the following scores on the dramatic, visual, technical, and musical clusters: 7.8, 4.1,

3.0, and 1.3. These are all standardized factor scores with a mean of zero and a standard deviation of unity. Hence, the order of these scores is the same as the overall predictive validity of the four clusters, with the dramatic cluster coming out on top and the music cluster coming out at the bottom. With respect to the dramatic cluster, the film received Oscars for best picture, best director, best actress in a leading role, best actress in a supporting role, best screenplay, and best film editing, as well as nominations for best actor in a leading role and best actress in a supporting role. Although there was no nomination or award for best actor in a supporting role, this was compensated for by the two nominations for best actress in a supporting role.

BUDGET, BOX OFFICE, AND
AESTHETIC SUCCESS

The foregoing conclusions might appear vulnerable to two main criticisms. First, one obvious criterion of cinematic success was omitted, namely, a film's box office performance. Movies vary greatly in how much money they earn during their theatrical release, and what makes a movie a box office success has unquestionable practical consequences. Yet the factors that are responsible for so-called "blockbusters" may not be the same as those that underlie movie awards and critical acclaim. Second, a crucial control variable may have been omitted from the statistical controls, namely, a film's production budget. Big budget productions may be able to purchase the services of the best screenwriters, directors, actors, and other contributors to the final creative product. Therefore, it is worthwhile to mention the results of a follow-up investigation that introduced these two variables into the analysis (Simonton, 2005).

In order to obtain reliable data on budget and box office, the inquiry focused on a sample of feature films released between 1997 and 2001. Besides obtaining the financial information, the study incorporated a composite measure of film reviews published by movie critics during the period of theatrical release and before movie awards are announced (in contrast to movie guide ratings, which come out after the awards and the video or DVD release). Although production costs were positively related to box office success (as measured by both first weekend and gross earnings), such expenditures had no correlation with best picture awards and were negatively correlated with critical acclaim as gauged by both favorable film reviews and movie guide ratings. Furthermore, even though box office performance displays a modest positive correlation with best picture honors, it exhibits slightly negative correlations with both contemporary film reviews and later movie guide ratings.

These divergent consequences could be explained in terms of how the budget and success criteria differentially correlated with the four creative clusters. Most strikingly, although critical acclaim and best picture honors are most strongly dependent on the dramatic cluster, production budget and box office both have minimal if any correlation with this essential component of the film product. Instead, these two financial aspects of filmmaking are most highly associated with the technical cluster. In other words, big budgets primarily go to paying for special effects, and these effects do attract lots of moviegoers. But these special effects do not impress those who vote for movie awards or who write film reviews. The latter are judging motion pictures mostly for the dramatic components. In a sense, there are two kinds of films. One kind aspires to be a form of art, and thus is centered in drama, an art form that can boast a long and secure pedigree. The other kind of film aims at entertainment, and accordingly emphasizes the spectacle of the circus arena rather than the subtleties of the drama theater.

This contrast between two types of motion picture can be illustrated using the films sampled for this investigation. The films with the biggest budgets were *Pearl Harbor, Harry Potter and the Sorcerer's Stone, How the Grinch Stole Christmas, The Perfect Storm, The Patriot, Lord of the Rings* (Part 1), *Ali, Gladiator, Planet of the Apes,* and *Black Hawk Down.* In contrast the films with the best critic evaluations were *Almost Famous, Gosford Park, Lord of the Rings* (Part 1), *In the Bedroom, You Can Count on Me, Traffic, Hedwig and the Angry Inch, Mulholland Dr., Memento,* and *The Deep End.* Note that only *Lord of the Rings* appears on both lists. Worse yet, some of the most critically acclaimed films had the smallest production costs. Specifically, *In the Bedroom, You Can Count on Me, Hedwig and the Angry Inch,* and *The Deep End* were among the 10 *least expensive* films in the sample. In contrast, *Pearl Harbor,* which was tops in budget, found itself in the bottom 10 in the judgments of film critics.

GENDER DIFFERENCES IN ACTING CONTRIBUTIONS

Gender differences permeate human behavior, including creativity and aesthetics. More specifically, there is ample reason for believing that gender may bear some relation with the cinematic product. For instance, it has been shown that women actors have shorter careers than men actors, earn much less money even at their career peak, and are obliged to perform in much less desirable roles (Lehman, 1941; Markson & Taylor, 1993). Yet another striking difference appeared in some of the investigations reviewed above: Exceptional women's performances may be less likely associated with outstanding feature films than is the case for exceptional men's performances. For example, in the investigation of creative clusters the factor loadings for female lead and supporting roles on the dramatic factor were lower than the loadings for male lead and supporting roles (Simonton, 2004c). Because the dramatic cluster is the main predictor of a film's success by the two criteria of best picture honors and movie guide ratings, this suggests that outstanding performances by women leave less of an impact than outstanding performances by men.

This implication was tested in two studies (Simonton, 2004a). In the first study 2,157 films that received Oscar nominations or awards between 1936 and 2000 were examined, whereas in the second study 1,367 films were investigated that from 1968 to 2000 had received awards or award nominations from seven professional, journalistic, and critical associations (the same seven as used in the preceding investigations). In both studies a significant gender discrepancy was found, a differential that persisted after the introduction of a large number of statistical controls and that showed no tendency to diminish over time. Specifically, the men's acting awards are more strongly associated with best picture honors and movie guide ratings than are the women's acting awards. This gap held for both lead and supporting award categories. So striking was the effect size that the male-female distinction was more important than the lead-supporting distinction. In concrete terms, an outstanding performance by a man in a supporting role is more likely to be found in an exceptional film than is an equally outstanding performance by a woman in a lead role. Thus, the best acting achievements of women are prone to be "ghettoized" in lesser films.

This phenomenon is perhaps best illustrated in the career of Meryl Streep. If we count both lead and supporting categories, she can claim more Oscar acting nominations than any other woman in the history of the Academy Awards, including both Katherine Hepburn and Bette Davis. Yet only a small proportion of these nominations were for films that were also nominated for best picture honors. In fact, her only award for best acting came for *Sophie's Choice,* a film that received no important best picture awards and only one best picture nomination (from the Hollywood Foreign Press Association). The films in which she received mere nominations did not do any better. Her main successes came early in her career, when she won Academy recognition for supporting roles in the award winning films *The Deer Hunter* and *Kramer versus Kramer,* the first as a nominee and the second as a winner. Yet later in her career this prominence in first-rate films gave way to acting nominations in films that were far removed from the running for best picture awards. Examples include roles in *Music of the*

Heart, One True Thing, The Bridges of Madison County, Postcards from the Edge, A Cry in the Dark, and *Ironweed.* Her stellar acting performances had become disconnected from the overall impact of the films in which she appeared.

Of course, the real question is why this gender difference appears in the first place. Although it is possible to conceive several distinction explanations, most prove to be inconsistent with various empirical findings (Simonton, 2004). For instance, because women actors are paid less than men actors they might appear in low budget films, and thus end up wasting their talents in inferior productions. Yet in opposition to this conjecture is the fact that expenditures are not positively correlated with best picture awards and are negatively correlated with movie guide ratings and favorable film reviews. Another possibility is that the difference reflects gender discrimination and prejudice. But this interpretation is contradicted by the fact that the differential has not decreased over the past several decades, as we would expect from increased gender equality in the workplace.

Yet another explanation is that the gender contrast is rooted in some intrinsic aesthetic properties of the feature narrative film. For example, male roles might be more strongly associated with great stories than are female roles. In support of this conjecture, one could point to the finding that best-selling novels, in contrast to unsuccessful novels, tend to have central male characters who are far more conspicuous than the female characters (Harvey, 1953). Perhaps this gender-based emphasis merely continues a long-term trend dating back to classic literary masterworks, such as the Babylonian *Epic of Gilgamesh,* Homer's *Illiad,* and Virgil's *Aeneid.* In a sense, according to this explanation "great films" are expected to include "great male actors" rather than "great female actors" because such films are most compatible with what may be styled an "epic prototype."

FUTURE INQUIRIES

The substantive issue raised in the preceding paragraph can become the subject of additional empirical research on cinematic creativity and aesthetics. Indeed, although the above four investigations have contributed a great deal to our understanding of this phenomenon, many more questions remain to be answered. For instance, a great many queries must concern the role that screenplay plays in a film's ultimate success. We already know that the quality of the screenplay serves as one of the main predictors of cinematic impact (Simonton, 2000, 2004c), but it is necessary to understand the details of that predictive utility. Does it make a difference whether the screenplay was adapted from a previous work rather than being written specifically for the production? If an adaptation, does the nature of the original work make a difference? For example, are adaptations from plays better than adaptations from novels? Whether or not the screenplay is an adaptation, are screenplays that present "true stories" or "biopics" more likely to be successful than those that represent pure fiction? And does it matter who is involved in writing a screenplay? If the director participates as either sole author or collaborator, does that enhance the film's prospects? Or if the screenplay is an adaptation, does it matter if the author of the original work is involved in making the conversion from paper to film?

Besides questions regarding the screenplay we can also pose the following issues: What is the contribution of film music, both score and song to cinematic success? Why was there a negative relation between music awards and movie guide ratings? What is the predictive validity of the various awards conferred at film festivals, such as Cannes, Venice, Berlin, and Sundance? Why are so many of the movies that won the prestigious Palm d'Or at Cannes totally obscure today? What about the supposed negative predictions of the Golden Raspberries or "Razzie awards" that are given to the worst films and cinematic contributions? Do these dubious honors operate in the same fashion as the bona fide awards but in an inverse direction? Finally, what are the factors that contribute to controversial films, cult favorites, or sleepers that take some time to catch on? Do such films feature a different set of predictors than mainstream products that receive wide-spread, immediate, and enduring acclaim?

It should be apparent by now that the research to date has only begun to scratch the surface of what needs to be known about cinematic creativity and aesthetics. The motion picture is often identified as the single most important artistic form to emerge during the twentieth century. It is therefore surprising that over a century after its emergence, we still know so little. Additional empirical analyses of award-winning movies may help reduce that unfortunate ignorance.

REFERENCES

Arnheim, R. (1957). *Film as art*. Berkeley: University of California Press.

Baumann, S. (2001). Intellectualization and art world development: Film in the United States. *American Sociological Review, 66*, 404-426.

Bazzini, D. G., McIntosh, W. D., Smith, S. M., Cook, S., & Harris, C. (1997). The aging women in popular film: Underrepresented, unattractive, unfriendly, and unintelligent. *Sex Roles, 36*, 531-543.

Corel All-Movie Guide 2 CD-ROM. (1996). Ottawa, Canada: Corel Corporation.

Dodds, J. C., & Holbrook, M. B. (1988). What's an Oscar worth? An empirical estimation of the effects of nominations and awards on movie distribution and revenues. *Current Research in Film, 4,* 72-88.

Harvey, J. (1953). The content characteristics of best-selling novels. *Public Opinion Quarterly, 17,* 91-114.

Holbrook, M. B. (1999). Popular appeal versus expert judgments of motion pictures. *Journal of Consumer Research, 26,* 144-155.

Internet Movie Database (n.d.). Accessed from http://us.imdb.com/Sections/Awards/

Jackson, J. M., & Padgett, V. R. (1982). With a little help from my friend: Social loafing and the Lennon-McCartney songs. *Personality and Social Psychology Bulletin, 8,* 672-677.

Lehman, H. C. (1941). The chronological ages of some recipients of large annual incomes. *Social Forces, 20,* 196-206.

Litman, B. R. (1983). Predicting success of theatrical movies: An empirical study. *Journal of Popular Culture, 16,* 159-175.

Markson, E. W., & Taylor, C. A. (1993). Real versus reel world: Older women and the Academy Awards. *Women and Therapy, 14,* 157-172.

Peary, D. (1993). *Alternate Oscars: One critic's defiant choices for best picture, actor, and actress from 1927 to the present.* New York: Delta.

Sedgwick, J., & Pokorny, M. (1999). Movie stars and the distribution of financially successful films in the motion picture industry. *Journal of Cultural Economics, 23,* 319-323.

Simonton, D. K. (2000). The music or the words? Or, how important is the libretto for an opera's aesthetic success? *Empirical Studies of the Arts, 18,* 105-118.

Simonton, D. K. (2002). Collaborative aesthetics in the feature film: Cinematic components predicting the differential impact of 2,323 Oscar-nominated movies. *Empirical Studies of the Arts, 20,* 115-125.

Simonton, D. K. (2004a). The "Best Actress" paradox: Outstanding feature films versus exceptional performances by women. *Sex Roles, 50,* 781-795.

Simonton, D. K. (2004b). Film awards as indicators of cinematic creativity and achievement: A quantitative comparison of the Oscars and six alternatives. *Creativity Research Journal, 16,* 163-172.

Simonton, D. K. (2004c). Group artistic creativity: Creative clusters and cinematic success in 1,327 feature films. *Journal of Applied Social Psychology, 34,* 1494-1520.

Simonton, D. K. (2005). Cinematic creativity and production budgets: Does money make the movie? *Journal of Creative Behavior, 39,* 1-15.

Zickar, M. J., & Slaughter, J. E. (1999). Examining creative performance over time using hierarchical linear modeling: An illustration using film directors. *Human Performance, 12,* 211-230.

CHAPTER 9

Creativity and Design: What the Established Teaches Us

Kees Overbeeke and Jodi Forlizzi

Design is creative in essence. It is about making innovative products. That is why it is often associated with the arts, and taught in Art Schools or Academies as they are called in Europe. As products became more technological as microelectronics crept in, design became associated with IT and computer sciences and it moved from Art Schools into Universities. This placed a new double burden on design: to become more technical *and* more scientific. Design is re-inventing itself. This causes lots of stress both within the profession and between the profession and the established sciences. Many people confuse design with styling, that is, making things beautiful. Or design is seen as unscientific or even anti-scientific within universities. Design, however, is a way of looking at the world and transforming it, just as physics or biology does. That is what we want to show in this chapter. We show through examples of our work how design borrows insights and methods from other sciences, uses them to shape physical hypotheses (prototypes of products), tests these hypotheses and so generates new, widely applicable knowledge. This is exactly what brought the two authors of this chapter together. From two widely different backgrounds (psychology and design, respectively) we met in the forum of interaction design. And we saw how we could help each other progress in our endeavors.

Design is about shaping meaning. In this chapter meaning is defined as knowledge-for-action: information about through which actions a person can access the product's functionality. To put it simply: which knob do I have to turn or push to start the washing machine?

The world around us, and the objects designers put into it, have a meaning: we know, or try to find out, what to do with these objects. And by using these products we reshape our lives and the way we interact with our community. It took some people time to learn to use an ATM machine. Older people might remember how on Friday afternoons they had to wait in line in a bank to get some ready cash for the weekend. Designers try to understand and predict what effect a new product will have on the individual and society: how it changes the experience of being in the world.

This led designers naturally to the psychological and philosophical underpinning of the experiential. Two major philosophical approaches include the European phenomenological approach represented by Heidegger (1962) and Merleau-Ponty (1963), and the American pragmatists approach represented by Peirce (1958) and Dewey (1980). Both approaches, although they have their differences, hold that information-for-action is created through interacting with the world. Information is a verb.

How, then is information-for-action created in the interaction with the world? In other words: how does the world invite us to act, even irresistibly so? Our sensory system is tuned to the world: it is apt to pick up signals from this world, and act accordingly; this changes the signaling world and, in turn, procures new signals. Gibson's theory of perception is based on this approach. He was influenced by European Gestaltists (the term affordance reminds us of Aufforderungscharakter) and the phenomenologist Michotte (Gibson, 1986; Michotte, 1963). Semiotics and the theory of signs also give us clues about signals in the world and the possibilities for meaning-for-action. Pierce's theory of semiotics is based on this approach. He attempted to explain the cognitive process of acquiring scientific knowledge through patterns of communicative activity (Peirce, 1958; Parmentier, 1987). These fields set up possibilities for scientific exploration of knowledge-for-action, including all of responses we have to products that are seemingly devoid of cognitive activity.

Let's return to design. Designers have to know how products derive interactive meaning—how they invite people—because designers have to materialize this meaning in products. Since the introduction of electronics in consumer products, design has become even more complicated. Everywhere you look these days you see people totally involved in pushing buttons on communication devices up to a point where they bump into a lamppost. Electronics need an interface. So, the user no longer does things with an object, but rather to an interface. This complicates matters. Scissors seem to easy to use because they fit my hand. The scissors' function fits my action possibilities. But what about a 50-button remote control? Sure, it fits my hand. But the movements we make are no longer creators of "meaning" (Dourish, 2001). We have to "know" which button to push to change the channel. And changing a channel requires the same action as turning up the volume, i.e., pushing. Interaction design, in a way, has come to a cul-de-sac.

We think the meaning-for-action approach offers a way out of the cul-de-sac. This is what this chapter is about.

INTERACTION SPACE

One of the essential concepts related to meaning-for-action is the interaction space. What is interaction space? The interaction space can roughly be defined as all of the possible signals that a product can give to invite its user or users to act. For example, a wine glass can be used because it can hold liquid to satisfy one's thirst, because it fits the hand, because it fits well in the experience of having wine, or because it fits in the social context of a dinner party. Clearly, variations in the appearance and behavior of a product define the interaction space and affect people's responses to any given product.

To this end, designers need to understand how human responses to products—whether "mindless" (or pre-cognitive), perceptual, habitual, or social—shape the interaction space and affect the design of particular products. To explore this phenomenon, we survey research in perception, semiotics, and pre-cognitive and habitual psychological responses. Perception is examined to explore how meaning is created through interactions in the physical environment. Semiotics helps us to understand what "universal" product elements allow for both subjective and objective interpretations of meaning. Pre-cognitive and habitual psychological responses help us to understand what responses to products are fast, automatic, stimulus-driven, and marked by positive affect.

PERCEPTION

According to Gibson (1986) perception is not an automatic brain process mediated by inference and memory, but rather an active sampling of the structured ambient light. Why active? The world unfolds itself in possibilities for action. The world affords actions to an organism on the scale of that organism—in an ongoing perception-action cycle. Doing things with a product as a result of the perceived action possibilities reveals new action possibilities. It follows that the world appears to us as inherently meaningful as we perceive action possibilities, i.e., affordances. Meaning is in the world, directly, not inferred through reasoning.

What are the consequences of Gibson's theory for design? Designers make objects and want them to mean something to the user. They, at least we may reasonably assume this, strive for ease-of-use, for natural or intuitive and for enjoyable human-product interaction. And Gibson's theory lends a helping hand here. His theory is about meaning in interaction with the natural environment, and thus by extension with the world of artifacts.

How has this theory impacted design and design research? The designer has to start by examining the user's perceptual-motor skills. From this analysis, i.e., what a user normally does, he can deduce how a product should work. If information for action is created in an ongoing action-perception cycle, we should design to support this cycle.

This is what the first author did about two decades ago. Using Gibson's idea that action is essential for perception, we devised a system to generate 3D images on a flat screen (Gaver, Smets, & Overbeeke, 1995). The basic idea of the system is that moving in front of a local monitor causes a remote camera to move analogously. When the onlooker moves, shifting his point of view, the camera moves accordingly and generates new information on the monitor. To see something out of view to the right, for instance, the viewer need only "look around the corner" by moving to the left; to see something on a desk, he or she need only "look over the edge," and so forth. The result is that the monitor appears as a window rather than a flat screen, through which remote scenes may be explored visually in a natural and intuitive way. The onlooker creates 3D information in a concerted action with the system.

Our early work upheld some basic assumptions from phenomenology and pragmatism. We delved into research on interaction design and emotional design. Our research has naturally merged in rich interaction design (Djajadiningrat, Wensveen, Frens, & Overbeeke, 2004).

The psychologist Donald Norman brought Gibson's concept of affordance to the design audience. Because of Norman's influence, affordance became a buzzword in the design community (Norman, 1988). However, Norman's concept of affordance was not complete. To quote Caroline Hummels (2000):

> Unfortunately, Norman and many other researchers outside the field of design have (. . .) interpreted the concept of affordances narrowly. They relate it only to the perceptual-motor skills of the user and the characteristics of the environment, but they

leave the intention and the feelings of the user outside the basic concept. (. . .) People are not invited to drink only because the glass fits their physical measurements. They can also be attracted to act, even irresistibly so, through the expectation of beauty of interaction. Temptation could be the goal. (pp. 1.21-1.22)

The point here is that product functionality alone does not suffice in creating meaning. If affordances are about meaning, they are not just about functional meaning; not only must they fit our perceptual-motor skills, they must also fit our emotional and cognitive skills. Man as a whole should be included if we want to come to true user-centered design.

For example, office chairs have many handles to heighten comfort when working. However, people use these handles rarely, i.e., when the chair is new. The handles are too difficult to use on a regular basis. Typically a person has a feel for his desired body posture. But translating this feeling into actually changing the posture of the chair is too big a bother. Different handles change different "dimensions" of the chair. And people are no good in handling different dimensions separately (Djajadiningrat, Overbeeke, & Smets, 1996). The chair requires them to construct a mental model with many degrees of freedom, i.e., to decompose a movement in its Cartesian components. Instead of adjusting the chair when discomfort is experienced, people start to move. The chair does not exploit our skills.

Why not design an office chair that changes its posture according to the way we sit in it, i.e., that senses how we feel and acts accordingly? This is what we mean by supporting the perception-action loop: I feel my desired posture; the chair feels it from the way I move and adapts. So we set out to design a conceptual chair that moves between four states, according to the situation the sitter is in and the task at hand (Figure 1). We chose two levels of communication with the environment (open-closed) and two levels of personal state (relaxed–concentrated) (see Figure 2). Furthermore, we wanted the chair to care for its user, and to prevent RSI. Our resulting design measures four user situations, and responds appropriately with four different positions (Overbeeke, de Looze, Vink, & Cheung, 2004).

The chair adapts its position to our behavior. We also conceived of and designed an alarm clock (Figure 3) that adapts to the way we feel from the way we dynamically, and thus expressively, interact with it (Wensveen, Djajadiningrat, & Overbeeke, 2004).

People express their emotions in the way they handle objects. If we give them the possibility to set the alarm clock in a myriad of ways, they will express their mood when setting the alarm. The alarm

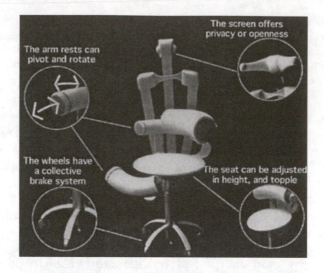

Figure 1. A conceptual office chair that senses and acts accordingly
(design: Kin Fai Cheung, TU Delft).

clock detects a person's mood by the way he interacts with the sliders. The clock then adapts its behavior in the morning by waking you up with a different tune. While you interact with the product to communicate "factual" information, the product senses your emotions from the way you handle it. There is a unity of cognitive (time), emotional and perceptual-motor skills.

SEMIOTICS

Semiotics can provide designers with knowledge for the design of interactive products, by showing how "universal" product elements allow for both subjective and objective interpretations of meaning. Semiotics as the understanding of communicable symbols can be applied at many levels in product design. For example, naïve, primitive, and even popular images have been used to create designs for a variety of products (Lin, 2003). The paper clip lamp by Designframe (www.designframeproducts.com) relies on the iconic paper clip and light bulb in its design of the Paperclip lamp. The humorous use of the paperclip form for stand and storage, and the silvered light bulb for light and lampshade is an example of the use of popular iconic images in the design of products for the home.

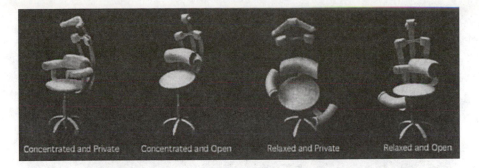

Figure 2. Shows a number of configurations for how the chair might look. When concentrated and open, e.g., the chair is high like a stool, does not support the arms or shields of the head. When relaxed and open the chair is low, turns away from the desk, and affords sitting in unconventional ways. Along with the usual office chair possibilities, this conceptual design offers more. Of course the chair knows things (and might even be equipped with learning capacities). But it has also new capacities. The armrest can be retreated or turned down to serve as a leg rest. A screen can shield you from the environment. The chair itself is mounted on a spring so that it can wobble, or, when the spring is de-activated, remain still.

NATURAL PERCEPTIVE RESPONSES
TO PRODUCTS

Another intriguing group of phenomena that relate to knowledge-for-action are our human abilities to generate natural perceptive responses to products. These responses are pre-cognitive, fast, and seemingly automatic. When related to product design, these responses are evoked in the absence of significant interaction with products.

These phenomena can be divided into two different processes. The first arises naturally and is often acquired in infancy, such as the human ability to quickly recognize faces. The second arises as we learn to respond habitually to stimuli in our environment. To relate these phenomenon to product design, we can think of two simple examples. The first could be natural responses to lifelike form or purposeful movement in designed products, such as a robotic dog toy. The second could be exemplified by driving a car. At first, using this product requires cognitive processing and memory, but later becomes an automatic skill.

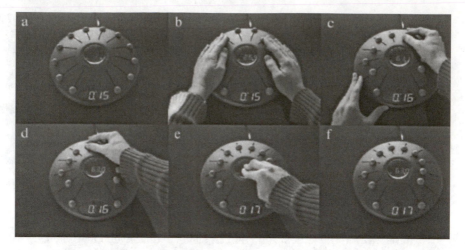

Figure 3. The prototype of the clock consists of two displays and twelve sliders. The front display shows the current time, the central display shows the alarm time. When the sliders are slid from the starting situation (a) toward the central display the alarm time appears in this display (b). With the first displacement of a slider, time is added to the current time to make up the alarm time. With each successive displacement, more time is added to (moving toward the center: c) or subtracted from (moving toward the edge: d) the alarm time. Each slider ranges from 0 to 60 minutes. Upon reaching the preferred wake up time the central display is pressed (e) and the alarm is set (f).

Natural responses to products leverage the skills of the human perceptual system. Research on visual perception shows that our perceptual system produces natural responses to even very simple two-dimensional displays (Scholl & Tremoulet, 2000). In early investigations of causal and lifelike movement in simple displays, it was discovered that viewers perceive various properties in simple displays that go beyond the movement properties therein (Heider & Simmel, 1944; Michotte, 1963). This work has inspired contemporary research on causality in order to generalize the basic phenomena in various ways. Subsequent studies have shown, for example, that viewers make attributions of animacy, causality, and intentionality to relatively simple displays. For example, a small set of motion cues was shown to be sufficient not only to determine whether or not a moving object was animate, but also to determine what intention motivated the object's movement (Dittrich & Lea, 1994; Blythe, Todd, & Miller, 1999). Interestingly, these attributions occur in childhood as well as adulthood, and are not culturally specific (Bruce, Nourbakhsh, &

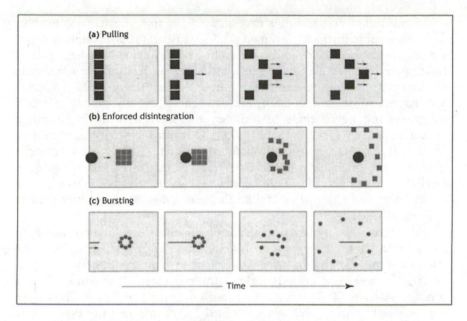

Figure 4. Displays that relate to functional relations such as pulling, enforced disintegration, and bursting, originally produced by White and Milne.

Simmons, 2002). Figure 4 shows snapshots from simple animations that resulted in viewers describing what they saw as pulling, disintegration, and bursting.

In the world of product design, natural responses have been capitalized upon in the form of biomimetic, lifelike, anthropomorphic, and zoomorphic product forms and product behaviors. For example, the Sorriso Chair, designed by Marco Marin, is a whimsical chair that cradles the sitter with a smile-shaped negative space in the contour of the chair. When empty, it greets passersby with the possibility of sitting in a friendly place.

Artists and designers have historically been interested in lifelike form and behavior in three-dimensional artifacts. Our anecdotal evidence suggests that people tend to unintentionally reference lifelike, human and animal characteristics when interacting with products, developing likes and dislikes, and even treating products as personalities or characters. For example, many drivers name their cars, describe the front of the product as having a particular "face" or character, and develop a long relationship through interacting with the car and creating attributions about its basic use.

Recent design research has investigated the use of anthropomorphic and zoomorphic forms in designed products. Bush (1990) concluded that we use anthropomorphic and zoomorphic constructs to help understand how human values play a role in interacting with a largely inanimate environment. Other research has found that subtle, barely perceived anthropomorphic and zoomorphic references are the most effective in generating perceptions of animacy and causality during product interactions (Ingram & Annable, 2004). Our earlier work has identified ways that designers use anthropomorphic form (DiSalvo & Gemperle, 2003)), how anthropomorphic form is created and used (Gemperle, Forlizzi, & Yonkers, 2003), and consistent emotional responses can be evoked through the use of lifelike form in a designed product (Mutlu & Forlizzi, 2004).

Quite often, designers use anthropomorphic form nearly unintentionally. In these cases, response activation often occurs without the user's awareness. The nature of the response depends on how a product matches a person's underlying mental representation, how often a product is used, and how these experiences of use are shaped by a person's own history. For example, in the case of a moving typography piece done by our research group shown in Figure 5, viewers interpreted the movement of the text as representing breathing (Ford, Forlizzi, & Ishizaki, 1997). This is most likely a post-attentional, pre-cognitive response to the quality of movement used in the piece. However, it is additional proof for how natural responses to product qualities can evoke emotion and knowledge-for-action.

Other types of perceptual responses to products develop through repeated exposure to that product. Psychological research has shown that repeated exposure to stimuli increases positive attitude to that stimuli (Zajonc, 1968). This finding has been supported with two basic models: the non-specific activation model and the perceptual fluency model (Buchner, Steffens, Erdfelder, & Rothkegel, 1997). The non-specific activation model shows that brief exposures to stimuli produce memory representations that can be activated again without any contextual reference. The perceptual fluency model shows that familiar stimuli are easier to perceive, code, and process, and increase feelings of pleasantness.

As designers, we are interested in understanding how attributions of lifelikeness, expressed through causality, animacy, and intentionality, might create natural responses for three-dimensional artifacts. We believe that we can capitalize on this hard-wired feature of the human perceptual system to design intuitive channels for knowledge-for-action.

Why?	Why?	Why?	Why?
Why?	Why?	Why?	Why?

Figure 5. Excerpt of still from a moving (kinetic) typography piece. Viewers interpreted the movement of the text as "breathing."

SUPPORTING NATURAL RESPONSES TO PRODUCTS

Motivated by a desire to contribute design knowledge to natural responses to products and a theory of meaning-for-action, our research group created The Hug—a conceptual design for a robotic product that facilitates intimate communication across distance (DiSalvo, Gemperle, Forlizzi, & Montgomery, 2003; Gemperle et al., 2003). Emphasizing the physical aspects of communication, The Hug uses expressive anthropomorphic form to impart a sense of presence, and relies on touch and voice for interaction and control (Figure 6).

Our decision to design The Hug was informed by our research on the experience of aging, where we saw a pronounced need for more accessible, appropriate, and compelling communication products for the aging population. Maintaining social and emotional bonds through intimate communication is an essential human activity and characteristic of healthy family life. Intimate communication is not only pleasurable, it is also profoundly important for maintaining mental, emotional, and physical health.

The physical shape of The Hug expresses the gesture of hugging. The shape is anthropomorphic, with two arms reaching slightly up and out from a stout torso. The body has rounded shapes suggesting a head and two feet. The form accepts the human body naturally and instructs the user how to interact with the product. When resting in its base or on a couch, The Hug reaches upward and outward, a gesture that begs for a hug. When cradled or hugged in the arms of the user, the curved form fits naturally with the human body, creating a

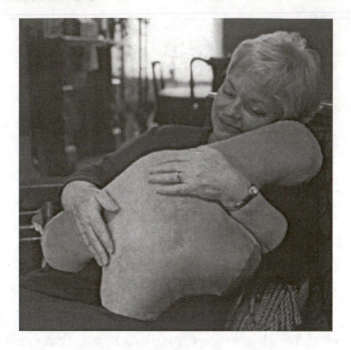

Figure 6. The Hug, an anthropomorphic product designed to
support social and emotional communication.

comfortable fit. When held in the lap, The Hug rests either facing
forward toward the upper torso or backwards sitting in the lap. The
scale of The Hug is similar to a pillow, creating a familiar relationship with the body and facilitating a number of alternate locations for
holding, hugging and resting on The Hug. The Hug activates responses
of pleasure, familiarity, and the human experience. There is a unity of
knowledge-for-action and resulting meaning.

Theories of natural responses to products and artifacts in the
environment offer new ways to understand and categorize action and
interaction with designed products. Beyond the concepts of familiarity
and liking, they will contribute to new design knowledge about
knowledge-for-action.

CONCLUSION

In this chapter, we have presented the idea that individuals can
experience products not only cognitively, but also in terms of the direct
experience of interacting with them. We have spent the last decade of

our careers understanding the breadth and depth of people's responses to designed products. This chapter presents integrated thinking about how action can be used to create meaning when interacting with products. To develop a deeper understanding of these issues, we hope to develop a much more detailed notion of knowledge-for-action and the interaction space.

The next question that naturally evolves is which qualities of products most readily lead individuals to action and meaning, and why? We hope that this issue will be addressed in the future of design research.

REFERENCES

Bush, D. (1990). Body icons and product semantics. In D. Vihma (Ed.), *Semantic visions in design*. Helsinki, Finland: University of Art and Design Helsinki Press.

Damasio, A. (1994). *Descartes' error: Emotion, reason, and the human brain*. New York: Gosset/Putnam Press.

Dewey, J. (1980). *Art as experience*. New York: Perigree Books.

DiSalvo, C., & Gemperle, F. (2003). From seduction to fulfillment: The use of anthropomorphic form in design. In J. Forlizzi (Ed.), *Proceedings of DPPI03* (pp. 67-72). New York: ACM Press.

DiSalvo, C., Gemperle, F., Forlizzi, J., & Montgomery, E. (2003, October). The hug: An exploration of robotic form for intimate communication. *Ro-Man 2003 Conference Proceedings*, San Francisco, CA.

Dittrich, W., & Lea, S. E. G. (1994). Visual perception of intentional motion. *Perception, 23*, 253-268.

Djajadiningrat, J. P., Overbeeke, C. J., & Smets, G. J. F. (1996). The importance of simultaneous accessible degrees of freedom. *Human Behavior and Information Technology, 16*(6), 337-347.

Djajadiningrat, P. J., Wensveen, S. A. G., Frens, J., & Overbeeke, C. J. (2004). Tangible products: Redressing the balance between appearance and action. *Personal and Ubiquitous Computing, 8*, 294-309.

Dourish, P. (2001). *Where the action is: The foundation of embodied interaction*. Cambridge, MA: MIT Press.

Ford, S., Forlizzi, J., & Ishizaki, S. (1997). Kinetic typography: Issues in time-based presentation of text. *CHI 97 Conference Proceedings*, Atlanta, GA, March 1997, pp. 269-270.

Gaver, W. W., Smets, G. J. F., & Overbeeke, C. J. (1995). A virtual window on media space. In I. R. Katz, R. Mack, M. Marks, M. B. Rosson, & J. Nielsen (Eds.), Human factors in computer systems, *Proceedings of CHI95*, pp. 257-264.

Gemperle, F., DiSalvo, C., Forlizzi, J., & Yonkers, W. (2003, October). The hug: A new form for communication. *DUX (Designing the User Experience) Conference Proceedings*, San Francisco, CA.

Gemperle, F., DiSalvo, C., & Forlizzi, J. (2004). Imitating the human form: Four kinds of anthropomorphic form. *Futureground 04 Conference Proceedings*, in press.

Gibson, J. J. (1986). *The ecological approach to visual perception*. Hillsdale, NJ: Lawrence Erlbaum. Reprint of the 1979 book.

Heidegger, M. (1962). *Being and time*. New York: Harper & Row.

Heider, F., & Simmel, M. (1944). An experimental study of apparent behaviour. *American Journal of Psychology, 57*, 243-249.

Hummels, C. C. M. (2000). *Gestural design tools: Prototypes, experiments and scenarios*. Doctoral dissertation, Delft University of Technology.

Ingram, J., & Annable, L. (2004). 'I see you baby, shakin' that ass: User perceptions of unintentional anthropomorphism and zoomorphism in consumer products. *Proceedings of Design and Emotion Conference*.

Lin, M-H. (2003). Archetypical icon and delightful design. In J. Forlizzi (Ed.), *Proceedings of DPPI03* (pp. 40-44). New York: ACM Press.

Merleau-Ponty, M. (1963). *The phenomenology of perception*. Chicago: Northwestern University Press.

Michotte, A. A. (1963). *The perception of causality*. New York: Basic Books.

Mutlu, B., & Forlizzi, J. (2004). Designing perceptually intuitive interfaces for social robots. *Submitted to ICRA 2004*.

Norman, D. (1988). *The psychology of everyday things*. New York: Basic Books.

Overbeeke, C. J., de Looze, M. P., Vink, P., & Cheung, F. K. (2004). Comfort by an emotion-aware office chair. In P. Vink (Ed.), *Comfort and design: Principles and good practices*. New York: Taylor and Francis.

Parmentier, R. J. (1987). Pierce Divested for non-intimates. In *RSSI*, Association Canadienne de Sémiotique, V7.

Peirce, C. S. (1958). *Collected papers of Charles Sanders Peirce*. C. Hartshorne & P. Weiss (Eds.). Cambridge, MA: Harvard University Press.

Scholl, B. J., & Tremoulet, P. D. (2000). Perceptual causality and animacy. *Trends in Cognitive Science, 4*(8), 229-309.

Wensveen, S. A. G., Djajadiningrat, P. J., & Overbeeke, C. J. (2004). Interaction frogger: A framework to couple action and function through feedback and feedforward. *Proceedings of DIS2004*, Cambridge, MA, pp. 177-184.

White, P. A., & Milne, A. (1997). Phenomenal causality: Impressions of pulling in the visual perception of objects in motion. *American Journal of Psychology, 110*, 573-602.

Zajonc, R. B. (1968). Attitudinal effect of mere exposure. *Journal of Personality and Social Psychology*, Monograph Supplement, *9*, 2-17.

PART III

ART AND COGNITION

CHAPTER 10

Emergence, Anticipation, and Schematization Processes in Listening to a Piece of Music: A Re-Reading of the Cue Abstraction Model

Irène Deliège

An overview and, to some extent, a re-reading of a model of cognitive processes involved in real time listening to a piece of music—the "cue abstraction model"—is given here. Music listening is considered as a schematization process based on cue abstraction where a fundamental principle—the principle of *similarity* and *difference*—comes into play in listening over long time spans. The basic lines of this model were proposed about 15 years ago (Deliège, 1987a, 1989, 1991) and specific experimental procedures were developed to test the validity of its different aspects.

Among these procedures, (i) the progressive emergence of the cued structures is demonstrated in two ways: first, by the results collected through segmentation approaches; second, by focusing on categorization processes for which the abstracted cues play a leading role. (ii) Anticipation mechanisms in listening will be approached by focusing attention on recognition of musical sequences. (iii) Finally, a number of different methods—the "Mental line" procedures—will afford a view on the role of memory of the cued structures involved in the schematization processes during listening.

THE CUE EMERGENCE

A study on rhythmic group processes (Deliège, 1987b), a test of Lerdahl and Jackendoff's (1983) grouping preference rules, had shown that, at the basis of those rules, there are main perceptual laws also put forth in vision by the gestalt theorists: namely the well known laws of similarity and proximity (see Figure 1). Inside the groups, musical structures are close to each other. Even if not all identical they show solidarity and share some degree of sameness. Therefore, in his recent book, *Music and Memory*, Bob Snyder (2000) likened the grouping effect to the identification of a metaphorical "«thing» that is «moving» . . . in a particular «direction»" (p. 113). On the contrary, the segmentations are always induced by strong contrasts (see Figure 1) generating boundaries between the groups. Consequently, the interplay between similarity and difference seems to be a most important organizational principle in music perception.

Starting from these preliminary remarks that are applicable to local musical structures, one might wonder if, and how, it is possible to generalize a grouping organization to apply to a complete piece? Some relationships with other fields of psychological investigation should be considered here. Psycholinguistics, from this point of view, might offer fruitful ideas applicable to the actual perception of music. Indeed, some analogies between text and music processing clearly exist since both extend over long temporal spans. Should listening to a piece of music, just as in listening to a talk, not result in an analogous cognitive treatment? To grasp the contents of a lecture, for example, one doesn't need to memorize the literal text but rather one focuses only on particular *salient points* of the message in order to reconstitute its contents. The same is true for music listening. Here too, it is impossible to keep all the incoming material in mind. It is thus necessary to collect specific elements of the piece to draw its general frame. But given that music, unlike a talk, does not refer back to a direct semantic support, the question is: what kind of tools should be selected in the piece of music to play the same role as the salient points in a lecture?

The hypothesis of cues abstracted during listening was put forth by this author (Deliège, 1987a, 1991). Cues are *emergent structures* playing a prominent role at the musical surface, an idea that brings us back to the well-known Gestalt notion of figure-ground discrimination. As pointed out by Bruner (2000) "All normal human individuals do perceive a world made up by figures dissociating themselves from a more general ground." And Bruner claims that "this is a universal process although cultural factors may intervene" (p. 7). Not all the figures appearing at the musical surface are memorized as cues. "Most

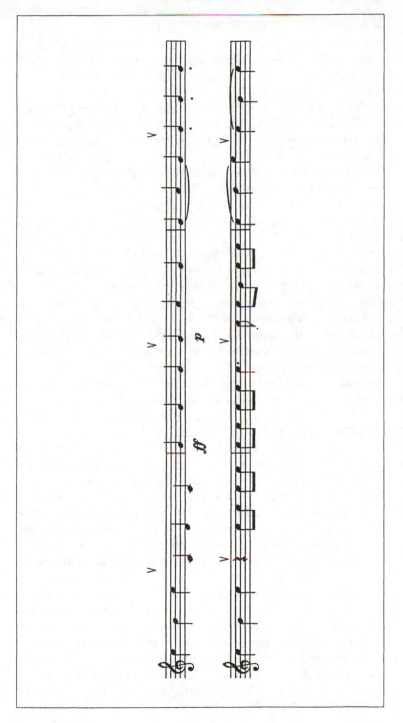

Figure 1. "V" shows examples of segmentation points:
1st staff: law of similarity (of register, 1st bar; of dynamics, 2nd bar; of articulation, 3rd bar).
2nd staff: law of proximity (interval of time given by a rest, 1st bar; by distance between attack-points, 2nd bar); by slurs, 3rd bar).

of them are temporary and fleeting" (Deliège, 1989, p. 214). *Emergence* precisely lies at this particular point; some kind of "natural selection" (Deliège, 1989, p. 214) occurs, a process in which only the strongest figures—the *emergent cues*—survive to define the actual progress of the listening.

The *emergent cues* contain invariant material, which points them out as being the initiating tools for the categorization processes of new entries. This is organized on the basis of the generalization of the interplay between similarity and difference. The emergence of the cues is always the result of some insistence on their main features by literal or varied repetition. As already pointed out, at the level of local rhythmic grouping formation, the principle of similarity and difference is again to be considered here. Similarity permits a grouping of groups to be extended for as long as a same type of invariant—the cue— is recognized: similarity generates adaptation: thus structures which share some degree of similarity are cemented together. Difference, on the other hand, records contrasting incoming features. As a result, a feeling of surprise is perceived and segmentation boundaries are established. This psychological tendency was already observed by Paul Fraisse (1967, p. 126) in relation to the perception of durations: small variations of a basic cell are generally minimized, while differences are overestimated. After a boundary, other cues will emerge to organize anew the categorization process leading to further groupings and seg-mentations until the end of the piece one is listening too.

Cue Emergence and Segmentation Processes

A specific procedure focusing on the categorization processes under-lying the segmentations perceived in a piece, was developed and applied on material selected among the contemporary repertoire (Deliège, 1989). The *Sequenza VI* for viola by Luciano Berio was chosen for a first experimental approach. Two expert subjects (young composers who were very familiar with this piece) were asked to perform a reference auditory analysis in order to compare the segmentations provided by the participants (musicians and non-musicians). These two composers gave the same general partitioning of the piece in six main sections in accordance with Berio's insistence on characteristic figures (the cues) together with the evolution of the perceived sound density (see Figure 2a). This compositional organization was also most obvious to the participants (see Figure 2b & c).

As a kind of anecdote, it is worth mentioning that one of the non-musician subjects provided spontaneously a sort of map of the piece (Figure 3) after the two experimental listenings that coincided with the

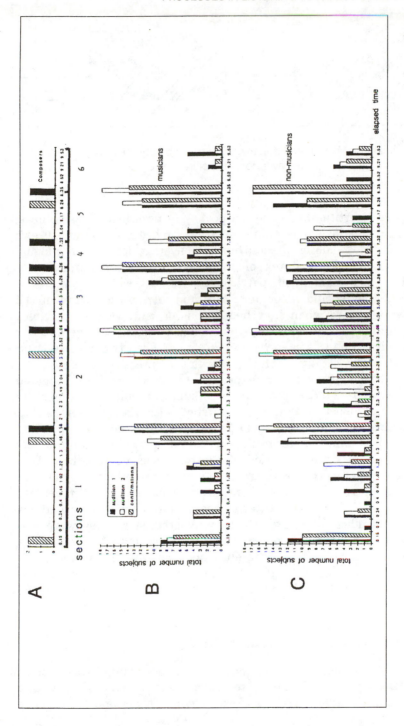

Figure 2. Segmentations perceived in the *Sequenza VI* for alto solo by Luciano Berio:
A – by 2 composers, B – by musicians, C – by non-musicians. Black lines = 1st audition, white lines = 2nd audition, hatched lines = confirmation of segmentations heard in both auditions.

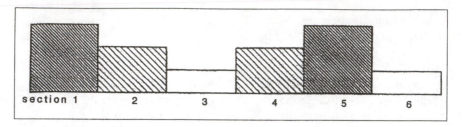

Figure 3. Map of the *Sequenza VI* for alto solo by Luciano Berio
drawn by a non-musician subject.

two experts' partitioning in all respects. He described it as follows: sections 1 and 5, insistence on a same figure in a strong sound context; sections 2 and 4, a similar process but in an average density; middle and end sections, 3 and 6, a context of single notes with soft dynamics.

For the experiment itself, participants were asked to listen to the piece as if they should listen to a talk and to press a button of the computer keyboard when they heard ends of sentences, paragraphs, indentations, and chapters. They first listened once to become familiar with the piece, and were allowed to take notes. Then two experimental listenings followed during which they had to press a button at the perceived segmentations. The experimental task was thus repeated twice (see Figure 2 b & c, black and white lines) to allow a comparison between the two performances (see hatched lines) and make sure that the responses were not given at random. It was expected that repetition of more or less similar material should be an intuitive indication for the listener that the ongoing period of the piece was not finished. This prediction was supported by the results: many more subjects segmented at the boundaries of sections where strong contrasting structures are introduced by the composer. Internal segmentations were recorded but did not contradict the cue-abstraction hypothesis, as they were less frequent and induced by local contrasting structures. It is important to note that there is little difference between Musicians' and Non-Musicians' results, which might indicate that the segmentation process is of a rather automatic nature and thus not greatly influenced by training.

Cue Emergence and Categorization Processes

The segmentation strategies described above cannot take place without the support of the ability to categorize; some kind of automatic classification of structures is performed which leads one to consider varied items as belonging to the same family. As early as 1947, Pitts and McCullogh were already puzzled by the capacity to recognize forms observed in animals and human subjects however varied their presentation. They thought that multiple transformations of the initial entry were needed to produce such a final canonical representation (in Bechtel & Abrahamsen, 1991, p. 4).

The categorization process of the musical material is also established on the basis of exact or varied repetitions of the abstracted cues. As put forth by Wilson and Sperber (1992), "since the representation and the represented object are two different things, they cannot, indeed, share all their properties: only some salient elements suffice. . . . If I am summarizing for you an article that I have just read you will assume that this summary is reliable to some extent and to certain respects, but in no way will you mistake the contents of my summary with the contents of the article itself" (p. 227, my translation). In the same way, speaking of the memory for temporal events, Fraisse (1967) pointed out that ". . . not everything from our past experience is transferred into memory. A large part is not fixed. There is a large discrepancy between the immediate richness of a perception and what we can recall a few seconds later" (p. 167).

Keeping these ideas in mind, I tried to appreciate the subjects' ability to evaluate the frequency of motifs in a piece they had just heard. The well-known *Allegro Assai* of the *Sonata for violin solo* in C major by Bach, a piece built on two main motifs, was chosen for this research (Deliège, 1996). After one complete hearing of the piece, participants were played Motifs A and B (see Figure 4) once and then asked to evaluate the frequency of appearance of these two motifs in the piece on a scale from 1 to 3. Surprisingly, the results of this evaluation was clearly in keeping with reality; musicians' evaluations were 3 for motif B and 2 for motif A; non-musicians' evaluations were 2.52 for Motif B and 2.16 for motif A. Then came the classification proper. Subjects first had to memorize both motifs. They were each repeated eight times, followed by a single recall repetition to make sure that the eight repetitions of motif B would not obliterate motif A, heard before. Then, for the experimental task itself, all the different variations of the two main motifs (see Figure 4) were presented three times in random. Subjects had to recognize the cue very quickly in whatever varied form in order to classify the sequences in their appropriate family. They were given 5 seconds to respond for each item. The accuracy of the responses was above 90% for non-musicians and reached 100% for musicians.

A similar experiment was carried out later with 9- to 11-year-old children, musicians and non-musicians (Deliège & Dupont, 1994). Easy pieces from Schubert and Diabelli were used. The average results

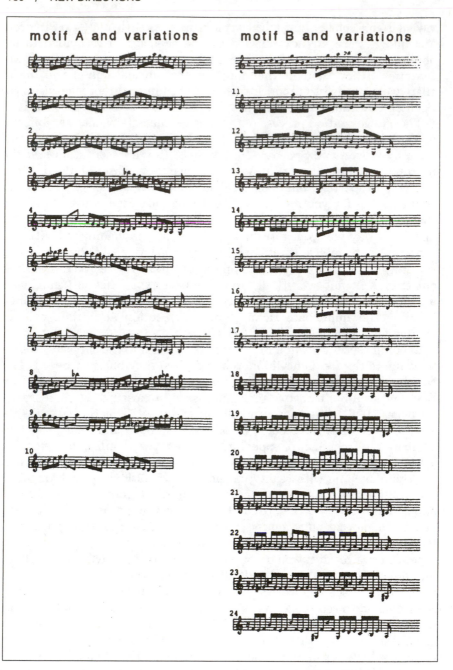

Figure 4. *Allegro Assai* of the *Sonata for violin solo in C major* by Bach.
Motif A and motif B and all the variations.

reached 75% for the non-musicians and 90% for the musician children. These very good performances allow us to assume that the classification strategies based on abstracted cues involve highly reliable automatic processes. It is even possible that these mechanisms are present very early in life. Woodfield (1992), for example, asserts that "The child is already equipped, at birth, by several micro-features detectors" (p. 277) and another French researcher, Lécuyer (1994), observed that 3-month-old infants already show categorization aptitudes (p. 199). Conversely, children were not very successful at evaluating motifs' frequency in the pieces. In relation to Fodor's (1983) theory of modularity of mind, this observation allows us to assert that classification strategies might be of a modular nature since these appear to be rather automatic, whereas evaluation processes should rely on more central cognitive structures that develop with growth (Deliège, 1995).

Cue Emergence and Imprint Formation

When we listen to the Bach piece, for example, we hear all the variations of the two main motifs. Nevertheless, this does not mean that all the multiple components of the different presentations will be stored. On the contrary, some sort of summary giving an "average value," will emerge progressively, which comprises the main coordinates of all the variations. This "average representation" is precisely what is here called an "imprint." The background of the concept is to be found in the notion of prototype developed in categorization studies (Rosch, 1975, 1978), the prototype being the most typical examplar that comes to mind for a given category, for instance a blackbird or a sparrow for the category of birds, but not an ostrich, nor a turkey.

The experimental procedure discussed here is inspired by prototype methodologies (Deliège, 1991, 2001) developed in the seventies (Bransford & Franks, 1971; Franks & Bransford, 1971; Posner & Keele, 1968). Participants first went through an acquisition phase and listened to the initial section of the piece by Bach (thus only the 42 first bars). Then a recognition phase followed in which subjects were presented with (i) items already heard in that first section; (ii) items belonging to the non heard section; (iii) items with pitch and rhythm modifications; (iv) items with only pitch modifications (Figure 5).

Four experiments were carried out: two (Experiments 1 and 2) with one-bar items and two others (Experiments 3 and 4) with two-bar items. For the modified items, experiments 1 and 3 presented pitch and rhythm changes; experiments 2 and 4, only pitch changes.

Six hundred adult participants (musicians and non-musicians) took part in the study. They were divided into three groups and listened to

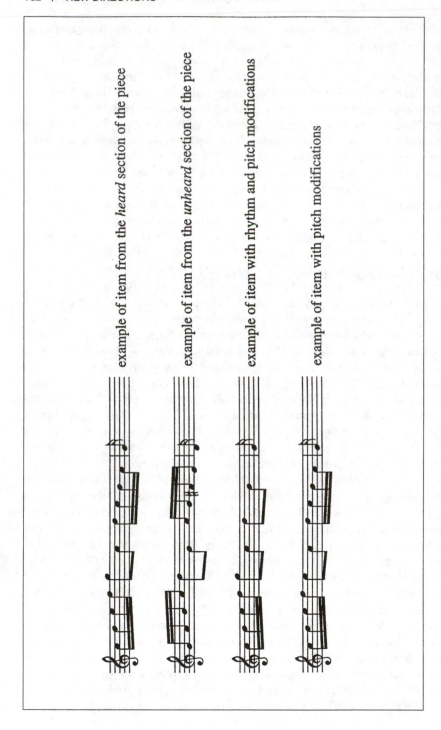

example of item from the *heard* section of the piece

example of item from the *unheard* section of the piece

example of item with rhythm and pitch modifications

example of item with pitch modifications

Figure 5. Emergence of the *Imprint*. Examples of the four categories of items set up for the experiment.

the first part of the piece either ten, six or two times during the acquisition phase. Then, in the experimental phase, in order to detect an imprint effect, they were asked to decide whether the items had been heard or not before and to indicate their level of confidence in their responses. The idea behind this procedure is that items very similar to those heard in the familiarization process would be erroneously felt as having already been heard. Consequently, it was hypothesized: (i) that modified items, especially those with rhythm changes, should be easily detected; (ii) that items even already heard, but too distant from the generated "average value" of the imprint, should also be rejected; (iii) that the length of the items (one bar versus two-bar items) and the number of previous familiarization processes should influence the accuracy of the responses.

As expected, for the most part, non-heard items were accepted as having already been heard and most modified sequences were rejected. This last result, particularly, is essential in relation to the stylistic characteristics of a piece. It shows that as soon as an imprint is stored, it acquires the value of an analyzer of the contents of the work, making a difference between what is, and what is not, the norm considering the style of that work. As a consequence, the role of an imprint becomes twofold: on the one hand, it is capable of keeping in memory long series of varied motifs by storing only a selection of major traits, but, on the other hand, since the stylistic characteristics of a piece are heard simultaneously, the imprint incorporates inevitably those aspects. Consequently, on the basis of a stored imprint it is possible to trace the limits of what can be perceived as acceptable or unusual in relation to a given style. An imprint is, in this respect, close to the concept of semantic memory introduced by Tulving (1972) in memory investigation, which stated that it becomes a "mental thesaurus," a recording of cognitive referents rather than perceptible properties (p. 386).

CUE ABSTRACTION AND ANTICIPATION PROCESSES

To be in a position to anticipate something, one needs to have experienced situations beforehand. Indeed, it is impossible to expect anything if you have no idea of what you are waiting for. As pointed out by Husserl in his phenomenological analysis (quoted by Dreyfus, 1972, p. 153), human intelligence signals itself by a continual search of anticipated situations. He asserts that the individual develops a mental representation—"the inner horizon"—which allows one to elaborate an "anticipated sketch" of the objects without necessity to experience things in full detail. For example, seeing the front of a house gives immediately some idea of its internal arrangements, etc.

Closely linked to the views of the phenomenologists are those of the Gestalt psychologists (in Dreyfus, 1972, p. 303) who also observed that the identification of objects does not require an exhaustive analysis of all the features. For example, a melody is not recognized by the addition of single notes, but as a whole even on the basis of a few initial notes that are always the "preferred cues" (Deliège, 2001, p. 400).

The concept of "frames," more recently developed by Schank and Abelson (1977), is another idea closely related to the notion of anticipation. To be invited for a Christmas dinner, for example, generates in mind a set of stereotypical situations that will probably happen in such circumstances.

Regarding the listening of music, what could one consider as an anticipation in relation to cue abstraction? The cue is a brief structure which signals the broader sequence from which it is abstracted and to which it remains necessarily connected. For this particular reason, the cue generates the possibility of *anticipating* that sequence while listening, thereby reducing recognition time and the weight of information to be stored. For example, to recognize *Riesen motif* in *Das Rheingold* by Wagner only small initial cues suffice (see Figure 6).

On the basis of this idea, a study of the recognition of Wagnerian leitmotifs was carried out (Deliège, 1992). The core of the procedure required participants to memorize one single target motif to be recognized later on in a long sequence of the opera in which their target motif appeared in various forms. The study focused on three different motifs (Figure 6) that made it possible to compare the performances in relation with the pertinence of the cues and the internal qualities of the musical structures in the recognition process. It should be stressed, at this point, that the possible cue structures do not always exhibit a similar level of efficiency in listening. What is decisive in this respect is the possibility to abstract clear rhythmic accents, namely strong *phenomenological accents* as defined by Lerdahl and Jackendoff (1983, p. 17). Regarding this particular aspect, the *Vertrags motif* is a long descending melodic line; no clear rhythmic accents are perceived making memorization thus less easy and recognition much slower. On the contrary, the *Wallhal motif* and, needless to say, the *Riesen motif* display strong rhythmic accents facilitating memory and recognition.

The results showed clearly the link between the accented structures with the number of repetitions required by the subjects to memorize their target motif. There is thus a strong relationship between the time required to memorize the information and the more or less clear presence of rhythmic accents to qualify the cues to be abstracted. This

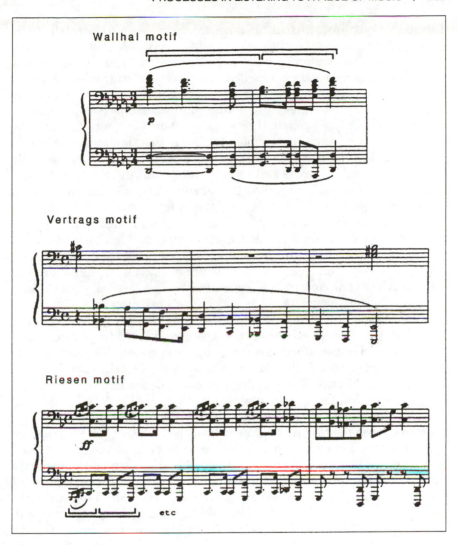

Figure 6. The three leitmotifs employed in the experiment. The brackets
in the *Wallhal motif* and the *Riesen motif* show the possible
segmentations given by the presence of an accent.

observation confirms conclusions made before in experimental research
on rhythmic groupings (Deliège, 1987b; Deutsch, 1982; Fraisse, 1967;
Povel & Okkerman, 1981).

Until now, in terms of anticipation, as stated by Daniel Dubois (1998),
it was observed that a cue makes it possible "to realize beforehand, to

foresee, to look forward, to act in advance, to prevent, to forestall" (p. 3, vol. 2). In addition, the author suggests two different aspects of the concept: *externalized anticipation* and *internalized anticipation* (pp. 4 and 5). By *externalized anticipation,* he refers to external events that can be anticipated: for example "to take an umbrella when one is anticipating rainy weather." This kind of anticipation is dependent on the environment. Of course, the weather may be sunny finally. The future is thus potentially *multiple* and the realization at each moment collapses all the possibilities to only *one:* present and past are actually *unique,* while the future is always potentially multiple, but *a posteriori* there is only one realized present state. *Internalized anticipation* deals with the *memory of the future.* For example, to plan a lecture for a conference some weeks in advance, means that you must write a paper, prepare the trip, buy a flight ticket, etc. Thus, during that period, one had to memorize the event and all necessary practical commitments. Such an anticipation creates its own future events and manages to meet what has been anticipated, the realization being practically a certainty.

Given these two aspects of the concept of anticipation, which one is most appropriate in relation to music listening? At first glance, listening to a piece refers to an external event: the piece played in a concert hall, for example. On the other hand, planning the concert in your diary is clearly an *internalized anticipation*, but as soon as you are sitting in the concert hall, the real-time listening process is dependent of an external event: the performance of the piece.

Regarding this twofold definition of the anticipation concept, let's go back to the segmentation experiment (Deliège, 1989) of the *Sequenza VI* by Berio (see Figure 2). In the two experimental listening sessions, subjects had to push a button to indicate the segmentations they identified. Clearly in such a situation, the listener is facing a potentially multiple future as defined in *externalized anticipation,* but each time the button is pushed, all the possibilities are reduced to only one and this until the end of the piece. What is interesting in relation to the *anticipation process,* lies especially in the comparison of the performances during the two listenings. Almost no difference was recorded which seems to indicate that the anticipation process based on the abstracted cues is rather *stable* and grounded in an intuitive knowledge of what should be done. Exactly as one has an intuition of the meteorologic features suggesting that an umbrella might be useful later in the day, the point here is that musical regions, inside which the musical materials acknowledge structural solidarity, should not be destroyed nor fragmented by major segmentations.

It should be also made clear that for all the experimental investigations of the different aspects of the model, real compositions that belong to the artistic domain were employed, *not* special material pre-pared for experimental use. Yet, an artistic message, by definition, has to convey unexpected events, in order to introduce surprising or innovating features capable to providing esthetic satisfaction. For this reason, as stated by Pachet (1999), perhaps "composers as well as listeners look for some compromise between repetition and sur-prise" . . . , some kind of "ideal position between . . . similarity and difference" (p. 140). Listeners' anticipation behavior is thus sometimes intentionally partly misled by the composer and the results show this clearly. The segmentations of the two expert listeners (see Figure 2a) have shown that before the main segmentations that close each section (see the black lines), there is often another one (see the hatched lines), defining what the two experts called a "dovetailed zone." The composer is giving there an anticipated feeling of the end of a section. Listeners' anticipation process was briefly disturbed and had to be readjusted immediately as experienced by both the musicians and non-musicians.

CUE ABSTRACTION AND SCHEMATIZATION PROCESSES

Schematization is a normal counterpart of any anticipation process. Indeed an anticipated event engraves some trace in memory: if you have taken an umbrella in the morning anticipating rain, if the weather is finally sunny, you will remember that you took it needlessly. Similarly when listening to music, anticipated events are counterbalanced by the elaboration of a schema allowing a retrospective glance on the memorized events: the "inner horizon" as suggested by Husserl (see p. 163). In the *cue abstraction model,* this process, called the *mental line* formation, is derived from the "cognitive map" concept put forth by Tolman (1948) in his research on rats. In the seventies, the French researcher, Pailhous (1970), who was developing a project on the representation of the urban space by taxi drivers in Paris, expanded on the cognitive map concept too. Both authors observed that the animal, as well as the human individual, builds such maps on the basis of some particular reference points, the out-coming schema being, by definition, a type of *reduction* of the complete information.

Similarly a *mental line* in music listening is a set of references marks that provides a feeling of durations and preserves the sensation of time elapsed between events. Such a schematization process also works out a reduction of the piece, largely built on *musical surface elements* in which the most immediately identifiable reference points lie. The idea of a cue-based schema might thus be generalizable to any musical system since the model has its foundations in general cognitive mechanisms. If each cue is an entry label which summarizes a longer sequence, it might be plausible to assert that such structures lead to developing "the ear of the mind" to paraphrase Haugeland's idea put forth in his book *Artificial Intelligence, the very idea* (1985, p. 223). This means that an image generated on this basis helps people to imagine mentally a melody, a piece, the sound of an instrument, etc. giving the sensation of some sort of auditive reality. Accordingly, I suggested that the temporal course of a piece might be symbolized by a *mental line* along which the structures would progressively take place (Deliège, 1991, 1993, 1998). It is a more or less faithful recording of events as experienced before by the listener, in relation with their time order and labeled by specific leading cues, a view close to what has been defined as *episodic memory* (Tulving, 1972, p. 387).

To investigate this proposal, three different versions of the procedure were developed. The first was applied to Berio's *Sequenza VI* (Deliège, 1989), where six main sections were recorded in the segmentation results (see Figure 2). Participants who had taken part in the segmentation experiment 3 or 4 weeks before, were informed that they would be presented with about 40 small segments to be located in their original section. The results were significantly above chance and slightly better for musicians.

In the second version, on Boulez's *Eclat* (Deliège, 1993), the subjects received 15 segments to be located on a horizontal line divided into 15 boxes symbolizing the complete duration of the piece. Just before, in the same session, the segmentation task was performed and subjects were only informed about the *mental line* task after the segmentation in order to observe how the cues act retrospectively in memory for time elapsed.

As for the mode, the segments location coincided better with the actual position in musicians' responses (see Table 1). Errors were more frequent for segments located in the middle of the piece that was in agreement with results observed a long time ago in research on memory for word-lists (Murdock, 1962). A *primacy effect* was observed for items presented early in the list that were well recalled. For items located in the middle of the series, a low recall success was recorded, while the last items of the series were most readily recalled, showing a *recency effect*. This is similar to the effect observed by Linton (1982) for memory in events of everyday life though the author insists on the greater effectiveness of *first* events in an on-going life sequence.

Finally, the third version of the *mental line* procedures (Deliège, 1998) consisted in reordering the complete material of a short piece divided into a number of segments. This procedure was applied to

Table 1. The Table Shows the Segments in the Order in Which They Appear in the Piece (1st Column). It Gives the Primary (Bold) and Secondary Mode Recorded for Each Segment in the Responses of the Musicians (2nd Column) and Non-Musicians (3rd Column).

Segment	Musicians locations	Non-musicians locations
1	**1**	**1**
2	**2** – 5	**2** – 12
3	**6** – 4	**11** – 12 & 5
4	**5** – 2 & 9	**3** – 7
5	**5** – 7	**12** – 5 & 3
6	**6**	**2** – 5
7	**9**	**9** – 7
8	**7** – 8 – 9 – 10	**4** – 6
9	**4** – 9	**3**
10	**12** – 7 & 3	**10** – 5 & 8
11	**11** – 10	**9** – 11
12	**12**	**9** – 12 & 10
13	**13**	**13** – 6
14	**14**	**15** – 14
15	**15**	**15** – 14

the *Tristan* cor anglais solo by Wagner, presented in 7 segments. Here again errors were few for the first and last segments. In addition, training and familiarization had a strong influence on participants' memorized schema. The number of previous hearings varied (3 or 5) and 4 different categories of participants were tested: Music Students (MS) and Music Professors (PM), Non-Musicians (NMS) and University Researchers (UR).

Table 2 shows the effect of familiarity on the level of the mode. After 3 hearings, only Musicians (students and professors) rebuilt the piece correctly. But after 5 hearings, the mode became correct for the 4 groups. Thus when the capacity of remembering is involved, performances were strongly improved by training and familiarity with the information perceived. This is not to say that non-expert participants have no sense of retrospectiveness at all, but their memorized schema is not that accurate without practice.

Table 2. The Table Shows the Segments in the Order in Which They
Appear in the Piece (1st Column). It Gives the Primary (Bold) and
Secondary Mode Recorded for the Location of Each Segment in the
Responses after 3 (3rd Column), and 5 listenings (4th Column), for the
Non-Musician Students (NMS), Musician Students (MS),
University Researchers (UR), and Professional Musicians (PM).

Segment	Participants	Primary (bold) and secondary mode after 3 listenings	Primary (bold) and secondary model after 5 listenings
1	NMS	**1** – 2	**1** – 2
2		**3 & 5** – 4 & 6	**2** – 3
3		**2** – 1	**3** – 2
4		**4** – 3	**4** – 5
5		**3 / 4 & 5** – 6	**5** – 3 & 4
6		**6** – 5	**6** – 2 / 4 & 5
7		**7**	**7**
1	MS	**1** – 2 & 6	**1**
2		**2** – 5	**2**
3		**3** – 1 & 2	**3** – 4
4		**4** – 3 & 6	**4** – 5
5		**5** – 4	**5** – 6
6		**6** – 3	**6** – 3 & 4
7		**7**	**7**
1	UR	**1**	**1** – 3 & 5
2		**6** – 3	**2** – 3
3		**2** – 3	**3** – 1 & 2
4		**4** – 3	**4** – 1 / 2 & 5
5		**4 & 5** – 3	**5** – 1 / 2 / 3 & 4
6		**6** – 2 & 3	**6** – 4
7		**7**	**7**
1	PM	**1**	
2		**2** – 6	
3		**3** – 2	
4		**4** – 3 & 5	
5		**5** – 4	
6		**6** – 5	
7		**7**	

BRIEF SUMMARY AND PERSPECTIVE

This re-reading of the cue abstraction model assumes that, in order to experience the form of a piece of music, the listener elaborates a mental schema of the work concerned, built on the progressive *emergence* of abstracted cues, a process broadly governed by the principle of the similarity and difference. But music listening is also supported by *anticipation* and *schematization* processes where the efficiency of the abstracted cues is particularly salient. As such, it was demonstrated that the schematization of a musical discourse might be compared to analogous processes arising in text comprehension. But, in the absence of a clear semantic content, the cues abstracted from the musical surface play a major role in such achievements. Consequently, future research on the way those who listen to music understand it, potentially relevant for any repertoire, should obviously rely on the structures of the *musical surface* to understand and demonstrate how a mental representation is progressively developed during listening.

REFERENCES

Bechtel, W., & Abrahamsen, A. (1991). *Connectionism and the mind. An introduction to parallel processing in networks.* Cambridge, MA & Oxford, UK: Basil Blackwell.

Brandsford, J. D., & Franks, J. R. (1971). The abstraction of linguistic ideas. *Cognitive Psychology, 2,* 331-350.

Bruner, J. (2000). *Culture et modes de pensée. L'esprit humain dans ses œuvres.* Transl. by Yves Bonin. Paris: Retz. (Preface to the French translation). Original publication (1986), *Actual minds, possible worlds.* New York: Harvard University Press.

Deliège, I. (1987 a). Le parallélisme, support d'une analyse auditive de la musique: Vers un modèle des parcours cognitifs de l'information musicale. *Analyse musicale, 6, 73-79.*

Deliège, I. (1987b). Grouping conditions in listening to music: An approach to Lerdahl & Jackendoff's grouping preference rules. *Music Perception, 4(4),* 325-360.

Deliège, I. (1989). A perceptual approach to contemporary musical forms. *Contemporary Music Review, 4,* 213-230.

Deliège, I. (1991). *L'organisation Psychologique de l'écoute de la musique. Des marques de sédimentation—indice, empreinte—dans la représentation mentale de l'oeuvre.* Thèse doctorale, Université de Liège.

Deliège, I. (1992). Recognition of the Wagnerian Leitmotiv. Experimental study based on an excerpt from "Das Rheingold." *Musik Psychologie, 9,* 25-54.

Deliège, I. (1993). Mechanisms of cue extraction in memory for musical time. In I. Cross & I. Deliège (Eds.), Proceedings of the 2nd symposium *Music and the Cognitive Sciences.* Cambridge, September 1990. *Contemporary Music Review, 9,* 191-207.

Deliège, I. (1995). The two steps of the categorization process. In R. Steinberg (Ed.), *Music and the mind machine, psychophysiology and psychopathology of the sense of music* (pp. 63-73). Heidelberg: Springer.

Deliège, I. (1996). Cue abstraction as a component of categorisation processes in music listening. *Psychology of Music, 24*(2), 131-156.

Deliège, I. (1998). Wagner "Alte Weise": Une approche perceptive. *Musicae Scientiae,* special issue, 63-90.

Deliège, I. (2001). Prototype effects in music listening: The notion of imprint. *Music Perception 18*(3), 371-407.

Deliège, I., & Dupont, M. (1994). Extraction d'indices et catégorisation dans l'écoute de la musique chez l'enfant. In I. Deliège (Ed.), *Proceedings of the 3rd ICMPC, International Conference for Music Perception and Cognition,* pp. 287-288. Liège, ESCOM Publications.

Deutsch, D. (1982). Grouping mechanisms in music. In D. Deutsch (Ed.), *The psychology of music* (pp. 99-134). New York: Academic Press.

Dreyfus, H. (1972). *What computers can't do. The limits of artificial intelligence.* New York: Harper & Row.

Dubois, D. (1998). Introduction to computing anticipatory systems. *International Journal of Computing Anticipatory Systems, 2,* 3-14.

Fodor, J. A. (1983). *The modularity of mind.* Cambridge, MA: MIT Press.

Fraisse, P. (1967). *La psychologie du temps.* Paris: Presses universitaires de France.

Franks, J. J., & Brandsford, J. D. (1971). Abstraction of visual patterns. *Journal of Experimental Psychology, 90,* 65-74.

Haugeland, J. (1985). *Artificial intelligence: The very idea.* Cambridge, MA: MIT Press.

Lécuyer, R. (1994). Nouveauté et organisation des connaissances. In R. Lécuyer, A. Streri, & M. G. Pêcheux (Eds.), *Le développement cognitif du nourrisson.* Paris: Nathan Université, tome 1, troisième partie.

Lerdahl, F., & Jackendoff, R. (1983). *A generative theory of tonal music.* Cambridge, MA: MIT Press.

Linton, M. (1982). Transformations of memory in everyday life. In U. Neisser (Ed.), *Memory observed* (pp. 77-91). San Francisco: Freeman.

Murdock, B. B. Jr. (1962). The serial position effect in free recall. *Journal of Experimental Psychology, 64,* 482-488.

Pachet, F. (1999). Surprising harmonies. *International Journal of Computing Anticipatory Systems, 4,* 139-161.

Pailhous, J. (1970). *La représentation de l'espace urbain.* Paris: Presses universitaires de France.

Posner, M. I., & Keele, S. W. (1968). On the genesis of abstract ideas. *Journal of Experimental Psychology, 77,* 353-363.

Povel, D. J., & Okkerman, H. (1981). Accents in equitone sequences. *Perception and Psychophysics, 30*(6), 565-572.

Rosch, E. (1975). Cognitive reference points. *Journal of Experimental Psychology: General, 104,* 192-233.

Rosch, E. (1978). Principles of categorization. In E. Rosch & B. Lloyd (Eds.), *Cognition and categorization* (pp. 28-49). Hillsdale, NJ: Lawrence Erlbaum.

Schank, R. C., & Abelson, R. P. (1977). *Scripts, plans, goals and understanding.* Hillsdale, NJ: Lawrence Erlbaum.

Snyder, B. (2000). *Music and memory.* Cambridge, MA: MIT Press.

Tolman, E. C. (1948). Cognitive maps in rats and men. *Psychological Review, 55,* 189-208.

Tulving, E. (1972). Episodic and semantic memory. In E. Tulving & W. Donaldson (Eds.), *Organization of memory* (pp. 381-403). New York: Academic Press.

Wilson, D., & Sperber, D. (1992). Ressemblance et communication. In D. Andler (Ed.), *Introduction aux sciences cognitives* (pp. 219-238). Paris: Gallimard.

Woodfield, A. (1992). Un modèle à deux étapes de la formation des concepts. In D. Andler (Ed.), *Introduction aux sciences cognitives* (pp. 273-290). Paris: Gallimard.

CHAPTER 11

Experimental Approaches to Reader Responses to Literature

David S. Miall

WHY EXPERIMENTAL APPROACHES?

The question I will pursue here is, at first sight, an obvious one to ask. What are readers doing when they read a literary text? Despite several decades of work on reception, however, including such notable books as Wolfgang Iser's *The Act of Reading* (1978), few literary scholars have thought of asking ordinary readers what occurs when they read. To ask a student in a literature class what occurs is, of course, likely to be a biased question, given the asymmetric balance of power created by the expectations and the assessments that govern classroom discourse (see, however, Steig, 1989). Yet plenty of anecdotal evidence suggests that readers are influenced or moved by the literary texts they read. Why is this apparently common and important experience so little studied? In this chapter I will discuss how systematic, experimental approaches to literary reading have been developed, and consider the questions raised by an empirical approach.

The paradigms within which literature is typically studied and taught have ruled against an experimental approach. Literary theorists, despite extensive theorizing, have been content to remain at what we might regard as a pre-theoretical level: literary theories cannot be right because they cannot ever be wrong. There is no evidence that could confute a literary theory, thus such writings are strictly speaking no more than interpretations. Literary theorists, like Galileo's inquisitors, refuse to examine evidence for literary reading in the empirical sense; offered a telescope, they rule that such an instrument cannot exist, or that it exists only as an ideological construct rather than a tool to aid perception. Thus Jonathan Culler (1981) argued:

> there is little need to concern oneself with the design of experi-
> ments, for several reasons. First, there already exist more than
> enough interpretations with which to begin. By consulting the
> interpretations which literary history records for any major work,
> one discovers a spectrum of interpretive possibilities of greater
> interest and diversity than a survey of undergraduates could
> provide. (p. 53)

No doubt the study of published interpretations has its own merit, but it is no answer to the question of how texts are actually read. Filtered out of printed interpretations are details of how a reader arrived at her understanding of the text; printed accounts are also likely to be subject to distortions and repressions of various kinds that misrepresent the act of reading. Above all, what is usually given in print is an interpretation, but this is not necessarily what a reader reading "non-professionally" is aiming to produce, thus a reliance on printed interpretations for a study of literary reading has little ecological validity (although it offers an interesting approach to the history of criticism: e.g., Zöllner, 1990).

The question of interpretation is, itself, a troubled one. Whether readers typically generate interpretations is, of course, an empirical question. Yet for academic study, it still seems to be the case, as Stanley Fish (1980) asserted over 20 years ago, that "like it or not, interpretation is the only game in town" (p. 355). Is this one reason why literary studies has lost its public role in the United States (and perhaps elsewhere)? Stephen Greenblatt (2003), when President of the MLA, commenting on the state of his profession, remarked that "in the public perception, it is as if we were cut off from the rest of the world, locked in our own special, self-regarding realm" (p. 8). At the same time, enrolments in literary studies have been steadily declining, whether in the United States, in Canada, or in Europe. Moreover, surveys of literary reading in the United States by the National Endowment for the Arts over the last two decades have shown a steady decline in the number of people reading literature. According to their report *Reading at Risk: A Survey of Literary Reading in America* (released on July 8th 2004), over the two decades from 1982 to 2002 literary readership at all ages has declined by 10%, with the steepest drop in the younger ages (18-24) of 28%; and the rate of decline has been accelerating. Whether this is related to "our society's massive shift toward electronic media for entertainment and information," as the NEA chairman suggests in his preface, is not clear from the survey.

If a decline in reading and in literary study is indeed in progress, then literary scholarship may in part be driving it. In our classrooms we may too persistently have called on readers to marginalize their personal experience of literary texts in order to participate in the game of interpretation. A survey I carried out 10 years ago showed that for student readers the requirement to interpret literary texts was often a major disincentive to further study (Miall, 1996). Thus, experimental research on reading, as a way of finding out what occurs during literary reading, can be regarded as an essential step to reconsidering our approach to literature, in particular, toward rethinking the emphasis given to interpretation.

The evidence against interpretation being an aim of the ordinary reader is rather strong. For Vipond and Hunt (1984), for example, literary reading was best characterized as "point-driven," in contrast to reading for story, or reading for information. But when they turned to empirical study, it proved quite difficult to detect point-driven reading. In their main study of the issue, a questionnaire survey of over 150 student readers of John Updike's story "A & P," only about 5% were found to be engaged in a point-driven form of reading; readers were more likely to adopt a story-driven approach, that is, to read for plot. While Vipond and Hunt note that a point is not an interpretation, it is clear that it represents a step toward interpretation. So it is important to bear in mind that student readers, who are likely to be closer to the ordinary reader outside the academy, do not usually derive points from their reading when reading normally. When we are reading for pleasure, we might aim to form a relation with the author, as Vipond and Hunt suggest, but this is not because we expect the author to make a point, but because we expect a literary author to offer a certain kind of experience.

Supporting evidence against interpretation comes from one of our studies (Miall & Kuiken, 1999). Thirty readers were asked to think aloud after reading each segment of a story that we had divided into 84 segments (the story was "The Trout" by Sean O'Faolain). The comments readers made were analyzed in detail and grouped into 14 types. Among these the most frequent type of comments (33.6%) related to explaining a character ("Julia will do it again for the excitement"); next came quotations from the text (21.5%), which we found to correlate highly with the presence of foregrounding in the quoted passages, suggesting that readers were savoring the quality of the writing and mulling over how to understand such passages; next were queries about local meanings in the text (10.1%), ("I wonder if Julia is afraid"); other types of commentary referred to style, expressions of surprise, or to the reader's emotions. One of the smallest categories, a mere 2.1% of all comments, was what we called "thematizing," e.g., "Again we have the symbolism of the trout in a prison." It is these comments that come the closest to what Vipond and Hunt mean by "point": they represent the moments when a reader is beginning to work out an interpretation of the story. In this example, the reader is elaborating her sense that the trout is like the main character, Julia, who is trapped in a prison of her parents' expectations; both will have broken free by the end of the story. But this analysis shows that during the course of reading such comments are quite rare. Readers appear to be engaged in a rather different set of activities: contemplating what characters are doing, experiencing the stylistic qualities of the writing, reflecting on the feelings that the story has evoked. In this particular study we also asked readers to make comments about their responses to the story as a whole after they had read it. Here, as might be expected, there were more comments consisting of points. Interestingly, though, these comments tended to refer to the personal meaning of the story for the reader, such as insights into aspects of the reader's childhood, or their enjoyment of the character. One reader, for example, says: "I can really respond to how the little girl must have felt. . . . I think it's neat that she can show that kind of compassion." Almost no readers began to offer interpretations of the story for its own sake, apart from any personal interest they might have in it.

Experimental studies, then, are unlikely to provide evidence for particular interpretations. But they do provide insights into what readers are able to tell us about their responses to literature, and in the next section I discuss some of the main types of research design employed in such studies. In the last section I will take up several issues raised by the experimental study of literature.

RESEARCH DESIGN AND SOME FINDINGS

In considering experimental approaches to literary reading, the first main difference in experimental methods to note is between studies that manipulate a literary text in order to isolate a particular effect, and studies with an intact text. The first approach is derived from the concept that different experimental conditions (i.e., different versions of the same text) will reveal how a particular aspect of the text influences readers. For example, in the studies by Vipond and Hunt (1984) I referred to earlier, the notion of "point" was made specific by identifying it with a specific type of feature that Vipond and Hunt termed "evaluations." They proposed that the narrator indicates how he or she "feels about an event, character, utterance, or other story element" by creating unexpected text elements, such as figurative language, an unusual word, deviant syntax, and the like. For the reader these evaluations are "deliberate invitations to share a meaning with the storyteller" (Hunt & Vipond, 1986, p. 58). In an experimental study they presented one group of readers with the original version of a short story, and another group with the same story with evaluations rewritten in neutral prose: e.g., the evaluative phrase "they camped around the room" was replaced with the more neutral expression, "they sat around the room." Shown a list of phrases taken from the story after each page and asked to indicate what they had particularly noticed while reading, readers with the original version chose the evaluation phrases significantly more often than readers with the rewritten version chose the equivalent neutral phrases (Hunt & Vipond, 1985).

Bortolussi and Dixon (2003) argue that "the careful manipulation of the text . . . allows one to identify covariation between features of the text and corresponding reader constructions and . . . allows much stronger and more precise inferences concerning causes" (p. 24). Although their own studies show the value of this approach, textual manipulation can also introduce unexpected, secondary side-effects that, while unrelated to the variance that the experimenter hopes to isolate, also influence readers. The elicitation of information from readers must be designed so as not to be confounded by the secondary changes in the text. In the Hunt and Vipond example the passages that are rewritten lose the connection they had in the original, where an aura of disorder and implicit violence, as in "they camped around the room," primes response to a series of "evaluations." To rewrite the passages introduces a series of questions about what literary qualities of the story may have been lost, not only the evaluative function. Although the general question to readers, what was noticed, provides an index of reader differences that is informative, it is not clear from this study what readers were noticing.

A study of a similar literary concept that we carried out (Miall & Kuiken, 1994) involved experiment without manipulation. Readers notice evaluations because they stand out from the local norm of the text. Similarly, we argued that the various stylistic features known as foregrounding also attract readers' attention. Our hypothesis was that paying attention during reading requires more time, and that readers would find passages rich in foregrounding both more striking and more evocative of feeling. To test this we analyzed a series of short stories for the presence of foregrounding, and developed an index of foregrounding in each segment (roughly one sentence) based on the presence of features at the phonetic, syntactic, and semantic levels. Instead of manipulating a text, each text itself provided a naturally varying level of foregrounding from low to high. If readers pay attention to foregrounding, then we can expect their reading times per segment to show covariance in line with its presence; and when asked to rate the segments for feeling or strikingness, higher ratings should correlate with elevated levels of foregrounding. In a series of studies with three literary short stories, these are the effects we found in each case. In addition, whether our participants were experienced senior students of English literature or beginning first year students of Psychology with little commitment to or experience of literary reading, our results were virtually the same, suggesting that response to foregrounding occurs regardless of degree of literary training—a finding that challenges the standard view that literary response depends on acquiring the relevant conventions and genre knowledge (e.g., Rabinowitz, 1998).

This study is an example of the use of single texts in which we hypothesize that intrinsic determinants influence the reader. A second type of study involves finding or creating extrinsic determinants that can be supposed to influence the reader. For example, Zwaan (1991) theorized that readers deploy "particular cognitive control mechanisms" specific to the genre they are reading. He proposed that literary reading would invoke a different set of controls from reading in a newspaper. He chose six short stories taken from either newspapers or from novels that could be read in either a newspaper or a literature condition. In other words, participants were told that they were reading from a newspaper or from a literary text. Participants read the texts on a computer which recorded reading times. As Zwaan predicted, the "literature" condition readers read more slowly than the "newspaper" readers—about 10% more slowly; in addition, when asked about their memory for the texts, it was found that literary readers had formed a stronger sense of the surface features of the texts, that is, of their stylistic features.

Another example of a frame approach is a supplementary study by Vipond and Hunt (1984). While looking for "points" among readers of a short story, they created a condition in which readers first read a supposed letter from an East German reader (this was in the 1980s) who claimed to find that the story illuminated understanding of his own position. Readers who received the story preceded by this frame generated more "points" in their comments.

While the studies I have mentioned suggest the existence of a specific literary form of reading, they leave open some important questions. Is reading in a literary mode (however we might define that) driven by the frame in which we encounter a text or by features of the text itself? Zwaan's (1991) study seems to point to the first possibility; the studies by Miall and Kuiken (1994) and Hunt and Vipond (1986) seem to point to the second. Given the rejection of literariness by recent literary theorists, the question is a critical one for empirical study. Terry Eagleton (1983) expressed a now common view: there can be "no 'essence' of literature whatsoever . . . any writing may be read 'poetically'" (p. 9). Thus given the right frame we would read a railway timetable as literature. It follows, says Eagleton, that we should

> drop the illusion that the category "literature" is "objective," in the sense of being eternally given and immutable. Anything can be literature, and anything which is regarded as unalterably and unquestionably literature—Shakespeare, for example—can cease to be literature. Any belief that the study of literature is the study of a stable, well-definable entity, as entomology is the study of insects, can be abandoned as a chimera. (pp. 10-11)

We read a text as literary, in other words, only because we find it in a literary frame (e.g., the back cover of a book tells us it is literary). The materiality of the book has also been held to influence reading. For example, N. Kathleen Hayles (2002) insists that "the physical form of the literary artifact always affects what the words (and other semiotic components) mean" (p. 25; cf. Genette, 1997). These views challenge the power of the literary text to preserve its meaning regardless of context: whether we find *Hamlet* in a leather-bound folio or on the computer screen, does *Hamlet* remain essentially the same? The question calls for empirical study.

A third kind of study involves comparison of two or more texts. A simple but effective method developed by Seilman and Larsen (1989) was applied to comparing a literary text (a short story) with a non-literary, or expository text (an essay on population growth). Their method required what they termed "self-probed retrospection," one of a class of methods that depends on the reader's self-report (such as the collection of ratings from readers in Miall and Kuiken, 1994) rather than an "objective" measure such as reading times. Larsen and Seilman (1988) argue that their method is less disruptive than the think-aloud method that requires readers to make comments after each sentence. In their study readers were asked to make marginal check marks while reading whenever a passage reminded them of something they had experienced. After reading the text participants were given a short questionnaire to complete about the experience related to each marked passage: its age, concreteness, perspective (from what position was the experience viewed), etc. On average they found that readers were able to remember 95% of the experiences. Although a similar number of "remindings" was elicited by both the literary and expository texts, twice as many "actor-perspective" remindings were elicited by the literary text, while the expository text elicited more "receiver" remindings (things read or heard about). Thus literary reading, they remark, "seems to connect particularly with knowledge that is personal in the sense that one is an agent, a responsible subject interacting with one's environment" (Seilman & Larsen, p. 174). Other measures of remindings (age, vividness, etc.) showed no significant differences. Interestingly, remindings were found to occur more frequently in the opening section of each text, and more frequently with the literary than the expository text. This suggests that readers initially need to mobilize specific personal information to contextualize the world of a literary text.

Readers of literary texts thus appear to draw more explicitly and frequently on their active personal experiences, a process that might be held to distinguish literary from other kinds of texts. Rather than attempting to define what is literary by a text's formal features (stylistic deviations, narrative form, or generic features), this points to an inter-active process underlying literariness: a literary text is more likely to speak to the individual through its resonances with the individual's autobiographical experiences. To learn more about such resonance and what it means for the reader, however, we must turn to the think-aloud method, despite the well-known problems that have been supposed to render verbal protocols questionable (Nisbett & Wilson, 1977; but see also Ericsson & Simon, 1980, 1984).

Thus, in a fourth kind of study, readers are asked to think aloud about a text during or after reading it. Either the text is presented section by section and readers comment after reading each section; or, in another model based on the "self-probed retrospection" of Seilman and Larsen (1989), readers make marginal check marks while reading whenever they find a passage striking or evocative; after reading they return to each passage and comment on what they were thinking while they read each marked passage. Both methods tend to generate lengthy protocols which must be transcribed and analyzed. Here, two alter-native strategies for content analysis are (1) to apply a previously designed category system to the protocols, or (2) to develop categories from whatever is found in the protocols themselves.

An example of the first type, the application of pre-prepared cate-gories, is a study of Andringa (1990). Readers of a Schiller short story were instructed to "think aloud" about all that came to mind after each of nine sections of the story; an interviewer was present to prompt and to question participants. Readers in the study ranged from beginning students of literature to professors. Two levels of analysis were applied when categorizing responses: first, speech acts (acts, metacomments, emotions, evaluations, arguments, references to text); second reception acts (emotive reactions, (re)constructive, forming bridges between constituents, elaborating, identifying). Among her findings, most notable was a sequence she found often among the less experienced readers: emotion, evaluation, then argument. This "seems to be a regular sequence": the emotion, as she put it, "initiates, selects, and steers the way of arguing" (p. 247). To refine this view of emotion has been one important aim of an alternative method that we have developed, called Numerically Aided Phenomenology (Kuiken & Miall, 1995, 2001).

In this method categories of analysis emerge from the readers' statements. Also, unlike standard psychological studies of reading, which are "laden with presuppositions appropriate to the study of reading comprehension rather than reading experience" (Kuiken & Miall, 1995), the method is designed to be as open to readers' descriptions of their reading experiences as possible.

The process involves a systematic comparison of statements made in all the verbal protocols (typically, we will collect responses from at least 30 readers) in order to identify similar expressed meanings; these are paraphrased, producing what we term "constituents." No preconceived categories are employed. The constituents, we argue, are natural kinds, not presuppositions brought to the study by the researcher. The constituents are then re-expressed at three different levels, from close to the original statement to the most general category. For example,

Level 1: Dogs do not say "bark bark"
Level 2: I negatively emotionally respond to literary style (phrase/word)
Level 3: I emotionally respond to a literary device

At the most general level, this enables us to count the proportion of responses that are made in a given category (here, emotional response to an aspect of style). But the method has at least two further analytical benefits.

First, the resulting categories can be used to create matrices of occurrences of constituent by reader, amenable to cluster analysis. These allow for the discovery of distinctive types of reader response based on similarities in occurrence of a range of different types of constituent. In one study, for example, we found four distinctive types of reading that we termed: 1. Reading resistance; 2. Emotional engagement; 3. Story-line uncertainty; and 4. Aesthetic coherence (Kuiken & Miall, 2001). Second, the development of meanings across a set of responses can be studied and their determinants examined. We have, for example, recently focused on the impact of reading on the reader's self-concept and how this manifests through what we term "self-modifying feelings." In several studies we have adopted the "self-probed retrospection" method in which readers are asked to choose several passages from the text they had marked and to think aloud in response to each passage. In a study of readers of Coleridge's "The Rime of the Ancient Mariner," comments by one group of readers were characterized by what we termed "expressive enactment." Here we found the emergence of comments involving resonance of the reader's feelings with the world of the text. In particular, "there was evidence of blurred boundaries between the reader and narrator, as though they were temporarily identified as members of the same class." This feature often takes the form of the use of the pronoun *you*, as in this commentary "So in a way you would be feeling kind of cursed and haunted" (Kuiken, Miall, & Sikora, 2004, p. 187). In a number of readers' comments we find the expression of an affective theme that is re-expressed and modified across the course of their commentaries on successive passages. We also found that readers in the expressive enactment group cited autobiographical memories less often in relation to the poem than readers in other groups, a finding that, in part, helped us distinguish two kinds of identification with the narrator of the poem: similes of identification (e.g., this emotion is like something I have experienced), and metaphors of identification (e.g., this experience in the poem is my experience—as with the use of the pronoun *you* to speak inclusively).

The fourth type of study, especially the phenomenological method I have just outlined, is at a considerable distance from the more typically "experimental" models, especially those involved in manipulating a literary text to create two or more experimental "conditions" that are expected to elicit differing responses from readers. The liability of this latter kind of study is the possible loss of what is distinctively literary when the variables influencing a reading are thus strictly delimited. The liability of the phenomenological type of study, in contrast, is its dependence on a degree of connoisseurship in categorizing and interpreting verbal protocols, and in the problem of its generalizability, i.e., what it would mean to attempt to replicate it. At the same time, the complexity of literary response, and the extraordinary variability in the texts that have usually been deemed literary, suggests that only a wide range of experimental methods will suffice to capture what, if anything, is distinctive to literary reading.

ISSUES FOR THE EMPIRICAL STUDY OF LITERARY READING

In my survey of experimental methods I have already mentioned several issues that face research in this field. In this section I will single out four for specific discussion.

What is Literary?

An ambivalence over literariness has influenced a number of scholars of reading. For example, in his book *Cognitive Poetics*, Peter Stockwell (2002) tells us that since "there is nothing inherently different in the form of literary language, it is reasonable and safe to investigate the language of literature using approaches generated in the language system in general" (p. 7). Similarly, in *Psychonarratology*, Bortolussi and Dixon (2003) indicate their acceptance of "the assumption [of discourse analysis] that literary language is not distinct from, but rather an instance of, ordinary language, and that consequently it is processed as such by readers" (p. 29). To assume that methods of literary analysis drawn from cognition will be adequate for all tasks forecloses the possibility of establishing what may be distinctive to the experience of literature. Whether literature can be distinguished is, properly, an empirical question, thus to develop experimental tools likely to elicit a specifically *literary* response must be a primary aim of research in this field. If "high" literature, as we might call it, calls upon characteristically different modes of reading, then it should be possible to demonstrate this (without, of course, disparaging the role of readers when reading popular fiction, which has its own values).

Delimiting the Literary

A separate question is how literature stands in relation to other forms of language, other media, or advertising. Since younger readers in particular are now likely to be exposed to such media from an early age, we must ask what influence these media may have on the skills or aptitudes required for literary reading. (So far, it appears to me, almost no research has yet been done on the literary aspects of other media.) Little is known about how ordinary readers choose their reading, what different kinds of media they choose, how they respond to it, how it compares in their view with other forms of leisure activity such as video gaming or going to the movies, what difference it makes to their lives, and what cultural or historical processes impact the activity of reading. Better information on this is important in its own right, but would also enable us to develop a more effective classroom environment for literary studies.

Normative Assumptions

We must ask whether in our studies of literary reading our research designs embed hidden assumptions about the kind of reading we think should be occurring. Should we, or even can we, avoid such assumptions? For example, in the phenomenological work I described, when comparing similes and metaphors of identification, it is tempting to pay closer attention to readers demonstrating metaphors of identification since these appear to involve a more radical commitment of the self to the text being read. But is this to argue that such readings are to be preferred, or are better than those of other readers whose protocols cluster in our other groups? This issue raises larger questions about the place of literary reading in society that are ethnically and historically inflected, and which have been little studied outside the troubled domain of literary theory.

Empirical Studies Require History

It could be argued that by studying readers now, and by studying only those narrow aspects of reading amenable to experimental study in particular, we have neglected to consider not only how reading may be determined by history, but have overlooked the possibility that reading in the past may have operated differently (Darnton, 1990). Here two additional contexts seem required, although neither so far has had more than a marginal influence on empirical studies of reading. First, we should attempt as far as possible to recover reading experiences from the past and subject the evidence to as much empirical rigor in our analysis as we do to verbal protocols collected now. For example, the recent work of Rose (2001) has provided rich information on numerous working class memoirs from the previous three centuries in which acts of reading and their effects are described, often in considerable detail. Second, developments in cultural analysis by evolutionary psychologists suggest that the evolutionary determinants of literary reading must now be seriously considered as a framework for understanding its present significance. What underlying, species-specific proclivities have led to the emergence of a literary culture in every human society in the world? Findings on this issue would lend stability and direction to the field of empirical studies of literary reading (Boyd, 1998; Miall, 2001).

Beyond Empirical Research

How, finally, might we make evident the relevance of empirical research and its findings, and how can we invite debate on its significance from our colleagues who teach literature in schools and universities? What difference might awareness of empirical findings make to how one teaches? As empirical study matures and takes account of a wider range of literary experiences and historical contexts, perhaps it will begin to influence the thinking of literary scholars in the mainstream. But at the present time of writing the likelihood of such a development is by no mean clear, especially as the field of empirical research is itself a mosaic of different methods and incompatible assumptions. To begin to resolve the declining status of literary studies and even of literary reading itself, however, empirical study seems the most promising candidate: it undertakes, after all, to give central place to the experience of real readers, placing on the agenda for the first time the richness, range, and personal significance of reading in our culture.

REFERENCES

Andringa, E. (1990). Verbal data on literary understanding: A proposal for protocol analysis on two levels. *Poetics, 19,* 231-257.

Bortolussi, M., & Dixon, P. (2003). *Psychonarratology: Foundations for the empirical study of literary response.* Cambridge: Cambridge University Press.

Boyd, B. (1998). Jane, meet Charles: Literature, evolution and human nature. *Philosophy and Literature, 22,* 1-30.

Culler, J. (1981). *The pursuit of signs: Semiotics, literature, deconstruction.* London: Routledge.

Darnton, R. (1990). First steps toward a history of reading. In *The kiss of Lamourette: Reflections in cultural history* (pp. 154-187). New York: W. W. Norton.

Eagleton, T. (1983). *Literary theory: An introduction.* Oxford: Basil Blackwell.

Ericsson, K. A., & Simon, H. A. (1980). Verbal reports as data. *Psychological Review, 87,* 215-251.

Ericsson, K. A., & Simon, H. A. (1984). *Protocol analysis: Verbal reports as data.* Cambridge, MA: MIT Press.

Fish, S. (1980). *Is there a text in this class? The authority of interpretive communities.* Cambridge, MA: Harvard University Press.

Genette, G. (1997). *Paratexts: Thresholds of interpretation.* J. E. Lewin (Trans.). Cambridge: Cambridge University Press.

Greenblatt, S. (2003). Introduction. *Profession 2003,* 7-9.

Hayles N. K. (2002). *Writing machines.* Cambridge, MA: MIT Press.

Hunt, R. A., & Vipond, D. (1985). Crash-testing a transactional model of literary reading. *Reader: Essays in Reader-Oriented Theory, 14,* 23-39.

Hunt, R. A., & Vipond, D. (1986). Evaluations in literary reading. *Text, 6,* 53-71.

Iser, W. (1978). *The act of reading.* London: Routledge and Kegan Paul.

Kuiken, D., & Miall, D. S. (1995). Procedures in think aloud studies: Contributions to the phenomenology of literary response. In G. Rusch (Ed.), *Empirical approaches to literature: Proceedings of the Fourth Biannual Conference of the International Society for the Empirical Study of Literature—IGEL, Budapest, August 1994* (pp. 50-60). Siegen: LUMIS-Publications.

Kuiken, D., & Miall, D. S. (2001). Numerically aided phenomenology: Procedures for investigating categories of experience. *FQS. Forum: Qualitative Social Research,* 2.1, February 2001.
http://qualitative-research.net/fqs-texte/1-01/1-01kuikenmiall-e.htm

Kuiken, D., Miall, D. S., & Sikora, S. (2004). Forms of self-implication in literary reading. *Poetics Today, 25,* 171-203.

Larsen, S. F., & Seilman, U. (1988). Personal remindings while reading literature. *Text, 8,* 411-429.

Miall, D. S. (1996). Empowering the reader: Literary response and classroom learning. In R. J. Kreuz & M. S. MacNealy (Eds.), *Empirical approaches to literature and aesthetics* (pp. 463-478). Norwood, NJ: Ablex.

Miall, D. S. (2001). An evolutionary framework for literary reading. In G. Steen & D. Schram (Eds.), *The psychology and sociology of literature: In honour of Elrud Ibsch* (pp. 407-419). Amsterdam: John Benjamins.

Miall, D. S., & Kuiken, D. (1994). Foregrounding, defamiliarization, and affect: Response to literary stories. *Poetics, 22,* 389-407.

Miall, D. S., & Kuiken, D. (1999). What is literariness? Three components of literary reading. *Discourse Processes, 28,* 121-138.

Nisbett, R. E., & Wilson, T. D. (1977). Telling more than we know. *Psychological Review, 84,* 231-259.

Seilman, U., & Larsen, S. F. (1989). Personal resonance to literature: A study of remindings while reading. *Poetics, 18,* 165-177.

Stockwell, P. (2002). *Cognitive poetics.* London: Routledge.

Rabinowitz, P. (1998). *Before reading: Narrative conventions and the politics of interpretation.* Columbus: Ohio State University Press.

Reading At Risk: A Survey of Literary Reading in America. Washington, DC: National Endowment for the Arts, 2004.

Rose, J. (2001). *The intellectual life of the British working classes.* New Haven: Yale University Press.

Steig, M. (1989). *Stories of reading: Subjectivity and literary understanding.* Baltimore: Johns Hopkins University Press.

Vipond, D., & Hunt R. A. (1984). Point-driven understanding: Pragmatic and cognitive dimensions of literary reading. *Poetics, 13,* 261-277.

Zöllner, K. (1990). 'Quotation analysis' as a means of understanding comprehension processes of longer and more difficult texts. *Poetics, 19,* 293-322.

Zwaan, R. A. (1991). Some parameters of literary and news comprehension: Effects of discourse-type perspective on reading rate and surface structure representation. *Poetics, 20,* 139-156.

CHAPTER 12

Studio Thinking:
How Visual Arts Teaching Can
Promote Disciplined Habits
of Mind

*Ellen Winner, Lois Hetland,
Shirley Veenema, Kim Sheridan,
and Patricia Palmer*

In the current climate of educational accountability, arts educators must answer two fundamental questions so that the arts will retain a place within public education: (1) What kinds of thinking skills do arts teachers strive to instill? (2) How can students learn these skills? It is not enough to say that the arts teach "how to paint or draw" or that the arts teach creative expression. We need to go beneath the surface and discover what underlying cognitive and social skills are imparted to students when the arts are taught well.

In the 1980s and 1990s, arts educators tried to skirt these fundamental questions and instead justified arts education by reference to what transferred from the arts to other "more basic" school subjects (Fiske, 1999). For example, a 1995 report by the President's Committee on the Arts and Humanities claimed that "teaching the arts has a significant effect on overall success in school," and notes that both verbal and quantitative SAT scores are higher for high school students who take arts courses than for those who take none. (Murfee, 1995, p. 3). According to these kinds of arguments, the arts should be in our schools because they help students learn to read, because they boost math performance, and because students who take more arts classes do better on their SATs.

WHAT THE EVIDENCE SHOWS ABOUT TRANSFER
OF LEARNING FROM THE ARTS

In a project called REAP (Reviewing Education and the Arts Project), our research team examined these instrumental justifications for arts education (Winner & Hetland, 2000). We conducted 10 meta-analyses of studies testing the claim that some form of arts education transfers to some form of non-arts learning (e.g., reading, math, verbal/math test scores, spatial reasoning). We first conducted an exhaustive, systematic search for all studies, published and unpublished, carried out since 1950, examining the relationship between arts study and academic achievement. We included only studies that assessed some kind of non-arts, cognitive outcome, and that compared children who received some type of arts instruction with those receiving either no arts instruction and/or some other form of non-academic instruction. We were able to identify almost 200 studies that met these criteria. We then sorted the studies by art form and outcome, and this sorting allowed us to conduct 10 meta-analyses.

Our findings were controversial because they revealed that in most cases there was no demonstrated causal relationship between studying one or more art forms and non-arts cognition. Below we summarize our findings: we found three areas where a causal relationship had been demonstrated and seven in which no clear causal implications can be drawn.

Three Causal Findings

Classroom Drama and Verbal Skills

Classroom drama refers to using acting techniques within the regular classroom curriculum (i.e., it does not refer to the formal production of plays). Podlozny (2000) found 80 studies that met the criteria for meta-analysis, and these studies all assessed the effect of classroom drama on verbal skills. In these studies, children who enacted texts were compared to those who simply read the same texts. Classroom drama significantly enhanced memory for and understanding of the texts, raised reading readiness and reading achievement scores, and improved oral language skills.

The most important finding of these meta-analyses on classroom drama is the demonstration that drama not only helps children to master the texts they enact, but also often helps them to master new material not enacted. The transfer of skills from one domain to another is generally not thought to be automatic; it needs to be taught (Salomon & Perkins, 1989). In the field of classroom drama, however, transfer appears to be naturally designed into the curriculum, even if teachers are not labeling it as such. If teachers of classroom drama did more to teach explicitly for transfer, these effects might be even stronger.

Listening to Music and Spatial Reasoning

In 1993, the journal, *Nature,* reported that spatial-temporal reasoning is temporarily enhanced in adults after listening to Mozart for 10-15 minutes (Rauscher, Shaw, & Ky, 1993). This finding, which became known as the "Mozart effect," captured the attention of the media and became distorted into the claim that exposing infants to classical music will improve their IQ (no such research has actually been conducted). The extreme media claims led researchers to reject the Mozart effect as bogus. However, Hetland (2000a) conducted a meta-analysis on 36 studies and demonstrated that listening to music does improve spatial-temporal reasoning temporarily when compared to listening to a relaxation tape or sitting in silence. However, the underlying mechanism has not yet been identified. In addition, this finding does not have direct implications for education, since no learning is involved, and the improvement in spatial reasoning lasts only a few minutes.

Making Music and Spatial Reasoning

Studies have also examined whether children who learn to make music in the classroom improve their spatial reasoning abilities. Hetland (2000b) meta-analyzed 19 studies in which young children were taught to make music in the classroom (e.g., by improvising, composing, experimenting with rhythm instruments or moving to music, or by learning to play a particular instrument), and found that the children who learned to make music significantly outperformed those who did not on a range of spatial temporal tasks (such as the Object Assembly test, in which the child must put together a jigsaw puzzle).

However, before policy-makers mandate music instruction as a means to enhance children's spatial abilities, some words of caution are in order. Because the spatial tests were conducted within a few weeks of the end of the music instruction, we do not know how long any enhancing effect lasts. We also do not know whether the effects of music instruction on spatial tests translate to better success in school. They might, or they might not. First, "real world" spatial problems, whether found in mathematics or the block corner or the ball field, may or may not be predicted by success on paper and pencil or table-task tests such as those used in these studies. Second, many classrooms do not give students a chance to use spatial skills, because instruction may not offer opportunities to apply spatial reasoning to school subjects. Third, because spatial reasoning is multi-dimensional (consider the differences in designing a bridge, packing a car trunk, or finding your way around a new city, for example), it is not clear where the effects of the specifically "spatial-temporal" tasks would show up. Thus, although this is a solid finding, its implications for educational policy are not self-evident.

One Equivocal Causal Finding

Music and Mathematics

In 1999, a study published in *Neurological Research* reported that piano keyboard training along with computer-based spatial training led to greater improvements in mathematics than when spatial training was combined with computer-based English language training (Graziano, Peterson, & Shaw, 1999). A meta-analysis of six studies testing the effect of music learning on math found a nearly significant effect, leading to the conclusion that there may be a causal link between some forms of music instruction and some forms of mathematics outcomes (Vaughn, 2000). More studies are needed before we can determine whether these findings are significant or not.

One Case of Near Transfer

Dance and Spatial Reasoning

Keinanen, Hetland, and Winner (2000) were able to find four studies assessing the effect of dance instruction on nonverbal, performance IQ scales and on nonverbal paper and pencil spatial reasoning tests. Meta-analysis of these four studies found a significant relationship and concluded that dance does enhance nonverbal skills. This finding, limited in significance because of the small number of studies combined, is one of "near transfer" given that dance is a visual-spatial form of activity.

Five Non-Causal Findings

Arts Rich Education and Verbal and Mathematical Achievement

Perhaps the most commonly heard instrumental claim for the arts is that they lead to enhanced standardized test scores, higher grades, and lowered high school drop out rates. Just what is the evidence for such claims? Winner and Cooper (2000) synthesized studies that examined the relationship between studying the arts (type of art course was not specified) and verbal and mathematical achievement. In these studies, students were either exposed to the arts as separate disciplines, or they received such exposure but were also given an arts-integrated academic curriculum. Unfortunately, few of the studies explained in much detail anything about the nature and quality of the arts instruction, or about what it really meant to study an academic subject with arts integration. Academic achievement in these studies was measured either by test scores or grades or academic awards.

When we examined the correlational studies—studies that compared the academic profiles of students who do and do not study the arts either in school or in after school programs, we found a strong general correlation between studying the arts and verbal, mathematical, and composite verbal/math test scores. Thus, students (in the United States) who choose to study the arts are students who are also high academic achievers. But because the studies on which these meta-analyses were based were correlational in design, they allow no causal inferences. Does art study cause higher scores? Or do those with higher scores take more art? Or, is there a third variable, such as parental involvement, that causes both greater arts study and higher test scores? We cannot tell. Unfortunately, however, studies such as these have often been used to support the claim that studying the arts *causes test scores to rise*.

When we examined the experimental studies testing the claim that studying the arts causes academic achievement to rise, we found no global effects. These studies compared academic performance before and after studying the arts and included studies that integrated the arts with academics as well as studies in which students studied the arts as separate classes. The lack of relationship between arts study and academic achievement held for the 24 studies testing verbal skills and the 15 testing math skills.

Thus we had to conclude that we had found no evidence that studying the arts, including the arts integrated with academic subjects, resulted in enhanced verbal or mathematical skills.

Arts Rich Education and Creativity

Does studying the arts lead to enhanced critical and creative thinking outside of the arts? All of the studies on this topic that we found assessed creativity via standardized paper and pencil creativity tests. A meta-analysis of these studies showed no significant relationship between arts study and creativity test scores (Moga, Burger, Hetland, & Winner, 2000). Perhaps the problem is with the outcome measures, and future research should examine more authentic and creative thinking outcomes, such as the ability to find new problems (Getzels & Csikszentmihalyi, 1976).

Visual Arts and Reading

Can studying the visual arts help remedial readers improve their reading? This is the assumption guiding several programs set up in New York City, such as the Guggenheim Museum's Learning to Read through the Arts, Reading Improvement Through the Arts, and Children's Art Carnival, where children with reading difficulties are given experience in the visual arts integrated with reading and writing. These programs consistently report that remedial readers improve their reading scores, and then go on to conclude, erroneously, that the improvement is due to the arts. However, because these programs did not compare the effects of an arts-reading integrated program with the effects of an arts-alone program, we cannot know whether the reading improvement that undoubtedly did occur was a function of art experience, art experience integrated with reading, or simply of the extra reading experience and instruction.

Burger and Winner (2000) therefore examined nine studies that compared an arts-only instruction to a control group receiving no special arts instruction and four that compared an art-reading integration treatment to a control group receiving reading only (four studies). The first group allowed us to see whether instruction in visual art by itself teaches skills that transfer to reading skills; the second group allowed us to test whether reading integrated with art is more effective than reading instruction alone.

We found no support for the claim that the visual arts enhance reading skills and were forced to conclude that programs that help remedial readers improve their reading through a reading-arts integrated program are likely to work well because of the extra intensive reading training that the children receive, independent of the fact that this training is fused with drawing.

Dance and Reading

In Chicago, a program called Whirlwind had sought to improve basic reading skills in young children through dance (Rose, 1999). One of the activities that children in this program engage in is "dancing" their bodies into the shapes of letters. By virtue of this activity, these children in fact improved their beginning reading skills significantly more than did a control group which did not get the same kind of "dance" instruction. However, the activity of putting one's body into the shape of letters is not authentic dance, though in fact it may prove to be an excellent way of helping children remember letters. Our meta-analysis on the four studies found that more authentic forms of dance showed no causal relationship between dance and reading (Keinanen et al., 2000).

Music and Reading

Music has also been claimed to be a way to improve reading skills, possibly because of the effect of learning to read music notation. Perhaps practice in reading music notation makes it easier to learn to read linguistic notation. In addition, perhaps listening to music trains the kind of auditory discrimination skills needed to make phonological distinctions. It is also possible that music enhances reading skills only when students learn to read the lyrics of songs. When Butzlaff (2000) located six experimental studies testing music's effect on reading and performed a meta-analysis on these studies, he found no significant relationship and concluded that there is no evidence thus far that learning music enhances reading in children.

The findings from our REAP meta-analyses showed that for the most part, there is only weak scientific evidence that arts education leads to better performance in other school subjects. The two clear exceptions to this were that classroom drama improved verbal performance, and that music improved spatial reasoning. Does this mean that studying the arts has no effects on non-arts cognition? We believe that the research on transfer to date is too flawed to allow us to draw conclusions. In the words of David Perkins commenting on the above-described meta-analyses, "it is important to stand back from their findings [about lack of transfer] and ask whether the game is essentially over. . . . Some would say that it had never really begun (Perkins, 2001, p. 117).

The most glaring weakness in the studies conducted thus far on arts transfer is that researchers have failed to document the kinds of thinking skills learned in the parent domain—learning about the arts. Only once we have determined what students actually learn when they study an art form does it make sense to test hypotheses about transfer. In none of the studies we found for our meta-analyses did researchers analyze what teachers were teaching in the arts, and what students were learning. Without knowing what is learned in art class, we cannot possibly guess at what might transfer outside of the arts.

The remainder of this chapter is devoted to a presentation of our current work, in which we have sought to identify the kinds of habits of mind that emerge from serious art study. Our model, derived from such documentation, provides art teachers a language for describing what they mean to teach and what students learn. Such a language should help advocates explain arts education to policy makers, help art teachers develop and refine their teaching practices, and help educators in other disciplines learn from existing practices in arts teaching. We have focused here on the visual arts taught at the high school level.

Our goal is three-fold: to document the kinds of habits of mind taught in the visual arts; to develop a teacher-friendly instrument to assess how well students learn these habits of mind; and to provide the ground work for better transfer studies by identifying particular kinds of thinking skills actually learned in the arts that might be useful in other disciplines. In what follows, we describe the findings from the first phase of our study—the documentation of the kinds of habits of mind taught in serious visual arts classes. The second and third phases of our work (developing an assessment tool and carrying out transfer studies) are not yet complete.

THINKING SKILLS PROMOTED IN
VISUAL ARTS CLASSES

In the fall of 2001, we began working with five visual arts teachers in two Boston-area high schools at which the arts are taken seriously. The Walnut Hill School for the Arts is an independent, residential, suburban school whose student body includes many students who are foreign nationals and non-native speakers of English (particularly from Korea). The Boston Arts Academy is a public, urban school whose students' ethnic, racial, and socio-economic backgrounds represent the demographics of the city of Boston. At both schools, students are admitted through audition into an art form (visual arts, dance, drama, or music), teachers are practicing artists, and students receive over 10 hours of arts instruction per week. During the 2001-2002 school year, we observed and videotaped 38 visual arts classes (some were two, most were 3 hours in length). After each class, we prepared video clips of what we thought were the most important teaching moments and then interviewed the teachers to find out what they meant to teach and why they had taught that as they had.

In addition to developing the eight "Studio Habits of Mind" through this methodology, we also documented the interaction patterns of teachers and students. We documented three major kinds of class-room structures used by studio teachers, all of which we believe are emblematic of studio arts classes: Demonstration-Lectures, Students-at-Work, and Critiques. Once identified, we coded the 38 classes in terms of when and for how long each structure was used in each single class session.

THE THREE STUDIO STRUCTURES

We found that studio art teachers interact with students in three primary ways. They generally begin classes with a Demonstration-Lecture (which emphasizes "showing" processes and information that is relevant to the tasks assigned for the class). Most of the class is then spent with students working individually on a project, with the teacher circling through the studio and talking to students individually (we refer to this section as Students-at-Work). In addition, teachers often have one or more Critique sessions per class in which students look closely, reflect on, and evaluate their work and that of their peers. Teachers of other disciplines could well learn from these practices, practices which allow teachers to teach to large classes of heterogeneous students and to practice ongoing assessment of student work.

THE EIGHT STUDIO HABITS
OF MIND

If you ask someone what students learn in visual arts classes, you are likely to hear that they learn how to paint, or draw, or throw a pot. This is tantamount to saying that students learn techniques specific to the arts in arts class, and would be analogous to saying that students learn writing skills in writing class. We tried to probe this question more deeply. Of course students learn arts techniques in arts classes. But what else do they learn? Are there any kinds of thinking dispositions that get inculcated as students study arts techniques? Careful study of the student-teacher interactions in the classroom helped us to uncover eight habits of mind which teachers were striving to instill.

We transcribed all the classes and interviews. We divided up the Students-at-Work segments into interaction units between a teacher and a student. An interaction unit could be one exchange or many, as long as the teacher remained in conversation with a single student or group of students. We then coded each unit for the kinds of thinking dispositions we saw being taught. As we watched the tapes over and over we refined our category definitions by working with four representative class sessions over a period of 18 months. After establishing eleven working categories of "studio habits of mind" (later collapsed to eight to facilitate ease of use), we achieved inter-rater reliabilities for coding of the remaining classes of between .71–.91 for two independent raters. We describe each habit of mind below, in alphabetical order.

Develop Craft

Perhaps the most obvious habits of mind that students are taught in an art class are about craft. Students acquire the skills needed to work in various media, and we refer to this as Develop Craft: Technique. Here is where students learn to use tools (brushes, pencils, viewfinders) and materials (charcoal, paint, clay). Students are meant to learn the varied properties of tools and materials and the range of ways these can be employed. Students also learn to care for materials and tools, and we refer to this as Develop Craft: Studio Practice. Here students develop a sense of which tools and materials to choose for the piece they wish to make. Whenever we saw students being taught to develop craft, we also saw one or more of the other habits of mind being taught as well.

Engage and Persist

Teachers in visual arts classes present their students with projects that engage them, and they teach their students to persist in their work and stick to a task for a sustained period of time. Thus they are teaching their students to focus and develop inner-directedness. They teach them to break out of ruts and blocks and to feel encouraged about their work so that they are motivated not to give up. This habit of mind is taught first and foremost by presenting students with challenging projects that engage them and require sustained work. But this habit is also taught by reminding students to stay focused, by pushing students to keep going, and by discouraging students from quitting. As one of our teachers said, she teaches them to learn "how to work through frustration."

Envision

Students in visual arts classes are meant to learn to envision what they cannot observe directly with their eyes. By envisioning we mean generating images of possibilities in one's mind. We saw envisioning taking several forms. Sometimes students were asked to generate a work of art from imagination rather than from observation. For instance, in one class the teacher asked students to paint an imaginary landscape. She asked them to think specifically about the light in the landscape. "Where is the light coming from? Is it day or night? What is the light like? Is it bright or foggy?" Sometimes students were asked to imagine possibilities in their works that are not yet there. For instance, our ceramics teacher told his students, engaged in making a ceramic tile project, "You need to know what each tile will look like before you start making it." Sometimes students were asked to imagine forms in their drawings that could not be seen because they were partially occluded. And sometimes they were asked to detect the underling structure of a form they were drawing and then envision how that structure could be shown in their work. In all of these cases, students are being encouraged to generate a mental image that will help guide their work.

Express

Students are taught to go beyond craft to convey a personal vision in their work. We refer to this as learning to express. Learning to express includes making works that exemplify properties that are not literally present, such as moods, sounds, or atmosphere (Goodman, 1976). Learning to express also means making works that convey a strong personal meaning. As one of our drawing teachers said, ". . . art is beyond technique . . . I think a drawing that is done honestly and directly always expresses feeling." Here is a quote from this same drawing teacher in which he makes it clear to students that the power of a drawing depends far less on technical skill than on how expressive the drawing is. Students are drawing from the model: two people are posing at opposite ends of the room, and the task is to capture something about the space between the two figures.

"You're going to have to include all this space, this empty space. Now that's going to be a big challenge in your drawing, because something is going to be in that space. . . . The strength of the drawing is going to depend very much on the evocative nature of this space." He draws students' attention to the expressive qualities of a Hopper painting to make the point that the evocative power of a picture hits us before the content does. About the Hopper painting, he said, "When they look at it, they don't think 'look at the figures.' They think 'wow, it's late mysterious night. . . .' That is the subject of the picture. It's not just a drawing of a figure."

Observe

"Looking is the real stuff about drawing," one of our teachers told us. The skill of careful observation is taught all the time in visual arts classes and is not restricted to drawing classes where students draw from the model. Students are taught, both implicitly and explicitly, to look more closely than they ordinarily do and to see with new eyes. Students are helped to move beyond their habitual ways of seeing and to notice things that might otherwise be invisible. Students are taught to look closely at their own works (the color, line, texture, forms, structure, expression, and style), at others works (whether by their peers or by professional artist), and at the world (when they are working from observation).

We saw drawing teachers using the view-finder as an observation tool. Students were given a view-finder to look through so that they could select a composition that they would then draw. As one teacher said to his students using the view-finder, "Instead of painting what we see, we're going to see what you would paint." Looking through the viewfinder is also meant to help students learn to see objects as only lines, shapes, and colors in a frame. "Forget that you are looking at a bucket or a person's hair, or a table and a chair. . . . Forget that these are objects that have any real definition. I want you to simply concentrate on the lines that are created and the depth in what you see." This teacher then went on to model the skill of observing through the view-finder. "Right here I am paying attention particularly to the way this line goes diagonally across this frame, and then there is another little line underneath it that I can see has a little bit of a distance. It's a different color, different texture, and the line is thicker because from my perspective this line is a little thinner than this line down here."

We also observed students being encouraged to look closely at the objects or forms from which they were drawing (e.g., ". . . get some of these straight verticals in, like maybe that big pedestal there, or maybe that box down there . . . so you can work these big diagonals against that") as well as at their drawing (e.g., "Where is your horizon line?"). They were encouraged to see the underlying geometry of complex forms. "Whether you're drawing a person or the most complicated thing in the world, you want to see it in simple terms first. . . . If you just think of chest and muscles and arms and everybody's different shape, it can be overwhelming. But if you think of someone as just a cube and another cube attached, it can really help to simplify it." In short, students were taught to look in a new way, and this took many forms.

Reflect

Students are asked to become reflective about their art making and we saw this reflection take two forms. Students are asked to think about and explain their process, intentions, and decisions, and we refer to this aspect of reflection as Question and Explain. Students are also asked to judge their own work and that of others, and we refer to this as Evaluate.

Question and Explain

Teachers often ask students to step back and focus on an aspect of their work or working process. We often noticed teachers asking students to explain *what* some part of their drawing depicted, *how* they had achieved a certain effect, *why* they had made something the way they did, and *what* changes they were planning in their work. These open-ended questions prompt students to reflect and explain, whether aloud or even silently to themselves. These kinds of questions help to foster an inner reflection. Our ceramics teacher explained to us that posing questions to students helps them become aware of the choices they make as they work. When students say, "this is the way I want it," he urges them to think about why.

Evaluate

Students in visual arts classes get continual training in evaluating their own and others' work. Teachers frequently evaluate student work informally as they move around the room while students are working, as well as more formally in critique sessions. Students can learn from these consultations and critiques how to evaluate themselves and others. Students are also asked to make evaluations themselves—they are asked to talk about what works and what does not work in their own pieces and in ones by their peers. Thus students are learning to make aesthetic judgments and to defend them. Because they are engaged in continuous self-assessment, they have the opportunity to learn to be self-critical and to think about how they could improve.

Stretch and Explore

Students are asked, implicitly and explicitly, to try new things and thereby to extend beyond what they have done before—to explore and take risks. When teachers encourage students to stretch and explore, they do not tell students exactly what to do. Instead, they urge students to experiment, to discover what happens, to muck around, and try out alternatives. Comments such as "See what would happen if . . . ," "How else could you have done this," "Don't worry about mistakes, be brave" were all ones prompting students to adopt an exploratory risk taking attitude and discover that instead of avoiding mistakes one should capitalize on them. As our painting teacher said, "You ask kids to play, and then in one-on-one conversation you name what they've stumbled on."

Understand Art World

Students in visual arts classes learn about art history and the practicing art world today and their own relationship to today's art world. They also learn to see art making as a social and communicative activity. We called all of this learning Understand Art World, and broke this learning into two components: Domain and Communities.

Domain

Students are meant to learn about the domain of art. While art history is not taught in a systematic fashion in studio arts classes, teacher often ask students to look at reproductions of works of art that relate in some way to the project students are engaged in. Students are meant to learn about their own relationship to the domain of art and consider the similarities between the problems explored in their own works and those explored by established artists. For instance, when students were engaged in drawing two figures standing far apart separated by an evocative lonely space, our drawing teacher asked them to study the same kind of atmosphere evoked by Diebenkorn and Hopper paintings.

Communities

Students are meant to learn about the community of people and institutions that shape the art world—the "field" of art (Csikszentmihalyi, 1988). By this we refer to galleries, museums, curators, gallery owners. These gate-keepers decide whose work will be exhibited and immortalized. Students are taught to think about their relationship to the art community and to consider ways that they might fit into this community if they want to become professional artists. They must learn how to present themselves as artists (e.g., by matting and framing their work, making slides, creating a portfolio, or hanging a show). All of these activities are ways in which students learn to become part of the *profession* of artists, if this is to become their career choice.

The community component of Understand Art World also refers to learning to work collaboratively with peers on group projects, as well as learning from others' work.

DO THE STUDIO HABITS OF MIND TRANSFER?

These eight habits of mind are important in a wide range of disciplines, not only in the visual arts. Students must learn a great deal about tools and materials in a science lab, and this kind of learning is analogous to *developing craft* in the art studio. The skills of *engage and persist* and *stretch* and *explore* are clearly important in any endeavor: students need to learn to find problems of interest and work with them deeply over sustained periods of time, and to experiment and take risks. The skills of *observation* and *envision* are clearly important in the sciences. The skill of *reflection* (including self-evaluation) is important in any discipline. Perhaps the least general of the eight habits of mind are *express* and *understand art world*. Yet even these might have broader reaches. Clearly learning to *express* is often important in any kind of writing that one does, even in analytical non-fiction. And *understand art world* may be more broadly construed as learning to see links between what one does as a student in a particular domain with what professionals in that domain do.

If a habit learned in the arts is a general one that would be useful in other domains, it does not follow that this habit transfers to other domains. The transfer hypothesis remains a hypothesis to be tested, but it is a plausible one. It is our plan to test the hypothesis that particular habits learned in the arts transfer to particular domains outside of the arts. For example, it seems reasonable to suggest that the habits of both observation and envision may transfer to a science class. It is possible that these habits would transfer only if students were explicitly taught to think about those that they had learned in arts class and to try to use them in biology class, for example. For each of the habits identified as learned in the arts, we can think carefully about how and where it might be deployed outside of the arts and then test for transfer. We need to assess how well each habit has been learned in the parent domain and then determine whether depth of learning in the arts for this habit predicts how well the habit is used outside of the arts. In our view, this is the only logical way to go about testing for transfer.

Michael Timpane, former university president and former federal education office policy director, was paraphrased as follows by Richard Deasy and Harriet Fulbright's "Commentary: The Arts Impact on Learning," *Education Week*, January 24, 2001. "Arts education research today is at an early stage of its development . . . [similar to] research on reading, where the accumulation of studies over time gradually honed the understanding of educators and policymakers as to the best policies and practices." It is our hope that our work will move arts education research up one firm notch.

REFERENCES

Burger, K., & Winner, E. (2000). Instruction in visual art: Can it help children learn to read? *Journal of Aesthetic Education, 34*(3-4), 277-294.

Butzlaff, R. (2000). Can music be used to teach reading? *Journal of Aesthetic Education, 34*(3-4), 167-178.

Csikszentmihalyi, M. (1988). Society, culture, and person: A systems view of creativity. In R. Sternberg (Ed.), *The nature of creativity* (pp. 325-339). Cambridge: Cambridge University Press.

Fiske, E. (Ed.). (1999). *Champions of change: The impact of the arts on learning.* Washington, DC: Arts Education Partnership and President's Committee on the Arts and Humanities.

Getzels, J., & Csikszentmihalyi, M. (1976). *The creative vision: A longitudinal study of problem finding in art.* New York: Wiley.

Goodman, N. (1976). *Languages of art* (2nd ed.). Indianapolis: Hackett.

Graziano, A., Peterson, M., & Shaw, G. (1999). Enhanced learning of proportional math through music training and spatial-temporal training. *Neurological Research, 21*(2), 139-152.

Hetland, L. (2000a). Listening to music enhances spatial-temporal reasoning: Evidence for the "Mozart effect." *Journal of Aesthetic Education, 34*(3/4), 105-148.

Hetland, L. (2000b). Learning to make music enhances spatial reasoning. *Journal of Aesthetic Education, 34*(3/4), 179-238.

Keinanen, M., Hetland, L., & Winner, E. (2000). Teaching cognitive skill through dance: Evidence for near but not far transfer. *Journal of Aesthetic Education, 34*(3-4), 295-306.

Moga, E., Burger, K., Hetland, L., & Winner, E. (2000). Does studying the arts engender creative thinking? Evidence for near but not far transfer. *Journal of Aesthetic Education, 34*(3-4), 91-104.

Murfee, E. (1995). Eloquent evidence: Arts at the core of learning. Report by the President's Committee on the Arts and the Humanities.

Perkins, D. (2001). Embracing Babel: The prospects of instrumental uses of the arts for education. In E. Winner & L. Hetland (Eds.), *Beyond the soundbite: Arts education and academic outcomes* (pp. 117-124). Los Angeles: J. Paul Getty Trust.

Podlozny, A. (2000). Strengthening verbal skills through the use of classroom drama: A clear link. *Journal of Aesthetic Education, 34*(3-4), 91-104.

Rauscher, F. H., Shaw, G. L., & Ky, K. N. (1993). Music and spatial task performance. *Nature, 365*(6447), 611.

Rose, D. (1999). *The impact of Whirlwind Basic Reading through Dance Program on first grade students' basic reading skills: Study II.* Chicago: 3-D Group.

Salomon, G., & Perkins, D. N. (1989). Rocky roads to transfer: Rethinking mechanisms of a neglected phenomenon. *Educational Psychologist, 24*(2), 113-142.

Vaughn, K. (2000). Music and mathematics: Modest support for the oft-claimed relationship. *Journal of Aesthetic Education, 34*(3-4), 149-166.

Winner, E., & Cooper, M. (2000). Mute those claims: No evidence (yet) for a causal link between arts study and academic achievement. *Journal of Aesthetic Education, 34*(3/4), 11-75.

Winner, E., & Hetland, L. (Eds.). (2000). The arts and academic achievement: What the evidence shows. *Journal of Aesthetic Education, 34*(3/4).

PART IV

ART, AFFECT, AND PERSONALITY

CHAPTER 13

Emotion in Aesthetics and the Aesthetics of Emotion

Gerald C. Cupchik

Modern scholars have argued that Descartes's distinction between a thinking mind and a mechanical body was a major setback for our understanding of human beings (Damasio, 1994). By extension, treating cognitive and emotional processes as if they were unrelated must be equally problematic given that the mind is the center of thought and the body is the peripheral locus of emotion. This is overcome by treating cognitive and emotional processes as complementary. You cannot have one without the other, but then what kind of cognitive process goes with what kind of bodily reaction? From a pragmatic and top-down *action* perspective, you cannot engage in purposive mental activity without having generalized bodily arousal to focus attention and facilitate objective evaluation while inhibiting emotional coloration. From a holistic bottom-up viewpoint, you can only have a bodily and *subjective experiential* response to culturally or personally meaningful events. It should not be surprising that these opposing and yet complementary perspectives have their respective traditions both in aesthetics and in the study of emotion proper.

EMOTION IN AESTHETICS

Enlightened Hedonism

There is a clear tradition in aesthetic theory that embodies the assumptions of a pragmatic, top-down *action* perspective. Frances Hutcheson (1725), a philosopher of the 18th century Enlightenment, gave us the important aesthetic principle of "uniformity amidst variety" to define an experience of beauty that could be cultivated as a special faculty of good taste. The same *tasteful* and rational process could also *manipulate* an audience's emotions through the selection of subject matter representing universally shared worlds. Richard Payne Knight, the late 18th century scholar, offered an associationist account of illusion in theater as a kind of passive response by an audience "in sympathy with increasing emotional stimulation until the reason surrenders to the force of the passions" (Burwick, 1991, p. 222). French Neoclassicism similarly stressed the importance of the "three unities" of time, place, and action in determining dramatic illusion (Burwick). According to these "Enlightened" viewpoints, subject matter can shape the emotional experience of drama in a detached and purposive manner (Cupchik, 2002). A similar emphasis on the power of the aesthetic stimulus was offered in the 20th century by T. S. Eliot and New Criticism theorists who maintained that literary text analysis could be as objective as positivist science (Eliot, 1975/1932; Richards, 1924; Wimsatt & Beardsley, 1998/1954). Experimental aesthetics, which was founded by Gustav Fechner (1978/1876) in the 19th century and reinvigorated by Daniel Berlyne (1971, 1974) in the 20th, empirically examined functional relations between isolated stimulus and response dimensions. Fechner proposed the "principle of the aesthetic middle," whereby people "tolerate most often and for the longest time a certain medium degree of arousal, which makes them feel neither overstimulated nor dissatisfied by a lack of sufficient occupation" (cited in Arnheim 1985; original, Fechner, 1978/1876, Vol. II, pp. 217 and 260). Berlyne (1971, 1974) provided an empirical framework for testing this proposition by manipulating structural or *collative stimulus properties,* such as complexity and surprisingness, to determine how they affect feelings of pleasure and interest. He showed that *interest value* or *arousal* increased linearly as a function of complexity while *pleasure value* was accounted for by an inverted U-shaped curve relating complexity and preference; subjects preferred moderate levels of complexity, as Fechner had proposed.

While *pleasure* and *interest* may appear to be characterized by distinct mathematical functions, they are in fact intertwined. A study examining the roots of pleasure and interest found dynamic, complementary processes underlying them (Cupchik & Gebotys, 1990). Subjects rated twelve paintings on six verbal scales (e.g., simple-complex, uninteresting-interesting, displeasing-pleasing) and then made pair-wise comparisons between them under contrasting instructional sets. The *interest set* encouraged subjects to adopt an intellectual viewpoint emphasizing objective analysis as a basis for making comparative judgments. Under the *pleasing set,* subjects were instructed to relate to the paintings subjectively and personally before making their comparative judgments.

There were two dimensions underlying intellectual and objective judgments of the *interest value* of paintings. The first had to do with a *search for knowledge and meaning* in the midst of *complexity* and was comparable to Berlyne's (1949) original "curiosity" dimension. The second showed that subjects found *unfamiliar* paintings to be more interesting. This was consistent with Berlyne's "variation" dimension which involved the *alleviation of boredom through mere novelty.* Two dimensions also accounted for *pleasingness* judgments. The first dimension, *emotional associations,* contrasted paintings depicting social interaction that were simple, warm and not emotionally intense with complex, cold, and emotionally intense paintings embodying negative themes, such as aggression and social alienation. This latter cluster was reminiscent of Berlyne and Ogilvie's (1974) set of "high arousal" paintings which captured the viewer's attention but created a sense of discomfort. The second dimension encompassed three scales which had appeared on separate dimensions in the *interest* solution; meaningfulness, unfamiliarity, and complexity. This dimension represented *aesthetic effectance,* the pleasure that comes from meaningfully interpreting challenging materials, an idea Reception Theorists have favored since the 1960s (e.g., Schmidt, 1982). While providing support for Berlyne's original notion of *interest,* this study also revealed two complementary aspects of *pleasure* that encompassed the *interest* dimensions; *emotional associations* and *aesthetic effectance.*

Psychology has also contributed to our understanding of the relationship between subject matter and form or style in aesthetic perception compared with everyday life. The pragmatic bias of everyday life leads us to automatically identify useful objects with the result that the physical/sensory features constituting their form are disregarded (Craik & Lockhart, 1972). In aesthetic reception, physical/sensory qualities are the stuff out of which *style* is formed. Indeed, artists are unique in their ability to attend to the structure of these physical/sensory qualities and recreate or transform their effects on canvas to shape viewers's experiences (Cupchik, 1992). Aesthetic materials therefore differ from the stimuli of daily life in that both subject matter and form (i.e., style) can shape aesthetic response. Berlyne (1971) and Moles (1968/1958) provided a formal way to talk about relations between subject matter and style as a contrast between *semantic* and *syntactic* or *esthetic information,* respectively.

Since people are used to focusing on subject matter in daily life, art educators are challenged to draw the attention of novice viewers, who typically search for literal meaning in art, to stylistic qualities (Cupchik & Gebotys, 1988a; Winston & Cupchik, 1992). The *cognitive bias* of everyday life is behind the overpowering effects of subject matter over style. This was shown in a study where participants made either "same" or "different" judgments between pairs of paintings when either subject matter or style served as a background foil (Cupchik, Winston, & Herz, 1992). Subjects found it easier to discriminate subject matter (e.g., still-life versus portrait) compared with style (e.g., impressionism, cubism, fauvism) and to make *difference* judgments (wherein a single incompatible feature terminates the comparison) than *similarity* judgments (which entails a comprehensive search of features). The most important finding was that subjects had difficulty discerning *similar* style (e.g., both Impressionist in style) when they had *different* subject matter (e.g., still-life versus portrait) as a background distractor. The salience of the different and therefore contrasting subject matter distracted attention from the visually similar style. Thus, viewers must learn to *see past* surface subject matter in order to appreciate the structure of underlying style. While Impressionist paintings might sell for incredible sums of money today, the bourgeoisie of 19th century Paris were slow to appreciate them because the broken brush stroke style interfered with a search for familiar subject matter.

What is the time course of aesthetic perception? How quickly do viewers respond to collative properties, such as complexity, and how much time does it take to respond to subject matter and stylistic qualities? The *Aktualgenese* tradition in Gestalt psychology would suggest that aesthetic responses occur even during the earliest moments of perception. A contrasting view holds that aesthetic reception involves a more profound "effort after meaning" (Bartlett, 1932) which takes more time. In a study conducted with Daniel Berlyne (Cupchik & Berlyne, 1979), subjects viewed paintings and patterns that varied in complexity and orderliness for 50, 500, and 5000 msec in a within-subjects design. This provided a framework for comparing "holistic"or "preattentive" processes taking place within a single glance (50 msec) with purposive or "focal attentive" processes (Neisser, 1967) that direct multiple eye fixations (500 and 5000 msec). Results showed that subjects could discriminate relative complexity and orderliness of both paintings and patterns *after only a single glance*. They also experienced aversive feelings after such a brief exposure which led them to avoid further exploration of *highly arousing* paintings (Berlyne & Ogilivie, 1974) combining discordant stylistic motifs (i.e., contrasting patterns of light and composition). This study clearly showed that the interaction of cognitive and affective processes in aesthetic perception take place holistically within the first glance. It contradicts Zajonc's

(2000) assumption that preferences are unmediated by cognitive processing in the *mere exposure* paradigm. In fact, preferences reflect, on-line, the earliest efforts at a search for structure in externally presented stimuli. The mere and early perception of relative complexity shapes emotional responses and thereby preferences.

The subjective experience of time is also a direct reflection of stimulus processing activity (Cupchik & Gebotys, 1988b). Subjects viewed slides of paintings that varied in complexity for 18, 36, and 72 seconds, estimated exposure duration and rated the stimuli on verbal scales. Results showed that they *overestimated* exposure duration as a direct function of stimulus complexity in accordance with Fraisse's (1963) notion of "filled time" which in this case implied perceptual/cognitive activity. In an earlier study on the reception of *impressionist* paintings (Cupchik, 1976-77), subjects viewed paintings by Manet, Monet, and Degas, then estimated exposure duration and rated them on verbal scales. They *underestimated* exposure duration for very orderly paintings in accordance with a notion of *empty time* reflecting the ease of perceiving structure in the work. Thus, residual feelings associated with the relative challenge posed by a painting have a direct effect on the subjective experience of duration. Intense processing activity makes time appear to pass more slowly, whereas relative ease of processing makes time appear to pass more quickly.

A study involving literary passages demonstrated the value of examining the effects on the time course of reading of collative stimulus properties as well as personal meaning. Cupchik and Laszlo (1994) exposed readers to short story excerpts that focused either on *action* or *experience* and measured reading speed as well as verbal scale ratings of the text. Results showed that "surprising" action-oriented segments were read quickly, whereas experience-oriented segments which "provided insight" were read more slowly. When encouraged to read the text subjectively in relation to their personal lives, subjects also slowed the pace of reading for passages that were judged to be "rich in meaning about life." The finding that a challenging search for personal meaning slowed the pace of reading, whereas suspense-based arousal increased it, was observed in another experiment focusing on rereading literary texts (Cupchik, Leonard, Axelrad, & Kalin, 1998).

These studies, based on the classical tradition of Fechner and Berlyne, showed that collative stimulus properties can affect processing activity and thereby modulate states of interest, arousal, and pleasure. In the second volume of this series on *Art and Emotion* (Cupchik & Winston, 1992), Andrew Winston and I (see also Cupchik, 1995) followed up on an implication of these findings. Specifically, it was proposed that people can *intentionally modulate* their states of pleasure or arousal by selecting stimuli that possess a needed quality. Thus, a person in need of love or social connection might want to experience sentimental pleasure and accordingly read a romantic book or view a film in which this quality was a central feature. Alternatively, someone who is bored might choose to enhance his or her state of arousal to a moderate level by viewing an action oriented film. The central point is that a person can purposefully choose to be exposed to a stimulus in which a critical affect modulating feature is salient. Thus, the relationship between stimulus features and affect states can be viewed as bi-directional depending on the potency of the stimulus or the need state of the person.

Imaginatively Constructed Meanings

The *objective* approach to aesthetic activity focused on art or literary works as stimuli to be analyzed using appropriate codes. Scholars of the Enlightenment stressed the powerful role played by *sensation* in shaping audience response. An emphasis on "correct" interpretations of the textual sources of these sensations was later evident in the writings of New Criticism theorists. Similarly, experimental aesthetics adopted an S-R behavioral approach applying information theoretic principles to account for the effects of artistic and literary stimuli. This top-down approach, with its belief in the constraining power of the aesthetic work, was challenged in the 1960s, 70s, and 80s by Reception Theorists who favored the active construction of meaning by individuals and communities (Fish, 1980; Holland, 1975; Schmidt, 1982). Rather than treating aesthetic materials as embodying a single meaning that could be uncovered in a quasi-scientific manner, they argued that aesthetic systems are "multileveled" (Kreitler & Kreitler, 1972) or "polyvalent" (Schmidt, 1982), and "open" (Eco, 1989/1962) to continuous interpretation.

Schmidt's (1982) contention that aesthetic pleasure results from interpretive efforts was echoed in the study by Cupchik and Gebotys (1990) on pleasure- and interest-based judgments described earlier. It was also supported by a recent study on poetry reception which favored the interpretive freedom offered in a private reading of poetry over hearing or seeing poems performed (Hilscher & Cupchik, 2005). Indeed, the bond that a person experiences with a work of art, literature, or drama reflects the personal meaningfulness of the subject matter and his or her identification with its main characters and themes (Braun & Cupchik, 2001; Cupchik, Oatley, & Vorderer, 1998; Vorderer, 1996; Zillmann, 1995).

These ideas were anticipated by German Romantic scholars such as Johann and August Schlegel who, along with the English poet Samuel Taylor Coleridge, placed a greater emphasis on the active and interpretive role of viewers and listeners (see Cupchik, 2002). Johann Schlegel was against the use of "crude naturalism with intent to deceive" (Wilkinson, 1945, p. 78) the spectator into believing that an the event on the stage is real, as was implied in the Enlightenment approach to shaping audience reactions. Instead, by selecting critical moments in life and expressing them in carefully fashioned dialogue, the playwright could expose the hidden workings of a character's mind. Providing a meaningful context to account for action lends coherence and meaningfulness to an audience's experience. Thus, *unity of action* was more important than the Neoclassical unities of time and place for these scholars of the Romantic period.

August Wilhelm Schlegel also disagreed with the Neoclassical principle that the unity of time, place, and action created powerful dramatic illusion, treating it instead as a "waking dream, to which we voluntarily surrender ourselves" (cited in Burwick, 1991, p. 194). He proposed that reality and illusion actually coexist: "The reality of the dramatic dialogue is that the text is written; the illusion is that dramatic dialogue is spoken spontaneously" (Burwick, p. 201). Schlegel grounded "aesthetic illusion in imagination" (Burwick, p. 193) and described the ways that illusion is shaped by events on the theatrical stage. Even the impossible might be accepted "so long as the *grounds* for impossibility are left out of the circle of our comprehension or are cleverly veiled from our attention" (Burwick, p. 210). He also included audience participation as an important aspect of theater, adding that knowing a seemingly spontaneous dialogue is put on serves to sustain the illusion.

Samuel Taylor Coleridge, critic and poet, similarly objected to mechanistic models that treated the mind as *passive*. Rather than the reception of sensation, he favored the logic of the imagination to foster the fluid continuity of conscious experience. Coleridge emphasized the role of *will* in adopting an aesthetic attitude and described aesthetic illusion as the product of a "willing suspension of disbelief for the moment, which constitutes poetic faith" (Coleridge, *Biographia Literaria,* 1817/1983, cited in Burwick, 1991, p. 221). Anticipating research in developmental psychology by more than a century, Coleridge argued that children can readily suspend the distinction between *artifice* and *reality*. Adults, on the other hand, are used to executing pragmatic comparative judgments and this makes it more difficult for them to use their imagination and accept the fictive as "real" when reading a story, or a "representation" as the "transaction itself" when viewing a play. Because excessive rational analysis can get in the way of aesthetic absorption, adults must learn to "willingly suspend disbelief." This anticipated the finding reported above that attention to subject matter, a habit of everyday cognition, interferes with the perception of style (Cupchik, Winston, & Herz, 1992).

Edward Bullough (1912) offered a psychologically oriented integration of Enlightenment and Romantic ideas in his classic paper on *psychical* or *aesthetic distance.* Elizabeth Wilkinson has suggested that Bullough's notion of *psychical distance* could be traced to Schiller's notion of *éloingment,* the idea that poets should not write in the moment of strong emotion but rather "in the tranquility of *distancing* recollection" (cited in Wilkinson, 1957). Bullough's approach to experience treated the notion of "psychical distance" as an "outlook," a "metaphor," a space that "lies between our own self and such objects as are the sources or vehicles" (Bullough, 1912, p. 89) shaping our "affections" defined as bodily or spiritual reactions involving sensation, perception, emotional states or ideas.

His analysis of aesthetic distance acknowledged that it has both a *"negative* inhibitory aspect—the cutting out of the practical side of things . . .—and a *positive* side—the elaboration of the experience on the new basis . . ." (Bullough, 1912, p. 89). The "distanced view of things is not, and cannot be, our normal outlook . . . and the sudden view of things from their reverse, usually unnoticed side, comes upon us as a revelation, and such revelations are precisely those of Art" (Bullough, pp. 89-90). The notion of "psychical distance" is not meant to "imply an impersonal, purely intellectually interested relation. . . . On the contrary, it describes a *personal* relation, often highly emotionally coloured, but of a peculiar character" (Bullough, p. 91) because the practical side is filtered out. Bullough articulated a *principle of concordance* to account for variations in taste whereby the *success* and *intensity* of a work's appeal stands "in direct proportion to the completeness with which it corresponds with our intellectual and emotional peculiarities and the idiosyncracies of our experience" (Bullough, p. 92). As applied to appreciating drama, the principle involves achieving the greatest concordance or "resemblance with his own experience—*provided* that he succeeds in keeping the Distance between the action of the play and his personal feelings" (Bullough, p. 93). The same principle applies to the artist who "will prove artistically most effective in the formulation of an intensely *personal* experience, but he can formulate it artistically only on condition of a detachment from the experience *qua personal"* (Bullough, p. 93).

The *central principle* is therefore the same for both viewers and artists. The goal is maximal involvement without excessive self-absorption; *"utmost decrease of Distance without its disappearance"*

(Bullough, 1912, p. 94). Bullough introduced the concept of a *Distance-limit*, "that point at which Distance is lost and appreciation either disappears or changes its character" (Bullough, p. 95). Two extreme conditions can be observed in relation to distance; *under-distancing* and *over-distancing*. Under-distancing occurs when the subject matter is "'crudely naturalistic,' 'harrowing,' 'repulsive in its realism'" and over-distancing takes place when the style "produces the impression of improbability, artificiality, emptiness or absurdity" (Bullough, p. 94).

In drama, various features of stage-presentation enhance the sense of Distance: "the general theatrical *milieu*, the shape and arrangement of the stage, the artificial lighting, the costumes, *mise-en-scene* and make-up, even the language, especially verse" (Bullough, 1912, p. 104). One factor that creates Distance for sculpture is its lack of color, and interestingly, pedestals serve to place a work in a space of its own and remove it from our own viewing space. Factors that contribute to distance in paintings are: the two-dimensionality and framing of pictures, the fact that "neither their space (perspective and imaginary) nor their lighting coincides with our (actual) space or light" (Bullough, p. 105), the reduction in scale of represented objects, and most importantly, "unification of presentment" effected by "such qualities as symmetry, opposition, proportion, balance, rhythmical distribution of parts, light-arrangements, in fact all so-called 'formal' features, 'composition' in its widest sense" (Bullough, p. 105). The "visibly intentional arrangement or unification, must by the mere fact of its presence, enforce Distance, by distinguishing the object from the confused, disjointed and scattered form of actual experience" (Bullough, p. 106). *Style therefore serves a dual role.* A high degree of finish reduces distance and makes a work more accessible, whereas salient stylistic qualities remove the work from the everyday world.

The effects of *aesthetic distance* were examined in a series of experiments using both visual and literary materials. What happens when you instruct readers of emotional of descriptively rich texts to be detached spectators who feel sympathy for the protagonist or to fully identify with and imagine that they are the protagonist (Cupchik, Oatley, & Vorderer, 1998)? Results showed that identification fostered the experience of "fresh emotions" in response to the descriptive texts, while being a spectator directed readers toward their own "emotional memories." The strong impact of emotional scenes was evident in this study as well. Emotional texts evoked both fresh emotions and emotional memories, and created robust situational models incorporating recognizable person and setting-oriented details.

These findings were also consistent with those of another study in which ratings were compared after first and second readings of the same short story excerpts from James Joyce (Cupchik, Leonard, Axelrad, & Kalin, 1998). In between readings, subjects either generated an interpretation of the meaning of the excerpt or received an expert interpretation of it. Emotional short story excerpts were read more quickly and judged more favorably on both text (e.g., challenging, complex, rich in meaning) and self-oriented scales (e.g., liking, expressive, personal relevance). The fact that emotional texts were read more quickly than descriptive texts, even though they were more challenging, shows how stimulating emotion can be even when embedded in complex structures.

When an aesthetic event, a drama for example, touches upon themes that are very close to the individual, the person can experience a powerful emotional response. If the experienced emotion is very negative, then the person might turn away from the work because it induces too much anxiety. This is an example of what Bullough (1912) called under-distancing. In the case of artworks, the viewer's attention might be re-distributed away from the aversive theme and toward innocuous stylistic elements (e.g., the color or composition). This defensive shift of attention, a kind of intellectualization, was found in a study comparing the reactions of lonely versus gregarious students to paintings of solitary figures (Cupchik & Wroblewski-Raya, 1998). When instructed to imagine being the figure in the paintings, "lonely" students generally preferred *stylistic* qualities over the subject matter which focused on a solitary figure who may have reminded them of their personal sense of isolation. On the other hand, viewers of sculptures which reminded them of personal life themes felt a strong bond with the works (Cupchik & Shereck, 1998).

In sum, the romantic tradition in philosophy stressed putting aside the critical criteria of daily life and suspending disbelief so as to imagine that an event on stage or in a narrative is "real." Conventions or cues in the setting which identify an aesthetic event as such can facilitate this imaginative process. People also bring to bear shared understandings and personally held meanings in an effort to understand the subject matter of a narrative. The more complex the narrative and the more multilayered the symbolism, the greater the challenge faced by the recipient to find coherent meaning in the whole. The interplay of manifest and latent meanings weaves a tapestry across conventional and personal symbolism enabling recipients to project themselves into the work and form a bond with it.

Cupchik and Winston (1992) described a *reflective mode* wherein the person construes a framework of understanding informed by general knowledge and personal life experiences. The projection of meaning onto an aesthetic event is complemented by the release of pent up emotion. It was Bullough who established the parameters of this process by noting that emotional involvement is fostered through an awareness that in the end it is only a story. Otherwise, the person might withdraw or engage in defensive activity when adverse feelings are brought to the fore. This personal engagement has been a theme in aesthetics reaching back to Aristotle's classical notion of *catharsis* and more recent discussions of identification with protagonists (Scheff, 1979; Vorderer, 1996; Zillmann, 1995). Miall and Kuiken (2002; see also Kuiken, Miall, & Sikora, 2004) have explored the implications of "expressive enactment" whereby the reader engages a text to produce metaphors of self-understanding. Viewers of art have similarly been observed to generate metaphorical understandings and retrieve personalized memories in responses to sculptural scenes involving grouped figures (Cupchik & Shereck, 1998). The reception of aesthetic materials thus provides an opportunity to plumb the depths of personal history and meaning, restructuring our appreciation of the work even as we sleep (Medved, Cupchik, & Oatley, 2004).

THE AESTHETICS OF EMOTION

How can we generalize from aesthetic theory to an understanding of relations between emotion and cognition in everyday life? The British philosophers of the Enlightenment period contributed to our understanding both of aesthetic activity and of emotion. Aesthetic appreciation (Hutcheson, 1725) is predicated on a "distinterested" (i.e., non-utilitarian) attitude and the development of a cultivated *taste* that enabled viewers to appreciate the subtleties of form or style as well as subject matter in the aesthetic *stimulus*. Good judgment in everyday life required the application of a *principle of utility* to govern practical *action* and an awareness of the *pleasure* that would be consequent to judicious decisions (see Danziger, 1997; Dixon, 2003). Thus, both aesthetic and everyday judgment involve the application of logical principles combined with attention to the resulting pleasure or pain. The difference was that everyday judgment focused on the *subject matter* of practical decisions while aesthetic judgment addressed primarily *form*.

This pragmatic attitude was carried forward in aesthetics by New Criticism theorists who emphasized the application of logical rules to decode the structure of aesthetic messages. Similarly, aestheticians in the behavioral/cognitive tradition examined relations between discriminable stimulus properties and response dimensions such as pleasure and arousal. The *Action* approach to emotion continued Darwin's functionalist emphasis on adaptation to environmental demands. This behavioral/cognitive perspective linked the objective analysis of challenging situations with the execution of *actions* needed to address needs and realize goals (see Oatley, 1992). The central principle of this *top-down approach* was incorporated in a "two-factor model"of emotion: **Emotion = Cognition + Arousal.** The seminal experimental paradigm, which involved injecting subjects with adrenalin, was developed by the distinguished Spanish physician and literary critic Gregorio Maranon in Spain in the 1920s and then replicated in America by Landis and Hunt (1932). The ideas were lost in the 1940s and finally rediscovered in the 1960s by Stanley Schachter (Schachter & Singer, 1962) who provided a theatrical framework for the injections (involving angry or happy stooges) as part of his explorations in the social evaluation of emotion evoking situations. Subsequent cognitive refinements (see Frijda, 1986) echo the early emphasis on a micro-analysis of threatening situations.

The Romantic approach to aesthetic processing in the early 19th century placed a greater emphasis on the role of imagination in appreciating a fundamental *unity* between subject matter and form in literature and drama. The underlying holistic perspective that shaped the Romantic approach echoed Leibnitz's law regarding the *continuity of consciousness*. This focus on the *response side* of aesthetic engagement was central to Reception Theorists of the mid-20th century who affirmed the interpretive role of individuals and groups in the effort after meaning. If the aesthetic work can be viewed as a hierarchy of layers combining form and subject matter, then aesthetic appreciation requires that a coherent pattern be found to unify them. This lies at the heart of the Gestalt approach to aesthetics expressed both in Iser's (1978) ideas about the *act of reading* and in Arnheim's (1971) holistic treatment of visual perception.

A similar pattern can be found in what might be called the *Experience* approach to emotion that incorporated William James's (1884) emphasis on the role of visceral feedback in giving form to emotion, a psychodynamic emphasis on unconscious responses to symbolically meaningful episodes, and phenomenology's analysis of the form of experience in terms of subjective distortions of time, space, causality, materiality, and connection (Straus, 1958). The Gestalt interplay between layers of subject matter and form in aesthetics is recreated here in the interaction between mind and body, and between conscious and unconscious meanings. The holistic experience of emotion encompasses perceived meanings that are shaped by culture and personal life circumstances and spontaneous physical reactions that echo conditioned memories of earlier episodes. This is a *bottom-up model* which values the spontaneity of bodily responses and the holistic form that they provide to emotion through the implicit transformation of its experiential parameters; time, space, materiality, and so on. The "uniformity amidst variety" that characterizes an aesthetic work (Hutcheson, 1725) is analogous to the unique interrelation between meaning and the bodily parameters of experience that we call "emotion."

Thus, the style of a painting as an expression of a unique perception of the world is analogous to the fabric of experience in everyday life and indeed shapes our experience during aesthetic episodes. Similarly, the form of emotional experience is projected out onto the world and we are not aware that the locus of transformations and distortions in the parameters of experience lies *sotto voce* within us. It is this implicitness that characterizes both the essence of style and the uniqueness of personal experience. The gift of artists and authors is that they tune to the subtle structure of experience, embodying it in a concentrated way in carefully crafted scenes, so that we can temporarily experience the world from their viewpoints. In this manner, emotion and cognition in everyday life and aesthetics are reconciled.

REFERENCES

Arnheim, R. (1971). *Art and visual perception.* Berkeley, CA: University of California Press.

Arnheim, R. (1985). The other Gustav Theodor Fechner. In S. Koch & D. Leary (Eds.), *A century of psychology as science* (pp. 856-865). New York: McGraw-Hill.

Bartlett, F. C. (1932). *Remembering: A study in experimental and social psychology.* London: Cambridge University Press.

Berlyne, D. E. (1949). 'Interest' as a psychological concept. *British Journal of Psychology, 39,* 184-195.

Berlyne, D. E. (1971). *Aesthetics and psychobiology.* New York: Appleton-Century-Crofts.

Berlyne, D. E. (1974). *The new experimental aesthetics: Steps toward an objective psychology of aesthetic appreciation.* Washington: Hemisphere.

Berlyne, D. E., & Ogilvie, J. C. (1974). Dimensions of perception of paintings. In D. E. Berlyne (Ed.), *Studies in the new experimental aesthetics* (pp. 181-226). Washington: Hemisphere.

Braun, I., & Cupchik, G. C. (2001). Phenomenological and quantitative analyses of absorption in literary passages. *Empirical Studies of the Arts, 19*(1), 85-109.

Bullough, E. (1912). 'Psychical distance' as a factor in art and as an aesthetic principle. *British Journal of Psychology, 5,* 87-98.

Burwick, F. (1991). *Illusion and the drama: Critical theory of the Enlightenment and Romantic era*. University Park, PA: Pennsylvania State University.

Craik, F. I. M., & Lockhart, R. S. (1972). Levels of processing: A framework for memory research. *Journal of Verbal Learning and Verbal Behavior, 2,* 671-684.

Cupchik, G. C. (1976-1977). Perspective théorique et empirique sur la peinture impressioniste. *Bulletin de Psychologie, 30,* 720-729.

Cupchik, G. C. (1992). From perception to production: A multilevel analysis of the aesthetic process. In G. C. Cupchik & J. Laszlo (Eds.), *Emerging visions of the aesthetic process* (pp. 83-99). New York: Cambridge University Press.

Cupchik, G. C. (1995). Emotion in aesthetics: Reactive and reflective models. *Poetics, 23,* 177-188.

Cupchik, G. C. (2002). The evolution of psychical distance as an aesthetic concept. *Culture and Psychology, 8*(2), 155-188.

Cupchik, G. C., & Berlyne, D. E. (1979). The perception of collative properties in visual stimuli. *Scandinavian Journal of Psychology, 20,* 93-104.

Cupchik, G. C., & Gebotys, R. J. (1988a). The search for meaning in art: Interpretative styles and judgments of quality. *Visual Arts Research, 14,* 38-50.

Cupchik, G. C., & Gebotys, R. J. (1988b). The experience of time, pleasure, and interest during aesthetic episodes. *Empirical Studies of the Arts, 6,* 1-12.

Cupchik, G. C., & Gebotys, R. J. (1990). Interest and pleasure as dimensions of aesthetic response. *Empirical Studies of the Arts, 8*(1), 1-14.

Cupchik, G. C., & Laszlo, J. (1994). The landscape of time in literary reception: Character experience and narrative action. *Cognition and Emotion, 8,* 297-312.

Cupchik, G. C., Leonard, G., Axelrad, E., & Kalin, J. (1998). The landscape of emotion in literary reception: Generating and receiving interpretations of James Joyce. *Cognition and Emotion, 12*(6), 825-847.

Cupchik, G. C., Oatley, K., & Vorderer, P. (1998). Emotional effects of reading excerpts from short stories by James Joyce. *Poetics, 25,* 363-377.

Cupchik, G. C., & Shereck, L. (1998). Generating and receiving contextualized interpretations of sculptures. *Empirical Studies of the Arts, 16*(2), 179-191.

Cupchik, G. C., & Winston, A. S. (1992). Reflection and reaction: A dual-process analysis of emotional responses to art. In L. Ya. Dorfman, D. A. Leontiev, V. M. Petrov, & V. A. Sozinov (Eds.), *Art and emotions* (Vol. 2, pp. 65-72). Perm, CIS: The Perm State Institute of Culture.

Cupchik, G. C., Winston, A. S., & Herz, R. (1992). Judgments of similarity and difference between paintings. *Visual Arts Research, 18,* 37-50.

Cupchik, G. C., & Wroblewski-Raya, V. (1998). Loneliness as a theme in painting. *Visual Arts Research, 24*(1), 65-71.

Damasio, A. R. (1994). *Descartes' error*. New York: Grosset/Putnam.

Danziger, K. (1997). *Naming the mind: How psychology found its language*. London: Sage.

Dixon, T. (2003). *From passions to emotions: The creation of a secular psychological category*. Cambridge, UK: Cambridge University Press.

Eco, U. (1989). *The open work*. Cambridge, MA: Harvard University Press. (Originally published in 1962.)

Eliot, T. S. (1975). Tradition and the individual talent. In Frank Kermode (Ed.), *Selected prose* (pp. 37-44). London: Faber and Faber. (Originally published in 1932.)

Fechner, G. (1978). *Die Vorschüle der Aesthetik* (2 vols.). Hildesheim: Georg Holms. (Original work published in 1876.)

Fish, S. (1980*). Is there a text in this class? The authority of interpretive communities*. Cambridge, MA: Harvard University Press.

Fraisse, P. (1963). *The psychology of time*. New York: Harper & Row.

Frijda, N. H. (1986). *The emotions*. Cambridge: Cambridge University Press.

Hilscher, M. C., & Cupchik, G. C. (2005). Reading, hearing and seeing poetry performed. *Empirical Studies of the Arts, 23*(1), 47-64.

Holland, N. (1975). *Five readers reading*. New Haven: Yale University Press.

Hutcheson, F. (1725). *An inquiry into the original of our ideas of beauty and virtue*. London: D. Midwinter and others.

Iser, W. (1978). *The act of reading: A theory of aesthetic response*. Baltimore, MD: The John Hopkins University Press.

James, W. (1884). What is an emotion? *Mind, 9,* 188-205.

Izard, C. (1971). *The face of emotion*. New York: Appleton-Century-Crofts.

Kreitler, H., & Kreitler, S. (1972). *The psychology of the arts*. Durham, NC: Duke University Press.

Kuiken, D., Miall, D., & Sikora, S. (2004). Forms of self-implication in literary reading. *Poetics Today, 25*(2), 171-203.

Landis, C., & Hunt, W. A. (1932). Adrenalin and emotion. *Psychological Review, 39,* 467-485.

Medved, M., Cupchik, G. C., & Oatley, K. (2004). Interpretive memories of artworks. *Memory, 12*(1), 119-128.

Miall, D., & Kuiken, D. (2002). A feel for fiction: Becoming what we behold. *Poetics, 30,* 221-241.

Moles, A. (1968). *Information theory and esthetic perception* (J. E. Cohen, Trans.). Urbana, IL: University of Illinois Press. (Original work published in 1958.)

Neisser, U. (1967). *Cognitive psychology*. New York: Appleton-Century-Crofts.

Oatley, K. (1992). *Best laid schemes: The psychology of emotions*. Cambridge: Cambridge University Press.

Richards, I. A. (1924). *The principles of literary criticism*. London: Kegan Paul Ltd.

Schachter, S., & Singer, J. (1962). Cognitive, social and physiological determinants of affect state. *Psychological Review, 69,* 379-399.

Scheff, T. J. (1979). *Catharsis in healing, ritual, and drama*. Berkeley, CA: University of California Press.

Schmidt, S. J. (1982). *Foundations for the empirical study of literature* (R. de Beaugrande, Trans.). Hamburg: Helmut Buske Verlag.

Straus, E. W. (1958). Aesthesiology and hallucinations. In E. W. Straus & B. Morgan (Trans.); R. May, E. Angel, & H. F. Ellenberger (Eds.), *Existence:*

A new dimension in psychiatry and psychology (pp. 139-169). New York: Basic Books.

Vorderer, P. (1996). Toward a psychological theory of suspense. In P. Vorderer, H. J. Wulff, & M. Friedrichsen (Eds.), *Suspense: Conceptualizations, theoretical analyses, and empirical explorations* (pp. 233-254). Hillsdale, NJ: Lawrence Erlbaum.

Wilkinson, E. M. (1945). *Johann Elias Schlegel: A German pioneer in aesthetics.* Oxford, UK: Basil Blackwell.

Wilkinson, E. M. (Ed.). (1957). *Aesthetics: Lectures and essays by Edward Bullough.* London: Bowes and Bowes.

Wimsatt, W. K., & Beardsley, M. C. (1998). The intentional fallacy. In D. H. Richter (Ed.), *The critical tradition: Classic texts and contemporary trends* (pp. 748-56). Boston: Bedford. (Originally published in 1954.)

Winston, A. S., & Cupchik, G. C. (1992). The evaluation of high art and popular art by naive and experienced viewers. *Visual Arts Research, 18*(1), 1-14.

Zajonc, R. B. (2000). Feeling and thinking: Closing the debate over the independence of affect. In J. P. Forgas (Ed.), *Feeling and thinking* (pp. 31-58). New York: Cambridge University Press.

Zillmann, D. (1995). Mechanisms of emotional involvement with drama. *Poetics, 23*, 23-51.

CHAPTER 14

Personality and Artistic Style: Patterns of Connection

Pavel Machotka

The role of personality in the arts—either in the making of art or in our responses to it—seems to me crucial. We do take personality more or less for granted in the making of art, and have done so since, perhaps, the Renaissance, when Vasari first took note of the characteristics of the personalities of the artists whose lives he was describing (Vasari, 1965, first published in 1550). But in the study of responses to art the role of personality has been equivocal; more common is the presumption that any difference between observers is an error term (a point to which I return below).

Here I will assume that, both in making art and in responding to it, individual differences are fundamental rather than an error term, and will focus on the specific internal mechanisms by which personality expresses itself. Although the research I will report will deal with the making of art, I will refer to responses to art as well, arguing essentially that the same internal mechanisms can be studied in the individual differences we observe.

It may be useful, in fact, to start with the seemingly harder case, that is, the importance of personality in responding to art. The most pertinent example is provided by studies of esthetic judgment where, one might assume, "good" judgment is a defining criterion and all else is an error term. On the contrary, research on aesthetic judgment (e.g., Child, 1965) shows that personality in fact helps explain why judgments, good or less good, are made. Although the criterion is the judgment of experts, observers who score well on the test differ in personality from those who score less well (with training in the arts controlled): they tolerate complexity and ambiguity, seek out active rather than passive oral experiences, and show greater independence of judgment. These qualities are differences in predisposition, that is, in what one seeks out in the visual and cognitive world and in how one then responds to it; under the right circumstances, one can find that the predisposition may be predominantly emotional (Machotka, 1982). Some people have better taste than others, to put the result simply, and the taste is determined in part by personality.

It might be argued, of course, that in more biologically rooted aesthetic matters there is either less individual variation, or that variation is indeed an "error" term—for example, in the question of what constitutes a beautiful face. Some research has shown that the most beautiful faces are average, and this finding is thought to be consistent with some biological assumptions about the rejection of atypical and unhealthy cases. The finding is similar in form, although different in details, to the arguments for prototypicality as the criterion of aesthetic quality in other objects. Unfortunately, more complex methods have isolated attributes of faces which, when exaggerated, make faces even more beautiful, and this puts into question the value of the typical. So does, of course, the observation that some very beautiful people in one's own experience are neither average nor even symmetrical, yet there is something about them that fascinates; and so does the everyday observation that people find different bodily proportions attractive, and the empirical findings that there are personality dynamics that explain these differences (Machotka, 1979).

But let me admit that there are typical preferences, that some things are more beautiful than others, and that there may be a biological or cognitive basis for this. The problem with the finding, when it can be made, is that it constitutes the discovery of a "winning formula"—a set of qualities that reliably attracts more people, as does youth, a smiling face, and certain movie and book plots. That, I would argue, is of limited interest; it may describe the routinely attractive but not the beautiful or the interesting or the overwhelming. And it certainly ignores legitimate and explainable differences in the aesthetic response, and I would submit that proper empirical study of the arts has to show as much interest in variability as it does in central tendency.

In studies of art making, the importance of personality is both assumed (in the world of art) and established in research; we know, for example, what type of person prefers complexity (Barron, 1953) or creates bold, exuberant architecture (Dudek & Hall, 1979). But we are still far from understanding why it should be so, if by "why" we mean some functional connection between the dynamics of individuals and the art they create or are attracted to. We are far from grasping the complex, and sometimes contradictory, paradoxical, and ambivalent aspects of our response to art.

For me, the point of departure that I do not wish to lose sight of is always this: aesthetic phenomena take place in the narrow moment that is jointly occupied by a person and his or her art; it is the point of creation or response, the moment itself when the art work and the individual are equally present, the work as the creation of the person, the person as absorbed by the work.

Now, it is obvious that for science such a moment is impossible to explain fully, because to do science, we need to abstract. The question is at what level we should pitch the abstraction, and it is this that I take as my topic here. What I wish to describe is what I consider a more optimal balance point between the abstract and the concrete, one that is closer to the point of encounter between the person and the work of art, and yet respects the need for going beyond the individual case. The point is one that I tried to maintain in a long-term study of the dynamics of art making (Machotka, 2003), where, with colleagues, I attended closely to the personalities and working methods of some 70 individuals. Although the study was lengthy, its dividends were considerable. They included a view of the many ways in which personality directs the production of art works, and support for the validity of the psychodynamic understanding of personality. Above all, here they allow me to offer an answer to the question posed in my title: what is it in the individual that is expressed in the substance and form of his art?

PERSONAL DYNAMICS AND THE MAKING OF ART

The full report on this research, with the relevant images, has appeared in book form, as *Painting and Our Inner World: The Psychology of Image Making* (Machotka, 2003), and here I will only outline its results and draw out its implications for understanding the role of personality in art. The starting point was the study of individuals who created images on the computer under instructions to "create a work of art." They had been trained by us in the techniques of Adobe Photoshop, and were then asked to choose from an array of photographs of landscapes one that interested them and to create a work of art from it. Some were art students, others were not, but given the equal training they had received in transforming images, none were inhibited by the request and all proceeded to create something that satisfied them.

While the participants worked, we took careful notes on each operation, and any comments on what they were doing. The time elapsed was also noted, and images in progress were saved in such a way that we could reconstruct the picture's development when we needed to. When they were done—as they saw it—they answered a series of questions about the process itself, their intentions, the image's possible meaning, and their past experience with the making or viewing of art. The whole research group would then analyze the images and the recorded protocol, attempt to reconstruct the painter's intentions, comment on the style and composition, and react to the image's aesthetic quality. We set this analysis aside, and gathered the personality data. We had asked the participants to come back for an interview, which was psychodynamically based and covered the issues that animated the individuals emotionally: their relation to their parents, the images and the reality of their romantic and other relationships, the patterns by which they had been disciplined, the parents' goals for them, their own ideas, goals, and hopes for the future, their profound needs, wishes and fears, and similar issues. Although relatively brief—about an hour and a half to two hours in length—the interviews always produced material that we could later connect to the analysis we had done of the images. We tested 72 individuals over a period of 5 years and wrote up a full analysis of each: we compared the themes and forms of the images with the themes from the personality interviews, and produced a clinical picture of each participant that was not dissimilar to the picture that a clinician forms of a client in psychodynamic therapy.

This was, however, only the beginning of the analysis, although it was an intuitively persuasive one. The important next step was to verify that the images indeed had the qualities we had attributed to them intuitively, and that the individual interpretations we had made and recorded had some validity. We went back to the images and rated each on a set of descriptive dimensions, and once we reached adequate reliability we submitted these ratings to a cluster analysis, whose purpose was to see how the images would group together with a purely statistical procedure. If we then found that the recorded interpretations were consistent within the clusters and different between them, then we could trust them: certain kinds of images will have been produced by people with similar makeups and concerns.

I lay stress on this verification because psychodynamic data have been held in suspicion; and indeed we wanted to be sure that we could allay these suspicions for ourselves. As it turned out, the cluster analysis yielded seven clusters, and these clusters revealed seven ways by which personality engaged itself in art making. The number seven, by the way, has no particular significance; it represents the finest distinctions that our population of 72 participants would permit. But each cluster does represent a unique approach to image making, a unique set of motives and visual ways of satisfying them.[1]

1. We encapsulated the characteristics of the first cluster under the name, *Narrative informality and compensatory longings*. In this cluster, the images the participants produced were narrative and without form; the images seemed to flow from their creators' hands but showed no concern for organization, texture, or composition. The psychodynamics of the image makers were highly consistent within the cluster: their childhoods were marked by inconsistency and loss or illness, and they grew up to dedicate themselves to improving the lives of others. The images they made were fantasies, attempts to create a better past than the one they had had. We saw their main impulses as wish-fulfilling and reparative, and so strong that they overwhelmed any desire—if there had been one—to think of their images in more detached, formal terms.

Notice that my emphasis is not on these participants' disappointing childhoods as such but on the manner in which they handled that disappointment: *by reparative wishes*. In this, as in all the work I have done, the manner of handling one's impulses turns out to be as important as the impulses themselves.

2. That the manner of handling impulses is important is seen in the second cluster, in which similarly disappointing childhoods were found, but where the images produced were above all disconnected from each other, and, in emotional terms, downcast and negative. In this cluster, presented in a chapter called *Inhibited, disconnected forms and downcast angry lives*, the participants did not feel reparative motives; they seemed mired in a kind of seething anger that allowed them neither consistent relationships with others nor coherent forms in their symbolic representations. The negative mood was clearly connected with an early pain, loss or deprivation. This was the earliest and deepest substratum of our artists' makeup, and it was followed by a childhood spent with a cold, or distant, or demanding and sometimes even frightening, father. The dark mood was joined by an inhibited, distant or dainty, mode of working—a mode that reflected an anger that either seethed or was being contained.

Now why in this cluster the response to a negative childhood could not have been more buoyant will have to remain unclear; the question is akin to the problem in clinical psychology of accounting for the particular defenses that a person may form, which is still a poorly understood process. But from the theoretical point of view—from the search for variables that connect personality to image making—we

---

[1] The images are reproduced in color on the author's Web site, www.machotka.com.

must, as a first formulation, insist both on *needs,* in this case a deficit, and *coping mechanisms,* in this case either reparative motives or a more resigned, impotent anger, expressed in a dainty defense that, technically, would be called manic.

But as I said, this accounts only for the mood of the pictures. We must also try to understand the episodic form of the images, and to do so, we must look at these same lives from another vantage point. Our painters related to others in a tenuous way—here living with conspicuous denial, there living with unreliability, elsewhere with clinging fathers. Some experienced attachment to partners or friends, but not a sexual one; others were sexual but separated their sexuality from attachment; none of them were both attached and sexual. Perhaps the best way to formulate the matter is not in terms of needs but in terms of emotional connectedness: *the disconnected form of these images seems to be a symbol of the incoherence of the subjects' connections with others.*

3. The third cluster re-introduced the relatively simple question of the ability to express emotion, but it also offered a refinement that addresses the matter of competence and organization. Its images were notable for their idiosyncratic handling—a kind of spontaneous originality—and for the emotional response which they stimulated in the viewer; there was also the sense that their forms moved diffusely and fluently within the frame, and it must be said that they were also made with an unhesitating and fluid process. These qualities described both the boldness and the flowingness by which the cluster was defined; what we found was a connection between a *Bold, flowing process and the direct expression of emotion.* It is as if the images had something to say—something immediate and direct, said without hesitation or perhaps with the certainty that it could be said. Looking at the personality of the members of this cluster, we found that few had adequate controls over the expression of their emotions; they either saw themselves as emotionally expressive in general, or told us that they were driven specifically by anger, and it seems reasonable to say that they seemed to translate emotional energy directly into something to say and/or a vigorous graphic gesture to say it with.

We must add that they had a parental model for the expressiveness—but it is significant that they had only one. That is, they told us that one of their parents was emotional while the other was organized. Perhaps it is this that accounts for the combination of freedom of expression and the direct, vigorous graphic gestures; it is as if *an emotional parent and an organized parent joined forces: the one provided the freedom of expression, while the other offered the encouragement of coherence.* In other words, we have to speak here both of the lack of constraints—in fact more: a drive for emotional expression— and the competence with which to express it.

4. Theoretically speaking, we have so far witnessed the power of compensatory wishes, angry constriction, and uninhibited emotional expression. Each of these pushes and pulls, sometimes combined with a strong sense of competence, explained the form of the pictures the subjects produced. But one can find that the dynamics that underlie other kinds of forms are purely defensive: that what governs the process of image making, or at least what explains the most significant part of it, is a nearly obsessive need to keep all aspects of the image under the image maker's control. This is what we found in the cluster called *Dense paintings and relentless control.*

All the images in this cluster seemed dense and closely assembled, most used some black, while a few were layered in strata. Whether the final product remained clearly readable or obscure, there was a sense of complexity or of piling up; one's gaze was not invited to move across the surface of the image by dynamic lines or into space by deep recession. Some of the images were made up of repetitive elements which by themselves suggested an obsessive process, and one picture maker in fact wrote his message out in words and repeated it throughout in different type sizes. There seemed little evidence anywhere of the painters' hands; rather, the images were cut up, assembled, multiplied, blurred, or transformed in their texture or color by the sophisticated electronic tools of the software. The photograph which served as the starting point had been for the most part obliterated, having served only as a springboard, perhaps even an excuse, for the work which the person "really" wanted to do.

We did see a clear dynamic operating in the interviews: all these individuals were highly controlled, and *all but one had a core issue which required a persistent exercise of the control.* Among these was a feeling of being driven by sex or love, which was in some cases combined with distance from people and in others with the need to manage the distance continuously. They spoke of love as a kind of ideal absolute, or as the equivalent of other people's religion. They were, in short, as compulsive in their life as they were obsessive in their ordered pictorial style.

Now, I have called this dynamic purely defensive, and said that the form of the images was determined by the form—and in this case the relentlessness—of the defense. That seems to me the right formulation for understanding the form the pictures took. But a fuller understanding of the person requires us to emphasize equally the needs that call for the constant use of these defenses, because the needs themselves are just as inexhaustible; and it might be asked whether it is not the needs that are being played out and symbolized in the pictures produced. Here I think we have a clear answer: it is not the needs but the defenses. Nowhere, for example, do we see the compulsive need for sex or for love symbolized; we only see the compulsiveness. *If the image is a symbol, it is a symbol of a relentless way of dealing with the inner life.*

5. Where the last cluster was driven and obsessive, the one we are coming to was inhibited, perfectionist, and as we shall see, in the grip of standards taken over from the parents. We described this cluster under the title *Imposed order, inhibition, and the acceptance of parental standards.* The images were timid, formal, and done in a disconnected, saccadic manner; their content and form were banal and failed to evoke an emotional response. The pictures were overly organized and subdivided, and expressed an intense preoccupation with establishing order and balance; they did not work by juxtaposition or tension, but by system, and in several of them the sole system, the sole organizing principle, was repetition. I must also add that many of the pictures overtly hid something, and thereby seemed to invite discovery: there were opaque, silvered windows, flowers missing from a bouquet, faces and eyes peering out of flowers.

The participants in this cluster all described themselves as meticulous, tidy, precise, or perfectionistic, and often self-critical. They told us that they had a clear model for this in their parents, one or both of whom were in technical, asocial occupations. And there were specific conditions which favored the acceptance of standards: the families the participants grew up in were intact nuclear families, and many felt close to at least one parent if not both. The parents, often emotionally distant, nevertheless presented a united front. All the painters, in short, grew up in conditions favoring the acceptance of adult standards. The interesting thing is that the standards they were asked to accept might be quite vague, as in the expectation that the children simply be respectful; invariably, what the young people identified with would reflect a process without an end-product: perfectionism.

Like the artistic style of the preceding cluster, then, the present style was determined by one's overall defenses. Yet the defense of perfectionism was not designed to cope with specific needs; it was without content, as it were, and served above all to *strengthen the identification with one's parents, or, more precisely, with their own need for perfection and order.* In the process, it also helped distance our subjects from their own inner world; they spoke of not knowing what they thought or felt. We were easily reminded of the quality of hiding that was present in many of the pictures; the subjects seem to be hiding from themselves, putting up barriers against self-knowledge.

6. Surely in a discussion based on the psychodynamic view of personality, an interplay between needs and defenses will figure prominently. But it may come as a surprise that we have so far seen little else. Some art work was defensive and inhibited, with form imposed artificially; other production was wish-fulfilling or impulsive, but then without any concern with form. In neither case did we see what we expect of art, namely an integration of form with substance.

Our analysis did, however, come up with a cluster—discussed under the heading *consistent style and the need to integrate*—in which the participants' wishes and concerns were given strong and appropriate form. It was a small cluster, consisting of five individuals, and all of them were artists. This was not the only cluster consisting of artists—the cluster based on the direct expression of emotions was, too—but they were artists with a different personality and mode of working. I shall mention the four on whom the data are the most complete.

One subject took the landscape photograph as a challenge to himself as a painter; it was a place that spoke to him "of a feeling of nature speaking to the painter." He set out to interconnect all aspect of the image, not by imposing a unique handwriting on it, but by searching for a kind of immanent unity within the scene and showing us his own connection with it. In fact, everything in his life was built on close connections: a Native American, he was taught to feel a close connection with nature, and now in his mid-twenties he was comfortable with his intimate connection with his brothers and his parents.

Another subject, used to seeking expressive consistency in her art but finding it only after a free exploration of her images, worked loosely, quickly and with vigorous gestures to loosen the photographic consistency of her chosen picture. She achieved a very colorful but utterly turbulent image rather quickly, and was unsatisfied with it—and then, almost as an afterthought, she picked up the tool called Pencil and drew a few lines within the leaves and added some outlines to their edges. The end result was unified and aesthetic, loose yet harnessed. She revealed that she was torn between the masculine and the feminine in her life—a step-father who was reserved and frightening, and a mother who was open, liberal, friendly and outgoing—and said enough about this conflict to suggest that the beginning of her work had the impulsiveness of her mother and the very end represented a kind of imposition of masculine control. The picture could be seen as an integration of her image of masculinity and femininity.

A third subject launched quickly into another kind of integration of her picture: she began to draw faces onto a photograph of persimmon leaves. She explained that whenever she tried to figure out what to draw she would start with human faces. But she also made clear that there was a deeper concern at work: to make a connection between nature and humans by adding heads. In the psychodynamic interview she told us that she, too, was concerned with integrating opposites—computers and creativity, which represent her diametrically opposed father and mother—and in fact believed in the unity of all living beings. "I guess we are all pieces of fruit," she commented. And then she added, laughing, ". . . I don't know how relevant this is, but my parents grow fruit, so I've grown up surrounded by fruit trees."

Our fourth subject produced another deeply integrated and balanced image, commenting that, as in his other work, his entire intention was to integrate the fluid, organic shapes with the more rigid, angular lines. He felt this process deeply; he said, "the physical building of the colors and the transparency really hits me, because as we grow, we don't forget what happened to us." What had happened to *him* was not clear until later, when he brought up his memory of his parents' divorce. The joint custody the divorce provided for meant that the children would travel back and forth between the two coasts each year, and, as he put it, "The worst part . . . was all the time spent in airports; we would say good-bye to our mom for the summer, and then we would be saying good-bye to our dad from the other end."

His need to interconnect and balance everything on the canvas, we can say, was in part aesthetic, but it was also a reflection of the painful dissolution of his family life; trying to bridge between distant poles was somewhat like wishing to reestablish the family's former togetherness. But unlike the reparative acts of the people in the first cluster, his picture recognized the actual separateness of the people involved and remembered the pain of separating.

I have mentioned these artists individually, because a general statement would not have conveyed what needed conveying: what it was that they felt the need to integrate, nor the way in which they worked the integration. It is surely clear with these four artists that their approach was more sophisticated than that of the other groups; they in fact splendidly illustrated the concept of sublimation. They showed just how complex sublimation is: more than mere displacement of a conflict to a higher-level, it is a free and integrative engagement with it, one that freely employs the artists' talents and creativity. And they illustrate, too, that sublimations come at a price: the artists deflect energy into art that they hold back from romantic relationships.

7. We turn finally to a cluster that was defined by a single dimension: abstraction. These pictures avoided both representation and narration; their space was flat, they were constructed by mechanical devices such as filters rather than hands-on methods, and all in all they seem more detached and avoidant than anything else. We noticed one other quality

in the pictures: they emphasized boundaries between objects either by blending them (this would be their one use of a hands-on method), or by giving them sharp outlines; they did this by cutting and reassembling, or using a filter appropriately called "Find Edges."

Clearly the psychology of this cluster was also primarily defensive. What leaped to the eye was the psychological distance that all these individuals maintained from others, from their parents as well as from their peers; one painter specifically remembered that she never saw her parents touch each other. The embodiment of that distance was the overall abstract form and the hands-off process; one could say that the abstraction expressed their avoidance of the emotional stuff of life. But the painters also seemed engaged in maintaining and defining their boundaries, and this, too, they explained in their life stories. Some called their parents "marshmallow," "wishy-washy," or "mushy"; they spoke of having come from families that were mixed up in their membership or having lived with parents who were inconsistent in their thinking, unconcerned about discipline, or intrusive into their child's space and thought. Whether the vague boundaries between themselves and their parents were reflected in their own woolly images, or in a confused superposition of sharply defined areas, seemed but two sides of the same coin.

BRINGING IT TOGETHER: PERSONALITY AND ART

I must say by word of caution that I neither intend to construct a concise framework nor think that one is possible or desirable. It would be of no help to reduce the data to a bipolar dimension (which the cluster analysis would have permitted); this would only send us back to the level of abstraction that I had criticized at the outset and lose all of the immediacy of creation that we had observed. But, having already gone from 72 individual ways of making art to seven styles, we can go a little further and discuss what seem to be the underlying mechanisms by which personality shapes art.

Patterns of defense are surely the clearest mechanism at work. We had generally seen them working in close conjunction with the impulses which they were designed to control, but in at least one instance they seemed to dominate the artist's production: in the case of the defense of avoidance. In cluster 7, an avoidance of the emotional stuff of life led directly to the abstract constructions of the images. In cluster 5, a similar defense pervaded the artists' work: a close identification with the parents' need for order, which led to the artificial imposition of orderliness on their images.

A more typically complex pattern was an *intimate connection between defense and need,* so intimate as to make it difficult to separate them. For example, in cluster 4, it was difficult to distinguish overdriven needs from the relentless defensive controls; all we could say was that, as closely related as needs and defenses were, it was the defenses which found expression in the form of the art work. In cluster 1, it was reparative motives that produced the highly informal images, and those motives were at the same time defensive. And in cluster 7, a search for boundaries could be seen as defensive at the same time as it became an expressed need.

We move toward greater complexity and greater flexibility as we consider mechanisms that seem to expand and enrich the image rather than constrict it; more broadly and positively they must be called *coping* mechanisms, and one of them is in fact sublimation itself. The images of the sixth cluster, which were based on a consistent style and showed a pervasive need for integration, were clearly the products of creative coping mechanisms; but we should also emphasize the creativeness of the third cluster, with its flowing forms, whose expressiveness was modeled on one expressive parent and shaped by the memory and example of an organized parent.

But we must also reach out toward a more metaphorical level of interpretation. Much of the data can be seen in another way, one that cuts across all the clusters: we can view the image making as a process that gives symbolic representation to the individuals' interpersonal world. We do know quite a bit about that world, and we only have to take full notice of it. In the book I have done this with all the clusters, and here I would offer two examples. Cluster 2, the one with disconnected forms, could be seen as symbolizing the unreliability of the artists' past and the disconnections in their present. Cluster 4, the one with the dense, repetitive forms, could also be seen as static above all, as if the repetitions in the artists' lives were more like standing than moving, and allowing oneself to be crowded would make sure that one would not move.

Now, no study, however thoroughly it tries to explore the many levels of personality that are involved, can pretend to be exhaustive. With other personality variables included, such a cognitive style, we might have come to see their role (Machotka, 1999). Under another experimental setup, one involving images of the human body, for example, one might have discovered identifications with one parent or the other, manic controls over depression, sensitivities to aspects of one's own body image, and other variables, all of which might also be symbolized; such patterns definitely appeared in a study I had done on the psychodynamics of preferences for the human nude (Machotka,

1979), and I see no reason not to expect them to be present in the creation of works portraying the body, if one were to do a study of that. Nor do I believe that I have explained what these artists may have done that is genuinely creative—but that is a limitation of all psychological science: we can only explain that which is determined.

REFERENCES

Barron, F. (1953). Complexity-simplicity as a personality dimension. *Journal of Abnormal and Social Psychology, 48,* 163-172.

Child, I. L. (1965). Personality correlates of esthetic judgment in college students. *Journal of Personality, 33,* 476-511.

Dudek, S., & Hall, W. B. (1979). Design philosophy and personal style in architecture. *Journal of Altered States of Consciousness, 4,* 83-92.

Machotka, P. (1979). *The nude: Perception and personality.* New York: Irvington.

Machotka, P. (1982). Esthetic judgment warm and cool: Cognitive and affective determinants. *Journal of Personality and Social Psychology, 42,* 100-107.

Machotka, P. (1999). *Style and psyche: The art of Lundy Siegriest and Terry St. John.* Cresskill, NJ: Hampton Press.

Machotka, P. (2003). *Painting and our inner world: The psychology of image making.* Boston: Kluwer Academic Publishers.

Vasari, G. (1965). *Lives of the artists.* New York: Noonday (first published in 1550).

CHAPTER 15

Pretend Play, Affect, and Creativity

Sandra W. Russ

We have known for quite awhile that pretend play relates to creativity in children (Russ, 2004; Singer & Singer, 1990). There are also studies that have shown that play facilitates creativity (Dansky, 1999). What we do not know much about are the mechanisms and specific processes in play that account for these relationships. This chapter will review the literature and speculate about the affective processes in play that may help set the stage for artistic creative work.

Play is important in the development of many of the cognitive, affective, and personality processes involved in creativity (Russ, 1993, 1999). Cognitive processes such as divergent thinking and affective processes such as affect-laden fantasy occur in play, are expressed in play, and develop through play experiences.

The type of play most important to the area of creativity is pretend play. Pretend play is play that involves pretending, the use of fantasy and make-believe, and the use of symbolism. Fein (1987) stated that pretend play is a symbolic behavior in which "one thing is playfully treated as if it were something else" (p. 282). She also stated that pretense is charged with feelings and emotional intensity. Affect is intertwined with pretend play. Fein viewed pretend play as a natural form of creativity.

THEORIES OF PLAY, AFFECT, AND CREATIVITY

Fein (1987) proposed an affect symbol system that represents real or imagined experience at a general level. After studying 15 "master players" (good pretend players) and categorizing her observations, she concluded that good pretend play consisted of cognitive characteristics such as object substitutions and the manipulation of object representations and an affective characteristic she called "affective relations." Affective relations are symbolic units that represent affective relationships such as "fear of," "love of," or "anger at." Fein proposed an affective symbol system that represented these complex relationships. These affective units store salient information about affect-laden events. The units are "manipulated, interpreted, coordinated, and elaborated in a way that makes affective sense to the players" (p. 292). These affective units are a key part of pretend play. Fein viewed play as symbolic behavior organized around emotional and motivational issues. This affective material is important in creative thinking and she proposed that divergent thinking in daydreams, pretend play, and drawing could activate the affective symbol system.

Russ (1999) pointed out that Fein's (1987) conceptualization is consistent with the psychoanalytic construct of primary process and creativity, another major theoretical approach. Primary process thinking was first conceptualized by Freud (1958/1915) as an early, primitive system of thought that was drive-laden and not subject to rules of logic or oriented to reality. Another way to view primary process thought is as affect-laden cognition. I have proposed that primary process is a subtype of affect-laden cognition (Russ, 1993). Primary process content is material around which a child experienced early intense feeling states (oral, aggressive, etc.). This content could be stored in the kind of affect symbol system proposed by Fein. According to psychoanalytic theory, primary process thinking facilitates creativity (Kris, 1952). Children and adults who have controlled access to primary process thinking should have a broader range of associations and be better divergent thinkers than individuals with less access to primary process. Freud's formulation that repression of primary process leads to general intellectual restriction predicts that individuals with less access to affect-laden cognitions have fewer associations in general. Research has supported the proposition that access to primary process thinking does relate to creativity in adults and children (Holt, 1977; Russ, 1993).

The primary process area is relevant to pretend play because primary process is expressed in play (Waelder, 1933). Play is a safe place where primitive emotional content can be expressed. Russ and Grossman-McKee (1990) did find a significant relationship between affect expressed in play and expression of primary process thought on the Rorschach in first and second grade children.

In 1993, Russ proposed an integrated model of affect and creativity, which was based on the theoretical, clinical, and research literature. I identified five affective processes important in creativity:

Access to affect-laden thoughts—the ability to think about thoughts and images that contain emotional content. Primary process thinking and affective fantasies in daydreams and in play are examples of this category. Thoughts that involve emotional themes such as aggressive and affectionate ideation illustrate this blending of affect and cognition.

Openness to affect states—the ability to experience the emotion itself. Comfort with intense emotion and the ability to experience a range of emotions and mood states characterize this openness.

Affective pleasure in challenge—enjoying the excitement and tension involved in identifying a problem and working on a task.

Affective pleasure in problem solving—taking deep pleasure in solving a problem or creating a product.

Cognitive integration and modulation of affective material—the cognitive regulation and control of emotional processes.

Pretend play is important in the expression, development, and facilitation of all five affective processes important in creativity. Both affect-laden fantasy and affect states are expressed in play. Children practice with the expression of a variety of feeling states and affective themes in fantasy. Also, the joy that most children experience when they become lost in pretend play may be similar to the flow (Csikszentmihalyi, 1990) experiences in creative work. The pleasure in play could also be similar to the intrinsic motivation so important in creativity (Amabile, 1990). Taking pleasure in the challenge and tension necessary in the process of identifying and solving problems is also evident in play. Children do scare themselves as much as they can tolerate in pretend play. They also use play to work on and rework internal conflicts and situational traumas (Erikson, 1963). Finally, through play, the child learns to master feelings and develop cognitive structure that aids in the modulation and regulation of emotion.

EMPIRICAL FINDINGS

A growing body of research has found a relationship between pretend play and creativity. Fisher (1992), in a meta-analysis of 46 studies in the play and child development area, found a modest effect size (ES) of .387 for the relationship between play and divergent thinking. Most of the research did not investigate specific processes in the play that accounted for the relationship, but the theories usually focused on cognitive explanations. For example, play is a place to practice with divergent thinking and recombination of objects.

There is some research evidence that links affect, play, and creativity and that provides support for the theories about affect and creativity. Lieberman's (1977) work supports a relationship between affect in play and divergent thinking. She focused on the variable of playfulness which included the affective components of spontaneity and joy. She found that playful kindergarten children did better on divergent thinking tasks than non-playful children. Singer and Singer (1990) also found that positive affect was related to imaginative play. Singer and Singer (1981) found that preschoolers rated as high-imagination players showed significantly more themes of danger and power than children with low imagination.

In a series of studies in my research program, we found that affect in play related to creativity. We used the Affect in Play Scale (APS; Russ, 1993) to assess affect in play. This scale codes fantasy and affect in play in 5-minute standardized puppet play samples. The play is videotaped and the raters code the tapes. For a full description of the scale, see Russ (1993, 2004). Russ and Grossman-McKee (1990) investigated the relationships among the APS, divergent thinking, and primary process thinking on the Rorschach in 60 first and second grade children. As predicted, affective expression in play was significantly, positively related to divergent thinking, as measured by the Alternate Uses Test. The correlation between affective expression in play and divergent thinking was .42. The correlation remained significant when IQ was partialed out. There was also a relationship between the amount of primary process thinking on the Rorschach and affect in play. This is important because it shows the consistency in the construct of affective expression across two different types of situations. Children who had more affect in their play had more primary process on the Rorschach.

The finding of a relationship between affect in play and divergent thinking was replicated by Russ and Peterson (1990) who used a larger sample of 121 first and second grade children. Once again, all of the APS scores significantly related to divergent thinking, independent of intelligence. With this replication, we can have more confidence in the robustness of the finding that a relationship exists between affect in pretend play and creativity in young children.

Russ, Robins, and Christiano (1999) carried out a follow-up study of the first and second graders in the Russ and Peterson study. Those children were fifth and sixth-graders for the follow-up. Thirty-one children agreed to participate for the follow-up study. This was a longitudinal study that explored the ability of the APS to predict creativity over a four-year period (five years in some cases , because the study took two years to complete). One major finding of the study was that the quality of fantasy and imagination in play was predictive of divergent thinking over a four-year period. Affective expression in play did not predict divergent thinking over time. However, the variety of affect score (range of affect expression) might have reached significance with a larger sample size ($r = .25$). It could be that processes of imagination and fantasy in play are more predictive of creativity over time whereas affect in play is important for creativity in the moment. Perhaps another creativity task where affect is more important, such as story-telling, would have resulted in affect being more predictive. Another important finding in this study was that most of the APS scores were stable over this four-year period. We had administered an adapted form of the APS to these older children (instructions were to put on a play with the puppets). The results showed good stability.

Russ and Schafer (2004) also found a relationship between affect in play and divergent thinking for emotion-laden objects. In a study with younger children, Seja and Russ (1999) adapted the APS for 4- and 5-year-olds. We found that frequency and variety of affect in play was related to divergent thinking and to teacher's rating of daily play behavior. Even in these young children, cognitive and affective processes in play were related to creativity.

An important question about the APS is whether it is measuring two separate dimensions of play—an affective dimension and a cognitive dimension—as originally conceptualized—or is measuring one dimension—an affect in fantasy dimension. This is an important question about play itself. Can we truly differentiate between the cognitive and affective processes in play or are they so intertwined that they are one process? In previous exploratory factor analyses (EFA) with the APS, using principal component analysis with oblique rotation, we did find two separate factors—one cognitive and one affective. In a recent confirmatory factor analysis with 342 six-year-old children, using AMOS with maximum likelihood method, we found that a two-factor structure was a better fit to the data than a one factor model (Russ, Min, Singer, Minnes, & Sacha, 2004). Consistent with the conceptual model and earlier EFA results, organization, imagination, and comfort loaded on a cognitive process factor; frequency and variety of affect loaded on an affect process factor. The two factors were significantly correlated. Results support the theory that pretend play involves both of these processes and that the APS measures both of these processes.

It is important that both cognitive and affective play processes be studied. They may have different roles in different types of creativity.

PLAY AND THE PROCESSING OF EMOTIONS

Children use play to express emotions and to learn to deal with and modulate emotions. Singer (1995) proposed that children, through play, create manageable situations in a pretend, safe setting where negative emotions can be expressed. Children can then increase positive affect and reduce negative affect through play. Play in therapy has been used for decades as a way to help children with emotional problems to express, integrate and master feelings.

Children who can express emotion in play should be able to express emotion in other situations. They should also have more access to emotional memories. Russ and Schafer (2004) proposed that children who had more affect in their play would be able to express emotion and think about emotion in other situations. Forty-seven first graders received the APS and an emotional memory task. Children were asked nine questions about their experiences. For example, "tell me about a time when you felt mad" and "Tell me about your first day in school." The results showed a significant relationship between the amount and variety of affect in play and the amount of affect in the memories. Quality of fantasy also related to affect in memories. Thus, children who were better players expressed more emotion when talking about their memories (independent of IQ and word count). We might speculate that, over time, the child who uses play well will be more open to affect themes and emotions. This openness to affect should effect the storage of emotional material in memory and retention of and access to those memories. More emotion could be included in those memories and the child would have a richer store of affect symbols (Fein, 1987) to use. Access to this emotional content should be especially helpful to the budding artist who draws upon emotion in writing, art, and acting.

FACILITATING PRETEND PLAY AND CREATIVITY

Can we facilitate pretend play and will that, in turn, foster creativity? This is a major question in the play area today. There have been efforts to improve children's play skills. For example, Smilansky's (1968) study was one of the first to demonstrate that teachers could teach play skills. She worked with kindergarten children for 90 minutes a day, 5 days a week for 9 weeks. The children who engaged in socio-dramatic play, with help from their teachers, showed significant cognitive improvement when compared with other groups. Dansky

(1999) concluded that there were consistently positive results in studies with adequate control groups that demonstrated that play tutoring, over a period of time, did result in increased imaginativeness in play and increased creativity on measures other than play.

Recently, Russ, Moore, and Farber (2004) investigated the effect of play intervention techniques on children's play skills and associations with creativity, coping, and life satisfaction. Participants were 54 first and second grade children in an inner city school. The school is 99% African-American. Children were randomly assigned to either an imagination play group, an affect play group, or a puzzle/coloring control group. Each child met 5 times with a play trainer in 30-minute individual sessions. A standardized play intervention was used with each play group.

Children in the imagination group were presented with a set of toys and asked to play out stories with high fantasy content (e.g., someone who lives on the moon) and high story organization (e.g., What someone needs to do to get ready for school). Children were encouraged to explore alternate endings for their stories and they were reinforced for being creative and engaging in object transformations. The play trainer used standardized prompts (model pretending; praise novelty).

Children in the affect play group had the same set of toys, but were told to express feelings and were asked to play out stories with affective content. They were given a different set of stories than children in the imagination group. For example, a child would play out a story about someone who was happy because she was going to a birthday party or sad because he lost his favorite toy. The trainer encouraged, modeled, and reflected expression of feelings.

The intervention with the control group of puzzles and coloring sheets was also standardized to control for amount of interaction with an adult and having a positive experience away from the classroom.

The major result of the study was that the play interventions were effective in improving play skills. The affect play condition was most effective in that, after baseline play was controlled for, the affect play group had significantly higher play scores on the APS on all play processes. The children had more affect in their play (both positive and negative), a greater variety of affect content, and better imagination and organization of the story than did the control group. The imagination group also had more positive affect and variety of affect than the control group. Another major finding was that there were significant effects for group on the outcome measures. Looking specifically at creativity, there was a significant group effect. Although the individual group contrasts did not reach significance, inspection of the profile plots indicate that the affect play group had the highest scores on the divergent thinking measures (number of alternate uses).

The finding that the affect play group increased both affective expression in play and cognitive abilities of organization and imagination suggests that involvement of affect also influences processes of imagination and fantasy. In order to express emotion, the child called on story-telling and imagination. Developing a narrative around an emotion may be a powerful process for children. That the imagination group improved positive affect and had a wider range of affect expression suggests that using one's imagination involves positive affect. This finding is consistent with results from the creativity research in which positive affect facilitates creativity and imagination (Isen, Daubman, & Nowicki, 1987).

The results suggest that improving play skills could improve creative thinking. Although the individual group contrasts were not significant, they may have been with a larger sample size. The results are encouraging and are consistent with previous research in the play area.

In a two to eight month follow-up study with these children, Moore and Russ (2004) found improved play skills for the imagination group. Although the affect play group had higher play scores than the control group, the results were not significant. Perhaps with a larger sample size, they would have been, Nevertheless, it appears that the focusing on cognitive processes in play may be more beneficial for long-term effects, whereas focusing on affect may be beneficial for the short-term. There were no significant effects over time for creativity.

The protocols developed for this play intervention study could be used in play intervention programs carried out by parents and teachers for children in kindergarten through third grade. We will be refining these protocols and carrying out research with them in the future.

Singer and Singer (1999) have developed a video-based program for parents and other caregivers of preschool children. The video and accompanying manual uses play and learning games to strengthen school readiness skills in children from three to five years old. The tape and manual provide very clear examples and instructions for parents and caregivers that model how to use play to help children use imagination and to learn through play. Singer and Singer (2002) also wrote a book for parents and teachers that reviews games and activities for imaginative play.

PRETEND PLAY, AFFECT AND
DOMAIN SPECIFICITY

Recently, there has been much discussion about whether creative ability is general and cuts across different domains or whether specific creative abilities are involved in each unique domain (science, art, music, etc.) (Sternberg, Grigorenko, & Singer, 2004). For example, Feist (2004) presented seven distinct domains. He also stressed the importance of fluid integration among domains. Creative talent is able to be flexible and cross boundaries of different domains.

Plucker and Beghetto (2004) took a hybrid position and proposed that all types of creativity involves both general creativity ability and specific creative ability unique to the area.

Russ (1993) proposed that there are many different profiles of creative ability. Different combinations of cognitive, affective, and personality traits and abilities could be associated with different types of creativity. Affect could be involved in different ways in different domains. Feist (2004) pointed out the importance of affect and intuition in scientific discovery. Passion and joy has been described in all kinds of creative pursuits. Russ concluded that artistic creativity involves the ability to have deep access to emotional memories and states. This in-depth involvement may not be so necessary in scientific creativity. For the scientist, good divergent thinking and flexibility of thought may be most important. Although even in these areas, as just reviewed, access to affect may be an advantage. For the writer, musician, artist, or actor, the need to get to basic affective content may be necessary for creative work that has universal aspects to occur.

Children who are able to express emotion in pretend play, and who can express and master negative affect and conflicts in play, may be at an advantage later in life when engaging in creative work. The artist would have a richer store of emotional memories to call on and would be better able to "sit with" the emotion while working with it. They would also have more experience with placing emotional material in a narrative and making things up in fantasy. Singer (2004) has proposed that pretend play is a forerunner for later specialization in creativity areas. He described the exciting reshaping of the world that occurs in play. I concur with this perspective, Root-Bernstein (2004) has found that a significantly greater proportion of MacArthur Fellows than a comparison group reported that as children they created miniature imaginary worlds in fantasy play. She concluded that play helped develop general creative skills. This finding was true for both scientific and artistic creativity.

CONCLUSIONS

In play, children can develop modes of expression of both positive and negative affect. In this safe world, children can express a variety of pretend mood states, memories and fantasies, and primary process themes. Negative affect can be expressed, worked through, and mastered. Children can then become more comfortable expressing negative thoughts and feelings. In play, positive affect can be expressed. Positive affect is important in creativity. Also, positive affect could be the precursor of the passion and intrinsic motivation often noted in creative individuals. Over time, as positive and negative affect-laden thoughts and affect states are expressed, the child develops access to a variety of memories, associations, and affective and non-affective cognition. This broad repertoire of associations helps in creative problem solving.

Future research in the area of play, affect, and creativity should:

- Investigate specific mechanisms and processes that underlie the play and creativity link. For example, exactly how does affect-laden fantasy facilitate divergent thinking?
- Investigate differential effects of different types of affect content on different types of creative tasks. Research suggests that positive and negative affect, and different content themes within those categories, may have different effects on various types of creativity.
- Carry out longitudinal studies that are necessary to determine how creative processes develop over time and whether early play predicts real-life creativity over the life span.
- Refine intervention techniques that facilitate play processes.

Finally, an important aspect of play may be that children are doing something they love in which they are free to be themselves, to express themselves, and to be creative. As adults, they may seek to recapture that experience by engaging in creative activities that recapture the joy and passion of play.

REFERENCES

Amabile, T. (1990). Within you, without you: The social psychology of creativity and beyond. In M. Runco & R. Albert (Eds.), *Theories of creativity* (pp. 61-91). Newbury Park, CA: Sage.

Csikszentmihalyi, M. (1990). *Flow: The psychology of optimal experience.* New York: Harper & Row.

Dansky, J. (1999). Play. In M. Runco & S. Pritzker (Eds.), *Encyclopedia of creativity* (pp. 393-408). San Diego: Academic Press.

Erikson, E. (1963). *Childhood and society.* New York: Norton.

Fein, G. (1987). Pretend play: Creativity and consciousness. In P. Gorlitz & J. Wohlwill (Eds.), *Curiosity, imagination, and play* (pp. 281-304). Hillsdale, NJ: Lawrence Erlbaum.

Feist, G. (2004). The evolved fluid specificity of human creative talent. In R. Sternberg, E. Grigorenko, & J. Singer (Eds.), *Creativity: From potential to realization* (pp. 57-82), Washington DC: APA Books.

Fisher, E. (1992). The impact of play on development: A meta-analysis. *Play and Culture, 5,* 159-181.

Freud, S. (1958). The unconscious. In J. Strachey (Ed. and Trans.), *The standard edition of the complete psychological works of Sigmund Freud* (Vol. 14, pp. 159-215). London: Hogarth Press. (Original work published 1915.)

Holt, R. (1977). A method for assessing primary process manifestations and their control in Rorschach responses. In M. Rickers-Ovsiankina (Ed.), *Rorschach psychology* (pp. 375-420). New York: Kreiger Publisher.

Isen, A., Daubman, K., & Nowicki, G. (1987). Positive affect facilitates creative problem solving. *Journal of Personality and Social Psychology, 52,* 1122-1131.

Kris, E. (1952). *Psychoanalytic exploration in art.* New York: International Universities Press.

Lieberman, J. N. (1977). *Playfulness: Its relationship to imagination and creativity.* New York: Academic Press.

Moore, M., & Russ, S. (2004). Follow-up of a pretend play intervention: Effects on play, creativity and emotional processes. Manuscript in preparation.

Plucker, J., & Beghetto, R. (2004). Why creativity is domain general, why it looks domain specific, and why the distinction does not matter. In R. Sternberg, E. Grigorenko, & J. Singer (Eds.), *Creativity: From potential to realization* (pp. 153-167). Washington, DC: APA Books.

Root-Bernstein, M. (2004, July). *Childhood play, adult play, and styles of creativity.* Paper presented at the meetings of the American Psychological Association, Hawaii.

Russ, S. (1993). *Affect and creativity: The role of affect and play in the creative process.* Hillsdale, NJ: Lawrence Erlbaum.

Russ, S. (1999). Play, affect and creativity: Theory and research. In S. Russ (Ed.), *Affect, creative experience, and psychological adjustment* (pp. 57-75). Philadelphia: Brunner/Mazel.

Russ, S. (2004). *Play in child development and psychotherapy: Toward empirically supported practice.* Mahwah, NJ: Lawrence Erlbaum.

Russ, S., & Grossman-Mckee, A. (1990). Affective expression in children's fantasy play, primary process thinking on the Rorschach, and divergent thinking. *Journal of Personality Assessment, 54,* 756-771.

Russ, S., & Peterson, N. (1990). *The Affect in Play Scale: Predicting creativity and coping in children.* Unpublished manuscript. Case Western Reserve University, Cleveland, OH.

Russ, S., Min, M., Singer, L., Minnes, S., & Sacha, T. (2004). *Confirmatory factor analysis of the Affect in Play Scale: Cognitive and affective processes.* Poster presented at Society for Research in Child Development, April, Atlanta.

Russ, S., Moore, M., & Farber, B. (2004). *Effects of play intervention on play skills and adaptive functioning.* Manuscript submitted for publication.

Russ, S., Robins, D., & Christiano, B. (1999). Pretend play: Longitudinal prediction of creativity and affect in fantasy in children. *Creativity Research Journal, 12,* 129-139.

Russ, S., & Schafer, E. (2004). *Affect in fantasy play, emotion in memories, and divergent thinking.* Manuscript submitted for publication.

Seja, A., & Russ, S. (1999). *Development of the preschool Affect in Play Scale.* Poster presented at the meeting of the Society for Research in Child Development, Albuquerque, NM.

Singer, J. L. (1995). Imaginative play in childhood: Precursor of subjunctive thoughts, daydreaming, and adult pretending games. In A. Pellegrini (Ed.), *The future of play theory* (pp. 187-219). Albany: State University of New York Press.

Singer, J. L. (2004). *Discussant, Symposium: Jack of all trades or master of one?* Meetings of American Psychological Association, Hawaii.

Singer, J. L., & Singer, D. L. (1981). *Television, imagination, and aggression.* Hillsdale, NJ: Lawrence Erlbaum.

Singer, D. G., & Singer, J. L. (1990). *The house of make-believe: Children's play and the developing imagination.* Cambridge, MA: Harvard University Press.

Singer, J. L., & Singer, D. G. (1999). *Learning through play* (Videotape.) Instructional Media Institute.

Singer, D. G., & Singer, J. L. (2002). *Make-believe games and activities for imaginative play.* Washington, DC: APA Books.

Smilansky, S. (1968). *The effects of sociodramatic play on disadvantaged pre-school children.* New York: Wiley.

Sternberg, R., Grigorenko, E., & Singer, J. (Eds.). (2004). *Creativity: From potential to realization.* Washington, DC: APA Books.

Waelder, R. (1933). Psychoanalytic theory of play. *Psychoanalytic Quarterly, 2,* 208-224.

CHAPTER 16

Strong Experiences Elicited by Music—What Music?

Alf Gabrielsson

Abraham Maslow, pioneer in humanistic psychology, asked subjects to describe "the most wonderful experience of your life; happiest moments, ecstatic moments, moments of rapture, perhaps from being in love, of from listening to music, or suddenly 'being hit' by a book or a painting, or from some great creative moment" (Maslow, 1968, p. 71). He found that such "peak experiences" were easiest to obtain through music and through sex. As regards music, he found peak experiences reported from classical music, "the great classics" (Maslow, 1976, pp. 169-170). Some of the criteria for peak experiences were a state of total attention or complete absorption by the stimulus/music; disorientation in time and space; perception can be ego-transcending, even mean a fusion of the perceiver and the perceived; the emotional reaction is characterized by feelings of wonder, reverence, humility and surrender before the experience as before something great. The peak experience is a unique instance, it is good and desirable, never evil or undesirable, and may occasionally be described as sacred (Maslow, 1968, chapter 6).

Following Maslow, Panzarella (1980) analyzed reports on instances of "intense joyous experience of listening to music" (p. 71) and identified four basic factors: *Renewal ecstasy*, an altered perception of the world; *Motor-sensory ecstasy*, various physical responses and quasi-physical responses; *Withdrawal ecstasy*, loss of contact with both the physical and social environment: and *Fusion-emotional ecstasy*, merging with the aesthetic object. In his study, too, most musical pieces triggering such experiences belonged to classical, "serious" music; however, some pieces were folk songs or rock'n'roll music. Earlier Laski (1961) found classical music as a common trigger of ecstatic experience.

There are reasons to believe that the almost exclusive reference to classical music in these studies may depend on the selection and rather limited number of people reporting on their reactions to music, possibly also on common views of classical music as "superior" to other music. As shown below, strong experiences may be elicited by music from a variety of musical genres. Moreover, it is an illusion to believe that music is the only responsible agent. Any experience of music is also influenced by many factors related to the person and to the actual situation. For further comments on these questions, see Gabrielsson and Lindström Wik (2003).

THE SEM PROJECT

Purpose and Methods

In the late 1980s I initiated a research project on *Strong Experiences of Music* (SEM for short). The primary purpose was to obtain a comprehensive and detailed description of the components—physical, behavioral, perceptual, cognitive, emotional, social, and others—contained in strong experiences related to music, and to explore the "causes" of such experiences and their consequences for the individual. Rather than suggesting a special character of the experience as Maslow and Panzarella had done, we avoided any suggestions or examples and simply asked people to describe, in their own words, "the strongest, most intense experience of music that you have ever had; please, describe your experience and reactions in as much detail as you can." They did so in interviews and, mostly, in written reports. They were also given supplementing questions concerning time and place of the experience; if they were listeners or performers; if this was the first time they heard the music in question, and if the same strong experience had recurred at a later meeting with the same music; what they thought may be the cause(s) of the experience; what the experience meant in a longer perspective; and how often they had such strong experiences.

Participants

After a pilot study comprising 150 participants, mainly recruited among personal acquaintances and students, some advertisements about the project in mass media resulted in hundreds of reports from persons of widely varying background and with different musical preferences. We also made active attempts, in many separate studies, to obtain good representation regarding gender, age, occupation, musical background and musical preferences; reports are still received now and then.

Presently some 950 persons have provided reports of SEM. Many of them have spontaneously described two or more experiences so that the number of reports is more than 1300. They vary in length from only a few sentences up to 10 pages; the typical report is 1-2 pages. Women have been more willing to contribute than men and comprise 62% of the sample compared to 38% men. The participants' ages range from 13 to 91 years. The distribution across 10-year-intervals, 10-19, 20-29, . . . 60-69, is fairly equal (12–19% of the total sample in each interval), while there are fewer participants above 70 years. Over one-half of the participants are musical amateurs of varying skill, ranging from simple performance at home to performance at a professional level. The remaining sample is about equally shared by professionals (musicians, music teachers, music therapists, a few conductors and composers) and non musicians. Musical preferences belong to many different genres: classical music, pop/rock, jazz, folk music, popular music, and others. (Some statistics on the number of participants in our previous papers differ from the present ones, because the number of participants has continued to increase).

Analysis and Results

The participants' SEM reports were subjected to content analysis in order to identify experiential and behavioral reactions mentioned in the reports, followed by attempts to sort the reactions into a number of appropriate categories. This required careful and repeated readings of each single report by two or more independent readers, a process lasting several years. It has resulted in an hierarchical three-level descriptive system comprising about 150 different aspects of SEM (Gabrielsson & Lindström Wik, 2003), too extensive to be included here. The upper two levels of the hierarchy are shown in Table 1. Although not all of our 1300 SEM reports would satisfy Maslow's criteria for peak experience, already the categories in this reduced representation of the system show apparent similarities to the characteristics proposed by Maslow and Panzarella, as well as to characteristics of Csikszentmihalyi's (1990) concept of "flow." An obvious exception, however, is that there are some SEM reports on strong negative experiences related to music (to be briefly discussed later). Further discussion of these questions is found in Gabrielsson and Lindström Wik (2003), which provides a far more detailed description of the SEM project. The present chapter will focus on what music appears in the participants' SEM reports.

Table 1. Descriptive System for SEM (Upper Two Levels)

1	GENERAL CHARACTERISTICS
1.1	Unique / Fantastic / Incredible / Unforgettable experience
1.2	Hard-to-describe experience, words insufficient
2	PHYSICAL REACTIONS, BEHAVIORS
2.1	Physiological reactions
2.2	Behaviors / Actions
2.3	Quasi-physical reactions
3	PERCEPTION
3.1	Auditory
3.2	Visual
3.3	Tactile
3.4	Kinesthetic
3.5	Other senses
3.6	Synesthetic
3.7	Intensified perception, multimodal perception
3.8	Musical perception-cognition
4	COGNITION
4.1	Changed attitude
4.2	Changed experience of situation, body and mind, time and space, wholeness
4.3	Loss of control
4.4	Changed relation / attitude to the music
4.5	Associations, memories, thoughts
4.6	Imagery
4.7	Musical cognition-emotion
5	FEELINGS / EMOTIONS
5.1	Intense / Powerful emotions
5.2	Positive emotions
5.3	Negative emotions
5.4	Different feelings / emotions
6	EXISTENTIAL AND TRANSCENDENTAL ASPECTS
6.1	Existence
6.2	Transcendence
6.3	Religious experience
7	PERSONAL AND SOCIAL ASPECTS
7.1	New possibilities, insights, needs
7.2	Music: New possibilities, insights, needs
7.3	Confirmation of identity, self-actualization
7.4	Community—communication

MUSIC IN SEM REPORTS

Classification

There is music from seemingly any musical genre in the complete set of SEM reports. To provide the titles of all pieces mentioned would require an enormous table. I have instead tried to sort them into a limited number of categories/genres. Any attempt at classification into genres meets with a lot of problems since one may use different principles for the classification and because it is hard to find mutually exclusive categories, not least regarding many of the recent newcomers in popular music. The categories proposed in the following do not pretend to be a perfect system, far from that, but represent one possible way to demonstrate the dispersion of music in SEM reports across many genres.

After many trials I decided upon a (quasi-)classification with 15 categories, each with a varying number of sub-categories:

(a) *Classical, non-religious music,* subdivided into early music, baroque, (Viennese) classicism, romanticism, "modern," and electronic/electro-acoustic; "modern" means 20th century music except such music that still essentially belongs to romanticism.

(b) *Sacred/Religious music,* with similar sub-categories as for classical music but also including categories for hymns, songs of praise, gospel songs, Christian pop songs, and the like.

(c) *Scenic music,* mainly opera music with similar sub-categories as for classical music, further operettas and musicals.

(d) *Folk music,* mainly subdivided into Swedish folk music (most examples) and folk music from other countries.

(e) *Jazz music,* including blues, traditional jazz, "modern" jazz (roughly from bebop to fusion and free form), at times also soul and funk or hybrids as jazz-rock or jazz-pop.

(f) *Rock music,* including rock in general, further hard rock, punk rock, symphonic rock, "synth rock," rock ballads, and sometimes hybrids as blues-rock, soul-rock, and the like.

(g) *Pop music,* including pop music in general, pop ballads, at times hybrids as pop-rock, pop-soul, pop-jazz, and the like.

(h) *Tunes,* non religious songs, traditional or newer, with or without instrumental accompaniment; evergreens and hits/schlagers may belong here, too.

(i) *Entertainment music,* traditional or newer.

(j) *Mixed genres,* a provisional category used to summarize many recent types of music, such as ambient music, new age music, disco, country, reggae, rap, techno, synth music, and the like; each of them usually appears in only a few reports

(k) *Dance music,* such as waltz, tango, salsa.

(l) *Improvised music,* performed by oneself or by others.

(m) *Artist/Ensemble* (mainly in classical music), when the SEM report focuses at least as much on the performer(s) as on the music performed.

(n) *Art music in other cultures,* such as Indian ragas, Indonesian gamelan music, flamenco.

(o) *Instrument,* when the SEM report focuses on the sound of a specific instrument, for instance, trumpet, drums, or the organ, rather than on the piece of music.

There are obvious overlapping categories in this proposal. Most pieces of music within Sacred/Religious music and Scenic music are usually regarded classical music as well. The borders between Rock and Pop music are very diffuse, as well as the borders between Tunes, Entertainment music, and Dance music, not to mention the many examples brought together under Mixed genres. There is much confusion concerning the proper musical terminology, not only among our participants but also among musical experts.

Distribution Across Genres

The number and percentage of SEM reports referring to music within each of the proposed categories is shown in Table 2 ($n = 1263$; precise information about the music was not given in 69 reports). Classical, non-religious music accounts for about 1/3 (34.2%) of all cases, Sacred/Religious music for 14.6% and Scenic music for 7.2%; these three may be said to form a "classical cluster" (except for gospel songs, Christian pop songs, and the like) that accounts for 56% of all cases. The categories Folk, Jazz, Rock, Pop, and Mixed each account for between 3 and 7%, together 27.3%, while Tunes, Entertainment music and Dance music together account for 11.5% (8.5 + 1.9 + 1.1). The remaining four categories (Improvised, Artist, Other cultures, Instrument) make up the remaining 5%.

However, these proportions differ depending on gender. As seen in Table 2, women's reports ($n = 784$) include higher percentage of Sacred and Scenic music and of Tunes than among men's reports. On the other hand, men's reports ($n = 479$) show a much higher proportion of Jazz and Rock music than in women's reports.

The proportions differ still more if we also include the age of the participants, as shown in Table 3. The percentage of SEM reports referring to classical music increases with increasing age for both men and women. The percentages of Sacred and Scenic music also increase

Table 2. Number, Cumulated Number, and Percentage of
All SEM Reports across Different Categories and
Percentage for Women and Men Separately

Category	Number	Cumulative	Percent	Women	Men
Classical	432	432	34.2	35.4	32.1
Sacred	184	616	14.6	18.1	9.0
Scenic	91	707	7.2	8.7	4.8
Folk	82	789	6.5	6.2	6.7
Jazz	75	864	5.9	1.5	13.2
Rock	91	955	7.2	4.2	12.2
Pop	58	1013	4.6	4.6	4.4
Tunes	108	1121	8.5	10.4	5.5
Entertain	24	1145	1.9	1.9	1.9
Mixed	39	1184	3.1	2.3	4.2
Dance	14	1198	1.1	1.0	1.3
Improvised	8	1206	0.6	0.6	0.6
Artist	32	1238	2.5	3.2	1.5
Other culture	6	1244	0.5	0.3	0.8
Instrument	19	1263	1.5	1.4	1.7

with age for women but remain at about the same level for men. For Folk and Jazz music the percentage is highest at middle age (30–49 years) for both genders; however, women's percentage for Jazz music is generally low. As regards Rock, Pop, and Mixed music the percentage is highest for the young participants and decreases with age. The highest percentage for Rock music (31.0) appears for young men; this value is higher than their percentage for Classical, Sacred, and Scenic music together (16.9 + 8.5 + 4.2 = 29.6%). Women's percentage for Tunes is highest for the youngest women and then decreases, whereas men's percentage regarding Tunes is highest at middle age (but always lower than for women). For Entertainment music and Dance music the differences are small and the percentages are low throughout; this also holds for the last four categories (Improvisation, Artist, Other cultures, Instrument) which are omitted here.

The largest difference between any of the six gender × age combinations is that between young men and older women. The classical cluster—Classical, Sacred, Scenic—occupies 75.5% of all cases for older

Table 3. Percentage of SEM Reports across Different Categories
for Women and Men in Three Age Intervals

Age	Women			Men		
	<30	30-49	≥50	<30	30-49	≥50
Classical	18.3	33.5	45.7	16.9	27.9	51.3
Sacred	15.4	18.5	19.9	8.5	9.9	8.4
Scenic	6.3	7.5	9.9	4.2	3.5	5.8
Folk	5.8	10.0	4.3	6.3	9.3	4.5
Jazz	1.9	2.5	0.9	9.2	15.1	14.9
Rock	13.0	2.0	0.6	31.0	8.1	0.6
Pop	13.5	3.0	0.6	7.0	5.8	3.2
Tunes	13.9	12.5	7.7	2.8	9.3	3.9
Entertain	0.5	1.0	3.4	0.7	1.1	1.3
Mixed	5.8	2.5	0.3	8.5	3.5	1.3
Dance	1.9	1.0	0.6	0.7	1.7	0.6

women versus 29.6% for young men; on the other hand, the cluster of Jazz, Rock, Pop, and Mixed music makes 55.7% of all cases for young men versus only 2.4% for older women. The difference between young women and older men is also considerable but less pronounced: 40.0% versus 65.5% as regards the classical cluster, 46.2% versus 9.0% for a cluster of Rock, Pop, Tunes, and Mixed.

These results should be considered in relation to the participants' age when their SEM occurred (see Table 4). Almost 40% of all SEM have occurred before the participant was 20 years old, 2/3 of them (66.2%) before 30 years of age. Of course, for the younger participants their SEM must have occurred in these early decades. However, including only participants who are 40-91 years of age—that is, the older half of all subjects, median age = 40 years—even then, about 1/3 of SEM has occurred before 20 years of age, and more than half of them (53.2%) before 30 years of age. In a separate study on participants older than 70 years (Gabrielsson, 2002), 57% of their SEM occurred before they were 30 years old. The highest frequency of SEM in any 10-year-interval occurs in the 10-19 interval, that is, during adolescence. This, in turn, means that for many of the older participants their SEM occurred long before genres such as rock, pop, and their "neighbors" had their breakthrough, in Sweden between, say, 1960 and 1970.

Table 4. Percentage and Cumulated Percentage of SEM
Occurring at Different Age, for All Participants and
For the Older Half of the Participants

	All subjects		Above median age	
Age	Percent	Cumulative	Percent	Cumulative
0 < 10	6.3	6.3	8.7	8.7
10 < 20	32.9	39.2	25.5	34.2
20 < 30	27.0	66.2	19.0	53.2
30 < 40	14.0	80.2	14.4	67.6
40 < 50	8.8	89.0	15.1	82.7
50 < 60	6.3	95.3	9.6	92.4
60 < 70	3.5	98.8	6.0	98.4
70 < 80	0.8	99.6	1.1	99.5
80 < 90	0.4	100.0	0.5	100.0

Some other observations are the following. Professional musicians show higher percentages of Classical (42.9%) and Jazz music (12.3%) in their SEM reports than amateurs or non musicians (29-37% for Classical, 4-5% for Jazz). On the other hand, professionals have lower percentages for Rock, Pop, and Tunes (1-3%) than amateurs and non-musicians (6-10%). These differences may reflect a view that Classical and Jazz music are "superior" to Rock, Pop, and Tunes. However, they may also simply reflect the fact that most of the professionals in this study were active in classical and jazz music, whereas performers of rock music were amateurs; the rock musicians were also much younger than performers of classical and jazz music. Non-musicians had very low percentage for Folk music (1.9% vs. 7-9% for professionals and amateurs) but higher percentage for Mixed genres (7.6%) than professionals and amateurs (1-2%).

Participants who had their SEM as listeners show higher proportions of Classical (37.3%) and Scenic (8.3%) music than participants who had their SEM when they were performers (20.4 and 2.2%, respectively). One may speculate that the demands on proper performance may diminish chances of experiencing SEM. On the other hand, however, the performers show a higher SEM percentage than listeners for Sacred music (31.4 versus 10.9%, respectively) and Rock music (11.5 versus 6.3%, respectively); whether this is due to less demands on the performance or on the character of the music itself must remain an open question. It should also be remarked that there is an imbalance in the number of reports: out of all SEM reports, 81% describe listening experiences versus only 18% in connection with performance of music.

EXAMPLES OF MUSIC WITHIN DIFFERENT CATEGORIES

Classical Music

In the "classical cluster," that is, Classical, Sacred, and Scenic music, there are numerous examples of the "great classics."

Works by J. S. Bach are mentioned in 55 SEM reports. Almost half of them (25) refer to sacred music: *St.John Passion, St.Matthew Passion, the B Minor Mass* and (to less extent) the *Christmas Oratorio*. The remaining examples include Bach's partitas for violin and for cello, two violin concertos, the second *Brandenburg Concerto*, the *Art of Fugue*, parts of the *Well-tempered Clavier*, the famous *Air*, and several works for the organ, among them the *Toccata and Fugue in D minor*.

Works by Beethoven appear in 50 reports. They include many references to *Symphonies Nos. 3, 4, 5, 7,* and *9; Piano Concertos Nos. 3, 4,* and *5; the Violin Concerto;* several piano sonatas, especially the so-called *Appassionata, Moonlight,* and *Pathétique* sonatas, and to the last sonata Op. 111 in C minor; his opera *Fidelio;* chamber music as the *Archduke Trio* and sonatas for cello.

Pieces by Mozart appear in 41 reports: his operas *Idomeneo, Cosi fan tutte, Don Giovanni, Le Nozze di Figaro,* and (especially) *Die Zauberflöte;* sacred music such as the *Requiem,* the *C minor Mass,* and *Ave verum corpus;* concertos for piano, for violin, the *String Quintet in G minor;* some piano sonatas and the well-known serenade *Eine kleine Nachtmusik.*

Schubert is also frequently mentioned (25 reports): The great *C Major Symphony* and the *"Unfinished" Symphony*; chamber music such as the *String Quintet in C major,* the *Trout Quintet,* the string quartet *Der Tod und das Mädchen,* pieces of piano music; the song cycle *Die schöne Müllerin* and lieder such as *Erlkönig* and *Heidenröslein;* music from *Rosamunde;* sacred music as *Ave Maria;* and one of the popular *Marche militaires.*

Works by Mahler are mentioned in 18 reports: *Symphonies Nos. 1, 3, 4, 5* (especially the *Adagietto), 6, 8,* and *10;* and to *Das Lied von der Erde* and *Kindertotenlieder.*

Handel appears in 17 reports, practically all of them referring to his oratorio *Messiah,* and especially the famous *Hallelujah* chorus.

Sibelius is mentioned in 17 reports: *Symphonies Nos. 1, 2, 4,* and *5;* the symphonic poem *Finlandia* and *En saga;* the string quartet *Voces Intimae.*

Verdi appears in 17 reports: Half of them refer to his *Requiem,* especially to the *Dies Irae* movement; and to his operas *Aida, Il trovatore, La traviata, Nabucco,* and *Un ballo in maschera.*

Brahms (15): Several references to *Ein Deutsches Requiem; Symphonies Nos. 3* and *4,* the *Double Concerto for Violin and Cello,* one of the piano concertos, the *Third Piano Sonata,* the *Piano Quartet in C minor,* and one of his waltzes for piano.

Chopin (14): his *Études, Mazurkas, Nocturne No. 1* in B Minor, the so-called *Raindrop Prelude,* and especially the *Fantaisie Impromptu* in C Sharp Minor, op 66.

Tchaikowsky (12): Practically all reports refer to either the *Sixth Symphony (Pathétique)* or the *Piano Concerto No. 1* in B flat minor; and to the *1812* overture.

Wagner (12): His operas *Tannhäuser, Lohengrin, Die Meistersinger von Nürnberg, Das Rheingold, Die Walküre, Tristan und Isolde,* and *Parsifal.*

Stravinsky (10): All ten reports refer to *The Rite of Spring.*

Numerous other composers with fewer mentions appear in Table 5.

As we have included operettas and musicals in the classical cluster, we should mention works by Léhar (the waltz in *Die lustige Witwe*); Offenbach (*La belle Hélène,* and the *Barcarole* in *Les contes d'Hoffmann*); Johan Strauss (*Zigeunerbaronen* and, although not scenic music, the famous waltz *An der schönen, blauen Donau);* Bernstein (*West Side Story*); Lloyd Webber (*Jesus Christ Superstar, Cats, The Phantom of the Opera;* also his *Requiem*); and Andersson and Ulvaeus (*Chess*).

Within Sacred music we also included hymns, songs of praise, gospels, and Christian pop songs. Several SEM reports mention two well-known Swedish chorales that are sung at the ceremony concluding the spring semester in school; these pieces become associated with summer and vacation. Other cited pieces are *Le Cantique de Noël* by Adam, *Amazing Grace,* several gospel songs as performed by singers as Mahalia Jackson and Cyndee Peters.

Most of the works mentioned in this classical cluster are considered masterpieces of western classical music. That they are frequently mentioned in SEM reports certainly confirms the results of Laski (1961), Maslow (1976), and Panzarella (1980) that "peak experiences" may be triggered by the "great classics." However, they do not exhaust the complete set of musical pieces mentioned in SEM reports. We now turn to examples from other musical genres.

Table 5. Composers and Works Beyond Those Mentioned in Text

Albinoni: *Adagio*

Barber: *Adagio for Strings*

Alban Berg: *Violin Concerto; Wozzeck*

Bartók: *Piano Concerto No. 3, Violin Concerto, The Miraculous Mandarine, String Quartet No. 6*

Berlioz: *Symphonie fantastique, L'Enfance du Christ*

Bizet: *Carmen, The Pearl Fishers*

Blomdahl: *Symphony No. 3, Aniara*

Britten: *War Requiem*

Bruch: *Violin Concerto No. 1*

Bruckner: *Symphonies Nos. 7* and *8*

Dvorák: *Symphony "From the New World", Cello Concerto, Serenade for Strings*

Elgar: *Pomp and Circumstance, The Dream of Gerontius*

Fauré: *Requiem*

Gershwin: *Rhapsody in Blue*

Grieg: *Piano Concerto*, music to *Peer Gynt*, piano pieces, in particular *Vaaren*

Haydn: *Die Schöpfung*, one of the cello concertos

Janácek: *Sinfonietta*

Kodály: *Psalmus hungaricus*

Larson: *Pastoral Suite, Förklädd gud ("Disguised God"), En vintersaga ("A Winter's Tale")*

Liszt: *Hungarian rhapsody No. 2, Liebestraum*

Lundsten: *Nordic Nature Symphony Nos. 3 and 4, Paradise Symphony, Tellus, Winter Music*

Lutoslawski: *Symphony No. 3*

Mendelsohn: *Violin Concerto*

Messiaen: *L'ápparition de l'église eternelle, Turangalila Symphony*

Mussorgskij: *Pictures at an Exhibition*

Nielsen: *The fog lifts*

Orff: *Carmina Burana*

Pachelbel: *Chaconne*

Pettersson: *Symphonies Nos. 7, 8, 10; Violin Concerto*

Poulenc: *Figures Humaines*

Puccini: *Bohème, Madame Butterfly*

Prokofieff: *Romeo and Juliet*

Table 5. (Cont'd.)

Pärt: *Johannes Passion, Spiegel im Spiegel, Tabula Rasa*

Rachmaninoff: *Piano Concerto Nos. 2* and *3*

Ravel: *Boléro*

Rossini: *Il barbiere di Siviglia, La gazza ladra* (the overture)

Saint-Saëns: *Samson et Dalila*

Schostakowich: *Seventh Symphony ("Leningrad"), Eighth String Quartet*

Schumann: piano pieces, in particular *Träumerei*

Sinding: *Frühlingsrauschen*

Smetana: *Moldau* from *Mà Vlast*

Richard Strauss: *Electra, Der Rosenkavalier, Salome, Vier letzte Lieder*

Webern: *Six Pieces* for big orchestra, *Op. 6*

Vivaldi: *The Four Seasons*

Folk, Jazz, Rock, Pop, and Mixed Music

Besides mentioning the piece of music, the SEM reports on classical music also frequently emphasize the importance of the performers (see Artists, p. 264). This is even more pronounced in SEM reports on Folk, Jazz, Rock, Pop, and Mixed music, in which the focus is on the appearance and qualities of the performers. When specific pieces are mentioned, if at all, it is more in passing.

SEM reports on Folk music mention a large number of Swedish, Norwegian, and Finnish folk musicians, performing on the violin (fiddle), the key harp, accordion, sometimes cow horn, especially female singers who use special singing styles with much ornamentation of the melodic line, stemming from local traditions. Most remarkable is the so-called *kulning* ("herding calls"), a very loud and high-pitched singing requiring a special vocal technique. It was, and still is, used to call cattle but is now increasingly used in professional singing. Other reports refer to folk music from various countries around the world, experienced *in situ* or when foreign ensembles were performing in Sweden. There are further reports that describe SEM during one's own performance of folk music, usually together with other musicians at folk music meetings.

SEM reports on Jazz likewise focus on experience, during concerts or in listening to recordings, of the performance by famous jazz musicians, representing various styles from blues and early jazz up to free-form and fusion. They appear here in alphabetical order:

George Adams, Louis Armstrong, Albert Ayler, Alice Babs, Chet Baker, Count Basie, Sidney Bechet, Betty Carter, Chick Corea, John Coltrane, Miles Davis, Delta Rhythm Boys, Duke Ellington, Gil Evans, Art Farmer, Ella Fitzgerald, Dizzy Gillespie, Benny Goodman, Bengt Hallberg, Coleman Hawkins, Quincy Jones, Johnny Mandel, Charles Mingus, Red Mitchell, Modern Jazz Quartet, Gerry Mulligan, Buddy Rich, Archie Shepp, Frank Sinatra, Toots Thieleman, Sarah Vaughan, Josh White, Lester Young, Niels-Henning Ørsted-Pedersen, and still others. There are also some reports by jazz musicians describing their experience during performances that were felt as unique events.

Most SEM reports on Rock, Pop, and Mixed music come from young participants. They describe their experiences during concerts, often giant concerts with many thousands of people in the audience, or in listening (often privately) to recordings by single artists or bands. As the borders between these genres are blurred, the mentioned musicians/ bands appear in alphabetical order with no attempts at further distinction between genres:

Alien, Beatles, Black Sabbath, David Bowie, Billy Bragg, Eric Clapton, Phil Collins, The Cure, Depeche Mode, Dire Straits, Duran Duran, Brian Eno, Eurythmics, Genesis, Guns'n Roses, Michael Jackson, Jean Michael Jarre, Kiss, Bob Marley, Paul McCartney, Metallica, Motorhead, Mike Oldfield, Pink Floyd, Dolly Parton, Elvis Presley, Prince, Rolling Stones, Bruce Springsteen, Sting, U2, Andreas Vollenweider, Stevie Wonder, Led Zeppelin; furthermore Jerry Williams, a well-known Swedish rock singer, and more locally known artists. There are also many vivid SEM reports from rock musicians who tell about their feelings during performance, often in a very "juicy" language.

SEM reports on Tunes include, for instance, songs by Jaques Brel, Leonard Cohen, Mikis Theodorakis, well-known Swedish songs by Bellman and Taube, and other familiar Swedish songs. This category also features some hits/schlagers of short lifetime.

Examples of Entertainment music are *Tango Jalousie* by J. Gade, *Champagnegalopp* by Lumbye, *Sæterjentens sondag* by Ole Bull, *In a Persian Market* by Albert Ketelbey, *Heinzelmännchens Wachtparade* by Kurt Noack, and the *Harry Lime Theme* by Anton Karas.

Among Artists in classical music, who were especially mentioned because of their performance, there were several singers: Martin Best, Jussi Björling (frequently mentioned), José Carreras, Kathleen Ferrier, Nicolai Gedda, Håkan Hagegård, Barbara Hendricks, Victoria de Los Angeles, Felicity Lott, Birgit Nilsson, Luciano Pavarotti, Fredrica von Stade, Joan Sutherland, Elisabeth Söderström; pianists: Vladimir Aszkenasy, Annie Fischer, Clara Haskil, Sergej Rachmaninoff (performing his own works), Svjatoslav Richter; violinists: Jascha Heifetz, Ann-Sophie Mutter, Endre Wolf; cello players: Frans Helmersson, Guido Vecchi; and guitar player André Segovia. Some Swedish choirs were mentioned as well.

Some SEM reports described exceptional experience due to the sound/timbre of a certain Instrument: the majestic sound of the organ, the sound of a shepherd's flute in a pastoral setting; the "divine" beauty of a solo trumpet in a church at a funeral, or in open nature at a Swedish summer evening sunset; and not least, the trance-like state reached in sustained rhythmic drumming.

Note on Negative SEM

Some 2% of the SEM reports described negative experience. In most cases the negative feelings were due to non musical factors; the music had become associated with negative events in life, such as unhappy love, divorce, separation from close friends, decease of relatives or friends, illness, attempts at suicide, war, other persons' dislike, and still other circumstances. In a few cases, however, the character of the music or the performance caused the negative reaction. For instance, a woman was scared by extremely loud, avant-garde organ music, and another woman the first time she listened to electronic music on the radio. Some performers' use of extreme, "ugly" sounds of their instruments also evoked strong negative reactions.

DISCUSSION

Although a lot of examples have been given above, a complete account of the musical material in SEM reports would require much more space. However, the examples given demonstrate that not only the "great classics" but also many other kinds of music, as well as special performance qualities and even special instruments/sounds, may elicit strong, unforgettable experiences.

By no means should the enumeration of composers, pieces, and artists be understood as a kind of ranking of them. What has been presented are simply the findings in a study on strong experiences related to music, conducted with some 950 persons in Sweden in the late 20th century and some years after the millennium. They have chosen to participate in the SEM project and have usually shown great interest and enthusiasm in sharing their experiences with others. Whether our results would be replicated in other countries or with other people is an open question. The primary purpose of the project was to develop a descriptive system for SEM, as published in Gabrielsson and Lindström

Wik (2003), here in an abbreviated form shown in Table 1. We do believe that most of the categories in the SEM descriptive system would recur in future studies. But it is very likely that the music eliciting the experience would be different, in different countries, with different samples, at different times, and so on.

An interesting question is if the music in SEM reports belongs to the person's usually preferred music or not. We asked our subjects which kind of music they usually listened to. Their answers were sometimes not easy to categorize because of differences in terminology and also because they often indicated many different genres, even that they were omnivorous regarding music. However, it is obvious that in the great majority of cases the music in SEM belonged to a musical genre that was familiar and usually preferred. On the other hand, there are many exciting reports of meetings with unknown or earlier neglected music that suddenly catches the person's total attention and leads to new discoveries in the musical universe.

A related question was if the music in SEM had been heard before or not. There were both "yes" and "no" answers at about the same rate, 34% "yes" and 38% "no" (no answer at all 28%). With "yes" answers, then, the music had been heard or performed earlier but it had not evoked a special reaction. This indicates that SEM is not only dependent on the music as such but also on many other factors related to the person or the situation—present state of mind, previous experience of music, education, personality, being alone or together with others, at home, abroad, and so on. This is also evident from the subjects' answers to the question if they had the same strong experience the *next* time they listened to or performed the same music. Out of 583 persons who answered this question, 63% said "no," 37% "yes." The dominance of "no" answers indicates that SEM was dependent on a unique combination of musical, personal, and situational factors, thus, it must be "the right music for the right person at the right moment," a condition that may not occur that often. On a question asking how often they had SEM, answered by 485 persons (a little more than 50%), the answers differed widely from "every day" (6 persons) to "once in my life" (36 persons). Among the remaining alternatives, the one that received the highest percentage (44%) was "once a year."

In conclusion, SEM may be elicited by many different types of music but it also always depends on extramusical factors in complex interplay. This results in large inter- and intra-individual variation that is overwhelmingly evident in our material. No statistical tables or graphs can do full justice to the experiences and the circumstances behind them, they do not become fully "alive" until one can read the participants' reports *in extenso*. Some 50 SEM reports or excerpts have been translated into English and published in various papers (Gabrielsson, 2001, 2002; Gabrielsson & Lindström, 1993, 1995; Gabrielsson & Lindström Wik, 2000, 2003) and more will follow.

ACKNOWLEDGMENTS

I express my gratitude to Siv Lindström Wik, my co-worker in this project, and to all participants who have generously shared their experiences with us. This research was supported by The Bank of Sweden Tercentenary Foundation and by The Royal Swedish Academy of Music.

REFERENCES

Csikszentmihalyi, M. (1990). *Flow. The psychology of optimal experience.* New York: Harper & Row.

Gabrielsson, A. (2001). Emotions in strong experiences with music. In P. N. Juslin & J. A. Sloboda (Eds.), *Music and emotion. Theory and research* (pp. 431-449). New York: Oxford University Press.

Gabrielsson, A. (2002). Old people's remembrance of strong experiences related to music. *Psychomusicology, 18,* 103-122.

Gabrielsson, A., & Lindström, S. (1993). On strong experiences of music. *Jahrbuch der Deutschen Gesellschaft für Musikpsychologie, 10,* 118-139.

Gabrielsson, A., & Lindström, S. (1995). Can strong experiences of music have therapeutic implications? In R. Steinberg (Ed.), *Music and the mind machine. The psychophysiology and psychopathology of the sense of music* (pp. 195-202). Berlin: Springer-Verlag.

Gabrielsson, A., & Lindström Wik, S. (2000). Strong experiences of and with music. In D. Greer (Ed.), *Musicology and sister disciplines: Past, present and future* (pp. 100-108). Oxford: Oxford University Press.

Gabrielsson, A., & Lindström Wik, S. (2003). Strong experiences related to music: A descriptive system. *Musicae Scientiae, 7,* 157-217.

Laski, M. (1961). *Ecstasy. A study of some secular and religious experiences.* London: Cresset Press.

Maslow, A. H. (1968). *Toward a psychology of being* (2nd ed.). New York: Van Nostrand Reinhold.

Maslow, A. H. (1976). *The farther reaches of human nature.* New York: Penguin Books.

Panzarella, R. (1980). The phenomenology of aesthetic peak experiences. *Journal of Humanistic Psychology, 20,* 69-85.

Index